LIFE & DEATH
DECISIONS

DR LACHLAN McIVER

LIFE & DEATH DECISIONS

Fighting to save lives from
disaster, disease & destruction

ENDEAVOUR

First published in Great Britain in 2022
by Endeavour, an imprint of
Octopus Publishing Group Ltd
Carmelite House
50 Victoria Embankment
London EC4Y 0DZ
www.octopusbooks.co.uk

An Hachette UK Company
www.hachette.co.uk

ISBN (Hardback) 978-1-91306-879-0
ISBN (Trade paperback) 978-1-91306-885-1

A CIP catalogue record for this book is available from the British Library.

Printed and bound in UK

1 3 5 7 9 10 8 6 4 2

Typeset in 12.5/18pt Garamond Premier Pro by Jouve (UK), Milton Keynes

This FSC® label means that materials used for
the product have been responsibly sourced.

For Dad

CONTENTS

CONTENTS

NOTES TO READERS

Author's Note

This book is based on real events and people. Most names and some details have been changed, partly for dramatic effect, but mostly out of respect for privacy and to avoid getting too many people into too much trouble.

Publisher's Note

Names and other identifying details have been changed to protect the privacy of individuals. Some events have been condensed, edited and altered for the book.

The book contains descriptions of the author's personal use of ayahuasca. Such descriptions do not constitute advice to others. Ingestion of any psychoactive substances should always be voluntary and under the guidance or direction of a suitably qualified person. It should be discussed with, and disclosed to, the relevant healthcare providers and medication or medical regimes should not be changed without prior discussion with such medical practitioners. The author and publishers are not liable for any injury or losses suffered from individuals choosing to engage in this practice.

ARCTIC OCEAN

NORTH
AMERICA

ATLANTIC
OCEAN

PACIFIC

OCEAN

SOUTH
AMERICA

DEMOCRATIC
REPUBLIC —
OF THE
CONGO

SOUTHERN
OCEAN

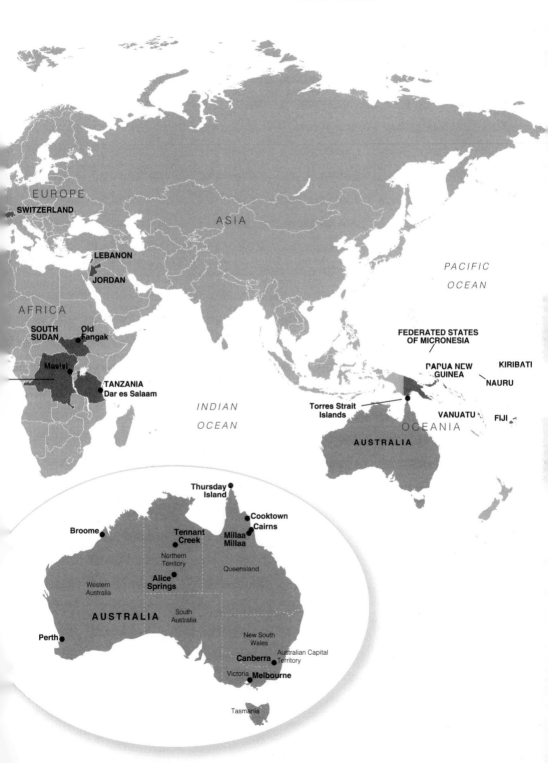

ARCTIC OCEAN

EUROPE

SWITZERLAND

ASIA

PACIFIC
OCEAN

LEBANON

JORDAN

AFRICA

SOUTH
SUDAN   Old
         Fangak

FEDERATED STATES
OF MICRONESIA

PAPUA NEW   KIRIBATI
GUINEA
              NAURU
Masisi

TANZANIA
Dar es Salaam   Torres Strait
                       Islands   VANUATU   FIJI

INDIAN   OCEANIA
OCEAN   AUSTRALIA

Thursday
Island

                              Cooktown
Broome   Tennant   Cairns
              Creek   Millaa
                        Millaa
              Northern
              Territory   Queensland

Western   Alice
Australia   Springs

AUSTRALIA   South
              Australia

                          New South
                          Wales
                                   Australian Capital
Perth   Canberra   Territory

              Victoria Melbourne

                      Tasmania

PROLOGUE

I found Dad dead on the side of the dirt road.

I was 16; he was 49. He'd left my sister and me at the house while he went out for his regular jog down to the bridge and back. Ma was away, working nightshifts as a midwife in the hospital two hours distant down the mountain range. The afternoon was cool and a light rain prickled as I wandered out onto the veranda to squint up through the mist towards the top gate to see if Dad was making his way down. He'd been gone a while now, so I assumed he must have stopped off to chat with our neighbours at their farm a couple of kilometres down the road. Shitty weather for socialising. I imagined him schlepping back in the cold and the mud and felt sorry for the old boy, so decided I'd go pick him up. It would give me the chance to take a quick little drive, too. My driving test was coming up soon, and even though I'd been driving the farm truck since I was 11, every bit of practice counted now. My little sister was in her room, doing whatever 15-year-old girls do on a wet weekend afternoon. I called out to her that I was going to grab Dad and headed up the hill in our sturdy white station wagon. With headlights and wipers on, crunching over the wet pebbles, I spotted something moving up ahead. It was Brydie, our Border Collie, running in small circles, clearly agitated. Although she was technically the family pet, she was completely devoted to Dad and accompanied him wherever he went around our cattle property. Why was she here, what was she so wound up about and where the hell was Dad? Then I spotted the still shape.

I slowed as I approached, foggily imagining that Dad might have just been worn out from the run uphill and had stopped for a quick siesta. Weird thing to do in the wet.

I pulled over, unclipped my seatbelt and opened the door, still half expecting him to stand up, stretch and show a bit of gratitude for the free ride I was offering back to the warm, dry house. No movement.

'Oi!' I shouted. No reaction.

I ran over, shook his shoulder and pulled my hands back, stung by how stiff and cold he was. I tried to lift him, but he was too heavy. *Fuck, fuck, fuck, fuck, fuck!*

Now properly panicking, I jumped back in the car, swerved around Dad's lifeless body and floored it to the neighbours' place, beeping the horn frantically as I hurtled down the concrete driveway to their farmhouse, screaming out of the window for them to call an ambulance. Jerry, our chain-smoking, ex-biker neighbour with the stiff leg from one too many accidents, followed me in his truck back to where Dad was lying while Meg, his wife, phoned for help. Jerry and Dad were mates who shared a dark sense of humour and a defiant approach to the effects of gravity on a hillside tractor, and I'd never seen either of them scared of anything. Jerry looked extremely worried as he instinctively rolled and licked a ciggie while he felt for Dad's pulse and paced around his body.

'Doesn't look good, mate,' he said, shaking his head and puffing nervously. 'Doesn't look good.'

We huddled in stunned, grim silence, perched on the edge of our driver's seats, the drizzle trickling down our bare legs, waiting for the hour or so it took for the ambulance to get organised and find us. The paramedics did some brief checks, spoke quietly to Jerry, then lifted Dad's body into the back of their vehicle and drove away.

'He's gone, buddy,' Jerry said, his brawny, tattooed arm over my skinny shoulders. He cleared his throat, sniffed a few times, pulled out his tobacco pouch and pivoted to face me, his oil-stained fingers once again working the sticky paper. 'Listen, you've got some tough jobs to do now. Is your mum home?'

I was paralysed. My vision was blurry.

'Breathe, mate. Is she home?'

I shook my head. 'She's at work,' I choked.

'Okay, you gotta go back to the house, phone her and tell her to come straight home. Is your sister there?'

I nodded.

'Well, you have to tell her too. Then call your grandparents and your aunts and uncles. They all need to know what's happened. I'll go home, get Meg and the girls and we'll come back with some food and stuff so you kids don't have to think about that.' He sniffed again, hoicked and spat into a tree fern, then stamped out his ciggie under a scuffed rubber flip-flop. 'This is some messed-up bullshit, that's for sure. I'm really sorry, Lach. You gotta be strong now, okay, bud?'

I nodded again.

'Get going then. Drive carefully. We'll be there soon.'

*

It would be wildly overstating things to say I became a man in that moment, but I definitely did a lot of growing up very quickly indeed. My sister, understandably, collapsed into hysterics and Ma broke off mid-sentence and dropped the phone when I eventually got hold of her and told her. I called my grandparents and asked them to pass the message on, so within a few hours our house was full of relatives and casseroles. The fire was kept crackling inside as the adults clumped around the dining room table, worn and worried hands clasped around countless cups of tea. Ma was almost catatonic for the first day or two but found the strength to rouse herself enough to decide on the casket, hymns and epitaphs and deal with the relentless phone calls.

Hundreds of people turned up to the funeral, far exceeding the capacity of the tiny church, so speakers had to be hastily erected outside for the unexpected crowd. The irony wasn't lost on many attendees, as they joked to each other gently about how hilarious Dad – the most cynical and non-practising of Catholics – would have found the whole scene. I blurted my way through the eulogy, my sister's fingernails digging fiercely into my hand as she stood trembling beside me. Later, after Dad's coffin was lowered into a hole in the damp red earth at the top corner of the local cemetery, we all traipsed over to the golf club for tea, beers, rum and sandwiches. I skulked on the first tee with my high-school buddies, knocking back vodka shots and muttering to them about how life was completely meaningless and we were all wasting our time doing anything. When someone shook out a packet of cigarettes, I took up smoking on the spot.

In the hazy, teary chaos of the days and weeks that followed, *things* still had to be *done*. Everyone said my sister and I needed to go back to school. I got my driver's licence and tried to be responsible when I had her or other passengers in the car, but I was prone to speeding and had increasingly intrusive thoughts of driving off the side of the cliff on the road we took every day to the town 70 kilometres away on the coast.

We also needed to sell the farm. That wouldn't be easy, as although it was an attractive property of historical significance, the land was too steep to be commercially viable for serious dairying or beef production. In any case, there was no way the three of us could run it without Dad, and while

I didn't know what my future had in store, I was pretty sure that it didn't involve being stuck in an isolated valley getting rained on for the rest of my life.

I had to consider my options. I was ambivalent about university and briefly considered applying to join the air force, but was laughed away at the interview stage when it became clear that I knew nothing about aeroplanes. That was lucky for all concerned, as I was definitely not cut out to be a military man. So, if I wasn't to be a farmer or a soldier and had no mechanical leanings that I could shape into a trade, it seemed I'd need to give university a go. When the time came, I took a scattergun approach to my submissions, applying for science, arts (not sure what the plan was there, given I'd studied nothing but maths, biology, physics, chemistry and English in my senior years), engineering and medicine in different states, and waited to see how the cards fell.

They fell in my favour. Despite my efforts towards self-sabotage through dark thoughts and drink, my final high-school exam scores placed me in the top fraction of a per cent in the state and I was fortunate enough to be able to select from my first-choice courses across the country. I still didn't know what to do, though, and – in retrospect – I was clinically depressed. I was experiencing suicidal thoughts on a daily basis, driving recklessly and intoxicating myself with blithe intent. At our last high-school party, when a couple of mates and I took a bottle of vodka down to the beach, I was single-mindedly committed to drinking myself to oblivion. Sure enough, I woke up the next morning in the back of a truck under a garden shower with sand in my mouth. I wasn't in a stable frame of mind.

Should I study physics – the only high-school subject that really interested me? What would I do with a degree in that? Or should I do something that led to a well-paid job like dentistry? One of Dad's friends was a dentist, and he had a nice house and his family stayed in hotels on their holidays, whereas we slept in tents on ours. But did I want to spend the rest of my days peering into and poking around in other people's mouths? Not if I could avoid it. Would I perhaps get my kicks studying history and languages? Then what?

In the end, more practical factors determined my fate. My mother would have walked through fire to help me on my way, but money was scarce, so when a medical school in Melbourne offered me a scholarship based on my grades, that effectively sealed the deal. Mentally, I shrugged and accepted that the universe had maybe given me the nudge I needed. I knew nothing whatsoever about medicine, apart from the snippets I'd picked up from Ma and her midwife friends over the years, and we didn't have any doctors in the family. But one thought did help motivate me to pack my two suitcases and say goodbye to Ma, my sister, our extended family, my friends and my high-school sweetheart. There was a burning inside me that I couldn't ignore.

Ever since Dad's death, I'd had the constant, aching pain of the thought that this wasn't right. Not just the scarcely bearable loss of a parent at that age, but the fact that Dad had been fit and strong and apparently healthy. Then he goes out running, has a massive heart attack – as the coroner eventually reported – and BANG! All over. No warning signs, no doctor, no hospital, no treatment, no recovery. His life ended in an instant and ours were changed irreparably, for ever. Piercing through the anguish, I felt outrage. This was Australia and the 1990s, for Christ's sake! In my furious teenage naïveté, I believed that something had to be terribly wrong with our country's health system if such tragedies could happen here, now. I put aside my plans for a blaze-of-glory car crash into a canyon and boarded the plane down to Melbourne by myself, determined to try and do something useful with my life that might help avoid this kind of shit happening to some other poor sod like me.

CHAPTER ONE

1973–81
Northern Territory, Australia

My origin story begins with Katherine. Not a person, but a place – the town in the Northern Territory where my parents met. My father, Ian, was a shaggy-haired, guitar-playing, race-car-driving teacher from the Victorian town of Ballarat, who'd just earned his pilot's licence and was the first 'flying teacher' for the Katherine School of the Air. Billed as 'The Largest Classroom in the World', this model of distance education enabled children living in remote locations to receive their lessons via radio, with their teachers getting flown in for visits a couple of times a year. It's still running now, having benefited from a few IT upgrades in the decades in between. Dad had desperately wanted to become an air force pilot but he failed the hearing test. He was a clever, adventurous, mischievous young man whose Plan B would have been to go to university if his parents could have afforded it, but they couldn't, so he went to teacher's college instead. His wanderlust, and his beloved burgundy second-hand panel van, took him up to the Top End* where, surprisingly, he met my mother.

It's not surprising that they met; it's surprising that she was there at all.

Ma was a pretty, demure country girl who'd led a relatively sheltered early life in the misty mountains of Far North Queensland. She adored

---

* The affectionate colloquialism for the northernmost, tropical part of the Northern Territory.

1

her family, but had no particular love for their daily life as dairy farmers. She had dreamed of being a home economics teacher, but her grades weren't good enough, so she followed in her mother's footsteps and trained as a nurse instead. She and a friend had followed a rather risqué path in circumnavigating half of Australia to do their midwifery training in Perth. Their journey included getting stranded for a fortnight in the middle of the Nullarbor Desert* when their car broke down. They had to wash dishes in a caravan park to pay for meals while they waited for the repairs, and they'd almost completed a lap of the continent by the time they arrived in Katherine. There Ma delivered babies – usually in the hospital but also often in Indigenous communities hundreds of kilometres away, requiring a packed lunch for the return trip in the bush ambulance – and had to scoop bits of people off the railway tracks every now and then when they'd tragically decided it was a comfortable and convenient place to sleep off a big night.

After meeting at a 'single's mingle' at the local bowling club, whatever initial enthusiasm Ma may have had for their first date was distinctly diminished when Dad announced he'd be coming to collect her in his 'hearse'. Their nascent relationship endured a night at the drive-in movies but foundered again soon after that, when on a subsequent outing Ma was forced to navigate for Dad on one of his airborne outreach visits to his students scattered on cattle properties around the vast region serviced by the School of the Air. Unaccustomed to light aircraft of any kind, let alone co-pilot duties, Ma's attempts to help Dad spot landing strips through the monsoonal fog were stymied by her vomiting onto the control panel every time the plane bumped through pregnant clouds and Dad banked to get another look down. The old man apparently had sufficient streaks

---

* Named – and famed – for its lack of trees, the Nullarbor also claims to be home to the longest stretch of straight road in our enormous, mostly empty country.

of charisma and/or persistence, though, as by Christmas that year they were engaged.

Far North Queensland, Australia

Ma took Dad home to meet her family. Both of Ma's parents had grown up in Millaa Millaa and each of their respective parents had been among the first generations of white settlers to the area. In the early twentieth century the government had gifted (or sold for a pittance) land to folks willing to fell the rainforest and build farms. The historical record is predictably lacking in what the traditional owners of the land – the Mamu people – thought about this, but it's safe to assume they were neither consulted nor compensated and almost certainly suffered as a consequence.*

My maternal grandparents each served in the Second World War – Grandad was a signaller who was almost killed and left partially deafened in an explosion in the Libyan desert; my grandmother, whom we all called 'Dede', was a hard-working and highly respected surgical nurse. Having survived their respective wartime experiences, they returned to their family's dairy farms before marrying and establishing their own. Neither had the opportunity to complete their schooling, but both were highly intelligent and over the decades became community leaders, historians, writers and award-winning gardeners.

It was armed with this deep local knowledge that my grandparents proudly showed their scruffy soon-to-be son-in-law around the district. Ma accompanied them contentedly, happy to see her fiancé's interest in her

---

* Over a century later, in 2013, the descendants of the Mamu people were recognised by a Federal Court Tribunal under the *Native Title Act* as the traditional owners of the land and granted 'exclusive rights to over seventy-five square kilometres'.

hometown and hopeful that she would be able to convince him to abandon his plan to return to Victoria and instead settle together in Millaa Millaa. Intentionally or otherwise, Grandad raised the stakes when he took them for a drive out of town, past the paddock by the creek where his childhood farm had been, then followed the dirt road winding up the hill. Down there in the valley, he pointed, hidden in the tropical overgrowth, was a little lost world.

The place had been a strange sort of commune in the first half of the twentieth century. It was once home to several hundred residents, mostly families with children who suffered from polio and other musculoskeletal disorders, who were treated by an eccentric Swedish chiropractor on a 'Come, stay, pay what you can and work off the rest' basis. Over the years that it was functional, the community sculpted the property into an elaborate homestead, with terraced gardens, orchards and undulating lawns. They were just normal, poor, hard-working families and it all seemed to run quite smoothly until the tax authorities found out about it and shut it all down. The terraces were then surrendered to the weeds, with the work of so many human hands disappearing into the bush. Enchanted, my parents offered to buy the property from the owner, a hoary old dairy farmer who was uncle to several of my mother's cousins, as well as her sister-in-law; it was that kind of town. He was happy to get it off his hands, as the country was too hilly for both his knees and his milkers.

My folks married at my grandparents' farm the following year. All of Millaa Millaa was invited and 57 chickens were beheaded, hung from the rafters, plucked and gobbled. Dad's not-quite-so-close family made the three-thousand-kilometre trek north for the occasion, as did a few of his unruly boozer teacher buddies. Dad turned up grinning in a maroon suit, Ma bit her bottom lip coquettishly in the single surviving photo, the priest ran off with one of the bridesmaids and thus my parents were hitched.

Ma took a part-time job delivering babies two nights a week. Dad reluctantly let his pilot's licence lapse, learned sign language and did extra training to specialise in working with children with disabilities. Over the next few years, they spent their weekends clearing the vines, bracken fern and prickly lantana, gradually uncovering the stone, concrete and terracotta treasures beneath. When they'd finally hacked away enough vegetation, they started building our house. It has always baffled me how Dad figured out how to do so many things. People generally seem to to me to have been far smarter in the pre-mind-melting internet era and evidently construction was one of the strings in Dad's bow, along with farming, auto repairs and the rest. He was laying bricks in the garage when I decided it was time to announce myself to the world and Ma went into labour. Dad asked her to hang on a bit, he just needed to finish this section of wall. 'That's fine,' Ma replied; she was monitoring her contractions and had a towel and a clamp for the umbilical cord at the ready, just in case. With the bricklaying complete, after the tortuous commute to the hospital and an otherwise uncomplicated labour, I was born. The paediatrician spanked me on the bum, inspected my sticky, squalling form and handed me over to my parents with the comment, 'He's a scrawny little bugger.' When I was presented to my grandparents, Dede – a huge-hearted but tough woman not known for her tenderness – had kinder words: 'I promise I will give him my time and the treasures of my mind.'

1981–98
Far North Queensland

My childhood was filled with farm work, adventure, family and fun. When we weren't helping Ma and Dad gardening, mending the fences, spraying the cattle or keeping the paddocks free of weeds, we were playing with our cousins, jumping off waterfalls, roaring around on the little red Honda 50cc motorbike Dad bought as a wreck and lovingly restored for us, camping by rivers or sleeping in our treehouse (officially named 'The Wolery', after Owl's house in the Winnie the Pooh stories). We got all but lost so many times on our expeditions in the rainforest that our parents taught us to tie string around trees to find our way home, and if all else failed to follow a creek downstream and we'd eventually reach the sea (fortunately it never quite came to that). Our property was pretty remote, even for rural Queensland. A cyclone struck in the days before I started pre-school, causing a landslide across our driveway, so to get me into town on my first day, Dad had to take me on the tractor up to the top gate where Grandad picked me up in his four-wheel drive.

When we lost power, we had to check the lines and phone the electricity company to report where the tree had fallen. Getting the phone fixed when those lines went down was trickier. When we lost water, we (usually I) had to walk from the little weir where our pump was, up the hill, through the scrub, with a torch, often in the rain, to find where the pipe had burst.

The farm butcher would come a couple of times a year to shoot, skin and slice up the pick of the steers. As soon as I was old enough to drive the tractor, I'd have to do the 'guts run'. This involved hauling the head, hooves and offal up to the far corner of the farm for the dingoes, stopping every now and then when a *thump-thump-thump* told me something had fallen off the carry-all and needed heaving back on again.

It wasn't all guts and gore. One morning as we crossed the creek on the way home from shifting the cattle, Dad scooped up a platypus in his hat and showed me the spurs on its hind legs that make it the world's most poisonous mammal.

Primary school was a bit of a shock to the system. It was in a town 50 kilometres away and, up until that point, I'd barely encountered children unrelated to me. I was a bright kid, but sometimes painfully shy. Ma had to bribe me with the gift of a microscope for me to pluck up the courage to do a talk in front of my class. I definitely stole the show one 'Show and Tell' day when I brought in a live echidna we'd found poking around our cattle yards. I was most interested in science – astronomy and palaeontology, in particular. A couple of my primary-school pals shared my passions, so we made nuisances of ourselves digging for dinosaur bones on our farm and in the school playground – whenever we had the opportunity and a trowel or two.

So, I was a bit of a nerd. That was fine, as I mostly enjoyed school, had a nice bunch of friends and was moderately capable at sports. I was taught piano by the Sisters of Mercy, which would obviously be a great name for a metal band* but by which I mean the nuns at the adjacent convent. Most of my teachers seemed to like me and a few (to whom I'll always be grateful) went out of their way to encourage me and keep me from getting bored. I got in trouble from time to time for fighting boys and kissing girls, and Ma was appalled at her darling boy's misbehaviour, but when Dad took responsibility for telling me off, I got the feeling his heart wasn't really in it. He was clearly a progressive thinker, certainly for his time, and his career was founded on a deep vein of compassion, particularly for children (although his tolerance for other adults was a different story). But he was – outwardly, at least – a strong, gruff, manly man, and I suspect that despite his liberal inclinations he still held some fairly old-school views on masculinity. I think my occasional displays of, shall we say, red-blooded behaviour, were therefore significant for Dad, because I must have been a disappointment to him in some other key respects. We shared a couple of

---

* I got curious after writing that, so I checked to see if it was taken. It is indeed the name of a British rock group. Good for them.

hobbies – playing guitar and water-skiing – but I showed very little interest in his other activities and shared nothing of his aptitude for mechanics. I barely disguised my lack of enthusiasm for spending my weekends and school holidays hauling timber, digging drains or pouring concrete, and I became increasingly gun-shy about the tractor driving I was expected to do on our property's vertiginous slopes after several near-death experiences. I preferred reading – chunky fantasy novels and physics textbooks, mostly – and anything with two wheels.

My first paid job was on a neighbouring relative's farm. I'd ride Dad's motorbike over and back – I was 13 by this stage so had graduated to the Honda 250cc, although it was a struggle to lift it when it fell on me. I'd putter through the paddocks and creeks, arriving mud-splattered on a Friday after school and spending that evening and the following morning getting pissed and shat on by the entire herd. I'd squelch bovine fluids into my gumboots down in the pit of the herringbone dairy, beneath the rows of ready-to-fire tails, labelling the milk samples he handed me as he yelled out their numbers, recognising each cow by the patterns on their backside. For this I was grateful to receive 20 dollars a month. I sent a typed letter enclosing my first month's salary as a deposit to the startled owner of the local bike shop (who told Dad he thought he'd received a summons from a solicitor) and carefully saved for another 11 months until I could afford a new 10-speed mountain bike.

My junior high-school years passed by without major incident. I played cricket and guitar, had braces on my teeth briefly like most of my friends, shoplifted a few magazines, learned important lessons about young love and heartbreak and, most importantly, discovered punk music. My mate Marco and I started a garage band and I've been slowly descending into deafness ever since.

Things started to get more interesting in my senior years. I was showing enough promise that some teachers were recommending extra coursework to keep me out of mischief and new opportunities were starting to appear, but I still had little idea of what I wanted to do with my life. I don't recall asking my parents for career advice, nor do I remember them offering it, except once. At the awards night towards the end of my penultimate year of high school, when I was 16, I'd managed to snap up most of the academic prizes on offer, having thankfully escaped the art and religion classes that were mandatory in our junior years. I was terrible at both subjects – the former for lack of ability and the latter for lack of belief. As we were driving home, I was wondering out loud about whether to apply for university the next year and, if so, what the hell I should do there. In a brief and rare moment of open encouragement, Dad looked over at me thoughtfully from the driver's seat and said, 'It's up to you, but for what it's worth, I think you'd be a pretty good doctor.'

I pondered that for a few moments, frowning out of the window. I wasn't convinced – about uni in general nor medicine specifically – but added it to the shortlist anyway.

Around that time, someone pointed out an intriguing line in the school's monthly newsletter and I applied to the programme it mentioned: the National Youth Science Forum. I was selected and spent a few weeks of the school holidays before my final senior year down in Canberra with a couple of hundred other horny young nerds from around the country. While there I somehow distinguished myself sufficiently that the following year I was invited to join the small group of staff. As part of that honour, along with five others, I was packed off to Russia as guests of *Soyuz* – the All-Russian Youth Aerospace Society. We got daytime drunk on vodka shots with our Russian hosts, hung out with former cosmonauts – still lionised by the Russian public – and donned our formal blazers to visit Mission Control in Moscow.

It was an incredible privilege, the radicalness of which was almost too much for my young brain to wrap itself around. It made the local newspapers back home. My high school was very supportive and surprisingly relaxed about rescheduling my end-of-year exams, and dozens of members of Millaa Millaa's little dairy-farming community passed the hat around to raise money for me to go. A ten-dollar bill in an envelope here, a mud-smeared cheque for twenty bucks there – all together, my family, friends and friends of friends crowd-sourced several thousand dollars to send me to the other side of the world, and I knew I was bloody lucky to be there.

It was wet and wintry when I returned from Russia, laden with stories and souvenirs. Ma reckons Dad kept on the Cossack hat I gave him for two whole days while he repaired my already-damaged chess set and I slept off my jetlag. They patiently listened to my ravings about snow-covered mountains, fairy-tale churches, mausoleums of dead Soviet leaders and the finer points of black bread and borscht. The following drizzly weekend, Ma went off for her two nights of work, and Dad took me to the lake to get my boat licence. I passed, and I knew he was pleased, particularly as that meant I could now drive while he was skiing.

Later that afternoon he went out for his run and never came back.

CHAPTER TWO

1999–2005
Melbourne, Australia

Having arrived in Melbourne with my two suitcases, I spent the first two years of medical school living in a little dorm room on campus. The residence was mostly full of other country kids, but they all seemed more worldly than me. They were certainly experienced drinkers. The engineering and medical students partied hardest. There were large-scale, organised piss-ups at least twice a week, and – as a guy at least – you were labelled a 'soft cunt' if you didn't turn up and get blind drunk. Soft I was not, so blind drunk I regularly got. I had very little interest in what was being taught in the lecture theatres and anatomy lab. If I turned up at all, it was in a hoodie and baseball cap, sitting up the back with my buddies, hungover and being generally obnoxious, frequently skipping classes to get stoned in the car park, play hacky-sack and scoff Subway. In my third year of uni I moved off campus and into a series of chaotic share houses, as I gradually developed my own extra-curricular interests. Friday nights were for bourbon and punk shows; Saturdays for ecstasy and techno. I dyed my hair blond and black and blue and pierced my ears and eyebrow and nipple. I drove the getaway car when we heisted some marijuana plants from a biker clubhouse, got several fines for drunken vandalism and spent a night in prison for 'Creating a public nuisance' after a champagne-fuelled rampage at the horse races. I mercifully managed to avoid any formal criminal charges, which could have torpedoed my career long before it began, but

I was blearily treading a very fine line between mediocre medical student and mild societal menace.

I did just enough studying to keep my grades where they needed to be to retain my scholarship, but found no appeal in physiology, cell biology, biochemistry or histopathology. A couple of subjects briefly interested me, and I got top marks for human evolution and an elective semester of sign language, but they did little to lift my overall grades. I was far more motivated by adventure, so I was constantly on the lookout for opportunities to escape from Melbourne's dreary weather and our endless, monotonous lectures. Towards the end of my first year of medical school, when I was 18, I heard about a bursary that covered travel and accommodation costs for med students to spend a couple of weeks of their annual vacation doing rural placements, I leapt at the chance.

Kimberley region, Western Australia

My application was accepted and I was assigned a genteel tourist town on the coast of South Australia. I politely declined. I knew enough to know that the top of Australia was where adventure lay. I phoned around and finally got permission to spend a few weeks in Halls Creek, a little desert town with a majority Indigenous population in the eastern part of the Kimberley – a vast region in the north of Western Australia, about the size of California. It took me three days to get there, but it was a liberating experience – ditching the fruit-picking gigs that usually occupied my summer breaks back home to fly up and across the continent into the tropics, where the turquoise, crocodile- and jellyfish-infested waters of the Indian Ocean caressed the golden shores. I stopped over in Broome – the largest town in the Kimberley and home to the region's main airport and some of its most spectacular beaches – long enough to get a taste for Emu Bitter, then took the overnight bus to Halls Creek.

I spent the first night in a caravan. The following day, as I was breast-stroking lazily around the caravan park's tiny swimming pool like a sunburnt frog in a salty soup, I met Digby. He was one of the three doctors in the town and was enjoying a round of Emu beers with a few of the hospital crew in the bar of the caravan park. It was a safer place to drink, they explained. The pub could get pretty rowdy on a Sunday afternoon. That was why it had a metal cage to separate the customers – by which, I realised, they meant the Indigenous patrons – from the staff. It wasn't as rough as the pub down the road though, they assured me. That place, a mere three hundred kilometres away, not only had a cage bar but was also rumoured to be frequented by a large pig, which slurped up beer from a bowl and was prone to getting quite pissed. (I later went to check it out for myself to find it all exactly as described.)

When he heard I was shacked up in a caravan, Digby, either out of hospitality, pity, or a bit of both, offered me the spare room in the house the hospital provided for him. I gratefully accepted. We dined on steak and chips, then he drove me and my backpack to his house. We were kicking back on the couch, Digby – to my astonishment – about to spark up a home-made bong, when the phone rang.

Digby answered, nodded, grunted and then shook his head in protest down the phone. 'But I'm not on call! Walter's working tonight, isn't he?'

I could hear the caller's tinny voice from where I was relaxing, absent-mindedly, cracking open a cold Emu from Digby's fridge. My attention snapped back as I heard Digby's reply.

'Shit, okay, well, if Walter's in that bad a shape, I'll have to come in,

13

I guess.' Digby glanced over at me. 'I'm bringing reinforcements,' he said, as he clunked the phone back on the hook. 'Duty calls,' he announced. 'Not ideal timing, I know, but I gotta go. You coming?'

I stumbled behind Digby out to the Land Cruiser for the two-minute drive up to the hospital.

'Axe to the head,' he muttered, rubbing his chin as he revved around the corners of the empty streets. 'This could be interesting.'

I blinked at him silently, uncomprehending.

The sounds of screeching in the little Emergency Department hurt my ears. A blood-spattered couple were bellowing at each other, in a mixture of English and what I later learned was Kija, as two policemen grappled to keep them apart. Digby directed the lady and her police escort into a side room and shepherded the male patient into the resuscitation bay, the man clutching at the side of his head. As I looked over Digby's shoulder, he gently took the patient's hand away. I nearly fainted. The guy's ear was upside down, dangling beside his neck, attached only by the lobe. There was a bloody hole where the ear was supposed to be. His wife, it transpired, had threatened to chop his head off if he didn't quit drinking. In a way then, you could say, he was lucky.

I watched in awe as Digby got to work. He briskly swathed the patient's head in bandages and over the course of several phone calls summoned a dishevelled second doctor and a couple of sleepy nurses, who transformed the single operating theatre into a hot little hive of activity.

'You're assisting,' Digby said, as he waved me into the change room.

I'd never set foot in an operating theatre before. I tried to follow his lead as he swiftly donned a set of blue scrubs, strapped on a theatre cap and marched out to the big sink to lather up to the elbows in iodine soap. I failed several attempts before finally getting the spin right to get tied into my sterile gown, then suddenly I was across the operating table from

Digby, staring down at the now-unconscious patient's draped, gaping head wound.

Digby looked around, surgical instruments aloft.

'Everybody ready?'

'Yep,' came the chorus.

Digby looked the part. It was an impressive transformation for a guy who'd been sprawled across his stained, tattered couch, chopping weed and listening to Tool blasting from a boom-box about half an hour earlier.

It was delicate work. I sweated into my gown as I cleaned off the caked blood and lifted bits of severed ear and scalp tissue with my forceps for Digby to stitch together, then snipped the ends of the thread and started again. Over and over and over. The ear was at least facing the right way up now, but I wasn't feeling good. It was stiflingly humid in the unventilated operating theatre and the heat and smell of blood weren't sitting too well with the beers from earlier that evening. I wobbled. Digby glanced up.

'Jeez, dude, you don't look too good. Need to step outside?'

I nodded and lunged for the doors, tearing off my mask, gown and gloves as I exited. With my head between my legs on the front steps of the hospital, I sucked in the warm night air. This was pretty full-on. But as my blood pressure came up and some circulation returned to my brain, my nausea subsided and I gazed up at the dazzling spectacle of the desert's night sky. An unfamiliar feeling stirred deep in my being. This was certainly a side of doctoring I'd never seen before. This was extreme medicine.

Our patient survived this initial salvage operation and he was flown three thousand kilometres south to the state capital of Perth for the subsequent rounds of specialised surgery he'd need to try and achieve the best possible cosmetic result and minimise hearing loss. I had a new-found respect for Digby and was surprised at my own enthusiasm when it came to tagging along on the ward rounds of the little hospital and seeing patients in the Emergency Department and outpatient clinic.

I was invited to spend a few days at Yura Yungi, the Community Controlled Health Service, where the husband-and-wife general practitioner (GP) team worked alongside health workers* to care for their patients. I was fascinated to see that this often involved a mix of medicine, social work and three-way translation. Over the sixty-five thousand years that Aboriginal peoples have inhabited the Kimberley region, more than fifty distinct language groups had emerged.

Over those two weeks, and on my annual return trips to Halls Creek, I learned an awful lot. I had my first genuine interactions with Indigenous Australians, both at the hospital and through home visits and outreach clinics in the various communities around the region. Each experience was deeply revealing. I was shocked at the conditions in which many people were living. I couldn't understand how such profound and widespread poverty could exist in a country as wealthy as Australia. The health workers did their best to explain to me the concept of 'connection to Country' – the fundamental reason that so many local people would never contemplate leaving the land to which they are tied. And the doctors and nurses I accompanied in their clinics and on their community visits pointed

---

* Health workers from Indigenous communities are a vital part of the health workforce in Australia, particularly in rural and remote areas, where they typically represent the first and most important point of contact for Indigenous people engaging with the health system. In mainland Australia, these professionals are often referred to as 'Aboriginal health workers'. In the Torres Strait, the same role is performed by Torres Strait Islander people. In this book, the term 'health worker' is used without specifying the ethnic or cultural origin of every individual. This term is also used to refer to the essential and roughly equivalent role carried out by community health workers in countries other than Australia.

out to me the links between many of the common health problems experienced by our patients, such as respiratory infections, diarrhoeal diseases and skin sores, and the dust and smoke they breathed, the kitchens where they cooked, the bathroom facilities they used and the mats on which they slept.

Some of the larger remote communities had a store, but when I wandered in to find some lunch one day, I was staggered at the price of food. The fruit and vegetables section included a bunch of brown bananas, three limp carrots, a bag of sprouting potatoes and four individually plastic-wrapped apples being sold for two dollars a pop. Next to that was a warmer with four quarters of roast chicken, some suspicious-looking crumbed sausages and several cups of hot chips.

As I strolled out, munching from my Styrofoam box of overpriced chicken and chips, Irene, the health worker waiting for me, shook her head and snorted.

'Healthy choice, hey, doc?'

'I'm not a doctor, you can just call me Lachie,' I reminded her. 'But yeah, I copped out in there I guess. Thought I might find a salad sandwich or something but the fresh stuff looked terrible and the fat and salt was too tempting!' I smiled at her, expecting her to share my little joke, but got another sad shake of the head instead.

'There's never any decent fresh food in the shop that most of the community here can afford. Shop owners reckon it's too expensive for them to transport up here and store properly. So guess what? People end up eating junk food 'cos they've got no other choice. And you fellas wonder why we're all getting type 2 diabetes!'

Melbourne

By the time I'd reached my third year of med school, back in Melbourne, we were required to spend chunks of time in the hospitals. This first taste of city hospital doctoring did not remotely inspire me. I found it extremely dispiriting. The tertiary-level hospitals where we were deployed were gigantic, soulless complexes full of doleful patients and harried health workers. As junior medical students we barely registered on anyone's radar and our main role appeared to be getting in everyone else's way. We were thrust upon patients to practise our history-taking and examination skills, which the kindlier of them tolerated, while the less beneficent told us to bugger off. We were condescended to by most of the staff, with the occasional welcome exception of a helpful nurse or one of the less cynical consultants. Many of the registrars – the early-career doctors training in the various specialties – clearly resented having to shepherd us around and teach us whatever was the topic *du jour*. Some others, whom I found far more frightening, appeared to regret their life choices. One poor bastard, a surgical registrar whose face and words I'll never forget, concluded his summary of the main causes of rectal bleeding with a heavy pause, a sigh, and a weary sign-off, 'Yeah, so, that's pretty much it, guys. That can be your whole career, if you want. Or, you know, there's still time to get out now.' With that, he hoisted his leather satchel and walked slowly into the elevator, head bowed, the doors closing as he disappeared into the bowels of the hospital once again.

I couldn't understand how so many of my fellow medical students already had their minds firmly made up when it came to their choice of specialty. Some had been determined to become cardiologists or orthopaedic surgeons from Day One. Others, including my drinking buddies, who'd seemed apathetic like me in the beginning, began earnestly discussing the various sub-specialty options within gastroenterology and the best places to train in trauma surgery and intensive care medicine.

The only thing by that stage that I could say I'd enjoyed at all in medical school were my experiences in Halls Creek, but that was a world away from Melbourne. The experiences I'd built up in those brief stints over the first three years had gradually caught the attention of some of my more industrious classmates, and I was invited to give, and subsequently organise, an annual lecture on Indigenous health at our university. I felt horribly underqualified but nevertheless sensed a strong responsibility to make sure the event was as interesting, informative and well attended as possible, and I ended up helping run the university rural health club for a couple of years after that.

Despite those flickers of interest, by the time I reached my fourth year of med school, I was having a major crisis of faith. On the golf course one afternoon, skipping lectures, I announced to my best mate, Harry, that I was going to take a break from uni. He narrowed his eyes at me for a moment, then shuffled into position and thwacked his ball down the fairway. After I'd taken a detour to hack my ball out of the rough, as I joined him on the green, he called out from where he was lining up his putt.

'So, what are you going to do then?'

I let him tap his ball in before replying. 'I'm thinking I'll probably hit the road. I've been giving extra piano lessons and maths tutoring to save up some cash. Might try and get a loan somehow, if I can convince a bank to give me one. I need to take a break, man. There's a whole fucking world out there and there's a bunch of other stuff I'd like to do. And to be honest, I'm just not sure medicine's the right thing for me.'

As we walked over to the next tee, he spat out his chewing gum. 'Like what other stuff?'

I glanced over at him as we pulled out our drivers. He wasn't a big talker, Harry, and I hadn't expected quite this level of interest.

'Well, I want to learn to scuba dive, for a start. And go hiking in the Himalaya, ride a motorbike around India, hit the Love Parade in Berlin, maybe take Spanish classes, spend a few months in Central America. That sort of shit. Live a little. Forget about medicine. Figure out what the fuck I want to do with my life.'

Harry smacked his ball straight and long and mine dribbled off the tee. We finished our round in companionable silence, then relaxed in the clubhouse with a couple of cold beers. Harry took a slurp, wiped the foam off his upper lip and announced, 'That sounds fun, mate. I'm in.'

Cheeky fucker hadn't been invited, exactly, but I was happy to hear it. We celebrated with a curry and started making plans.

Asia–Africa–Europe–Latin America

We packed our backpacks and took off for a year. The bank was surprisingly forthcoming with a loan, which was clearly premised on me finishing med school and paying them back on a doctor's salary, although I chose to ignore the small print for the time being. I kicked things off with a couple of months hiking and volunteering with a small aid organisation in Nepal, then met up with Harry in Bangkok. We did the full-moon party circuit in Thailand and a camel safari in Rajasthan. We were extras in a Bollywood movie in Mumbai – completely failing to recognise the Indian megastars with whom we were sharing scenes as we sweated last night's booze and hash through our ill-fitting suits – and rode motorcycles between the acid raves around Goa. We sailed on a felucca down the Nile, ran with the bulls in Pamplona, attempted to open a hostel in Dubrovnik, hiked the Inca Trail in Peru and studied Spanish in Guatemala. Harry and I eventually

peeled off on separate adventures, but we both ended up training as PADI*
Divemasters – a useful backup career, I thought, as I whiled away pleasant
weeks getting paid just enough for food and lodging by leading small groups
around the reefs off the Caribbean coast of Honduras and Nicaragua.

I also figured this was the one time in my life where I could be completely
irresponsible, so I did a bunch of adrenaline-junkie, safety-defying fun
stuff (backflipping off waterfalls in subterranean caves and such) and got
as fucked up as possible pretty much everywhere I went. I smoked opium
out of a human skull in a mountain village in Laos, escaped a flash flood in
the Mexican jungle while tripping on magic mushrooms and did so much
cocaine in Costa Rica that I woke up one morning and didn't know where
I was or how I got there, so I ditched my travel buddies, skipped the border
to Panama and locked myself in a cheap hotel room with air-conditioning,
a TV, a carton of beers and some sandwiches until I got my head together
and the coke, at least, cleared out of my system. I was so broke by the end of
it, I had to borrow money from the Israeli girls I was travelling with to catch
a bus to the airport to fly home. After a year on the road, I still couldn't
roll a decent joint, but I did at least take back to Australia the realisation that
I needed some purpose in life. I spent a repentant summer picking limes
and reluctantly returned to medical school to finish what I'd started.

Australia

With a renewed sense of purpose came a slightly higher level of motivation
for my studies than I'd had prior to my sabbatical. It was mostly a case of
'too little, too late' when it came to improving my grades, but I'd been out

---

* PADI stands for Professional Association of Dive Instructors. It's the largest scuba-
   diving/training organisation in the world.

and seen a bit of the world and had come back with a broader perspective of what was important. I'd experienced a reawakening of my childhood love of the outdoors, which led me to pay more attention to the environment and what was happening around me, including in politics. Some friends I'd kept in touch with from the National Youth Science Forum suggested I apply to join the Prime Minister's Youth Roundtable. I did so, suited up, was selected and ended up being the spokesperson for the environment working group, presenting the outcomes of our year-long deliberations to Prime Minister John Howard at the programme's final dinner in Canberra. It was, of course, a completely tokenistic exercise on the part of the politicians, but the futility of it wasn't evident to me so couldn't depress me at the time. I was getting more interested in the fields of governance and decision-making, even wondering if I should take my medical career in the direction of health policy or administration. I bored myself quickly on the brief occasions when I thought about it out loud, but it nevertheless held some sort of strange, big-picture appeal.

I spent as much as possible of my final year of uni out of Melbourne, racking up the rural placements in the hope of finding something that seemed like a career. My attendance peaked during a six-week stint doing an elective rotation in tropical medicine up in Darwin, the capital of the Northern Territory. The consultants I trailed around the hospital were as preposterously clever as ever, while I was true to my hitherto indifferent form as a medical student, but their work with infectious diseases and the care they provided for Indigenous patients fanned my previous flickers of interest into a tiny flame.

During our final few months of med school, with our main exams safely out of the way, our class coordinators rattled through the last few topics on their list of things to teach. Those topics included global health and general practice. For the former, a spiky-grey-haired guy with rolled-up shirtsleeves was introduced to us as having worked for 'MSF' – the abbreviation for Médecins Sans Frontières, or Doctors Without Borders. He peppered us with questions about what we knew about the causes of and mortality from the First and Second Congo Wars. None of us had a clue what he was on about, and I squirmed in my seat, ashamed of my worldly, political pretensions, as he wearily recited devastating statistics about the millions of deaths from the worst humanitarian catastrophe since the Second World War. What he was describing seemed so different from the glimpses I'd seen of what doctors usually do. I was fascinated. Médecins Sans Frontières even the name rang with adventure.

During my general practice rotation, I sat silently and obediently in the corner of the consulting rooms of the private clinics in which I was placed around Melbourne, watching the clock and wishing I was in the pub, or at least seeing more interesting stuff like I had in Halls Creek. Then, in our last week of GP lectures, as most of us were already picturing ourselves drunk on a beach somewhere in a post-graduation haze, up popped an overweight, bushy-bearded, excitable professor called Ray. Ray was a real old-school rural doctor, who could do a bit of everything. Having a heart attack in the middle of nowhere? He was your man. Need an emergency appendicectomy, your diabetes treated or your skin cancers cut out? No sweat. He could do it all, and probably all at once, while driving a tractor and shearing a sheep. He was the kind of jack-of-all-trades doctor that was common not so long ago in countries like Australia but was by this stage at risk of extinction. Ray showed us photos from his years working in Papua New Guinea as a district hospital doctor, doing everything from delivering babies to taking out spleens, hammering nails into broken bones, walking for days to do clinics in remote mountain villages and occasionally having to hide with his family when hostilities between warring tribal groups got out of hand.

This was nothing like the suburban general practices I'd been witnessing over the previous weeks. Of course, that was important – every patient and all of their problems had to be treated with respect and care – but the type of doctoring Ray was describing was some kind of punk-rock cross between Halls Creek and the Congo Wars.

When the time for questions came at the end of his lecture, I did something I'd rarely done in six years of medical school: I raised my hand.

'How did you get into doing that kind of thing?' I asked. 'Does it involve some sort of specialty training?'

Ray gave a mischievous smile. 'It's not about specialty training, young man, it's a question of one's appetite for adventure. There are certain types of foreigners one finds working in wild places like PNG. Some of them have hearts as big as oxen, but others aren't so admirable. There's an expression you might have heard,' he said, pausing, with a smirk and a sly twinkle in his eye. 'They say we're mercenaries, missionaries, martyrs or madmen, and often a combination thereof!'

That was it. I was hooked. I was 24, about to finish medical school and I'd finally seen the light, or at least some dim, distant glimmer of it. Whatever Ray's job was, that was what I wanted to do. I wasn't so sure about that expression of his, though. Was he joking? Mercenaries and missionaries? Fuck those two for a start. Money didn't motivate me – only slippery pricks got rich in such interesting places anyway – and I'd long ago forsaken organised religion, much to my darling mother's dismay.

Martyrdom and/or madness it was to be for me, then.

CHAPTER THREE

2006–7
Perth, Western Australia

Flushed at long last out of med school, I loaded up my Honda Civic and headed west. I was finally escaping the spirit-crushing drudgery of my student experiences and was kicking off my career as an intern in Perth – the sunniest state capital in Australia. I rolled out of Melbourne, leaving my friends and the worst of my sins behind, as Ma joined me on a week-long road trip, following the same route she'd taken some thirty years earlier across the Nullarbor. I was dimly aware that I hadn't paid sufficient attention to my studies over the previous years to be of much use as a junior doctor, but they'd let me graduate, so I could only assume that must have meant I was ready enough.

I was fortunate to have relatively relaxed and amiable registrars for my first two rotations in general medicine and surgery. They seemed willing to overlook the many gaps in my knowledge for the fact that I was polite to them, compassionate with our patients, respectful to the nurses and able to learn on the job. The role of an intern isn't intellectually stimulating; one's main responsibilities are administrative, ensuring that patients get the tests and treatments that the bosses order and keeping track of each patient's progress, results and plans. I was rarely able to make sense of the consultants' discussions and diagnostic decisions, but (mainly thanks to Ma) I did at least know how to be organised. I was also pleasantly surprised – and greatly relieved – to find I quite liked being a doctor after all, even the lowly shit-kicker kind. That discovery inspired a reasonably solid work ethic that enabled me to figure most things out on the fly and get through my first few months unscathed.

The realities of the job proved harsh at times, such as when a lovely elderly gentleman we'd been caring for over several weeks as his hip fracture and subsequent surgical repair led to a blood clot and hospital-acquired pneumonia suddenly – at least it seemed to me – died one afternoon. He was a cheerful, avuncular fellow of whom I'd grown quite fond, and I'd often linger to chat with him when I'd pop by to update his medication chart or replace his intravenous (IV) cannula. One of the many quotidian responsibilities of interns is 'certifying' deaths – a rather macabre procedure whereby one must examine a patient, who is typically very clearly dead, going through the motions of feeling for a pulse and listening with a stethoscope for breath sounds for several minutes, in order to then be able to write a solemn final entry in the patient's record and complete the official death certificate in triplicate. This painful piece of theatre is often done in the presence of family members, and the weight of hope that inevitably hangs in the air until the final pronouncement is made is difficult for all involved to bear. I will for ever remember this gentleman as only the second person I'd ever seen both alive and dead.

I also had my first encounters with individuals on the brink between both worlds. There were few things more terrifying to me as an intern than to be carrying the Medical Emergency Team (MET) pager – which one intern on each ward was required to have at all times – and have it buzz shrilly into life on my belt. This meant I had to drop whatever I was doing and hustle to the bed number displayed on the little screen, trying to walk fast enough to show serious intent but slow enough that someone more senior would beat me to the bedside. Being the first doctor on the scene of a resus is a daunting prospect, as it usually means that a nurse is giving cardiopulmonary resuscitation (CPR) while another wheels in the crash cart (a trolley loaded with the emergency drugs, airway gear, ventilator and defibrillator) and it's expected that the doctor(s) present will have a clear idea of what to do next. As an intern, the only procedure I could capably perform was inserting IVs, so I usually tried to busy myself fiddling with that while fervently hoping that the medical, anaesthetic or intensive care unit (ICU) registrar would turn up sharpish and sort things out. Some patients survived such resuses – the slim chances of you making it back from a cardiorespiratory arrest are slightly better if it happens while you're in hospital. Many others didn't make it.

Becoming accustomed to death on a near-daily basis was a strange cognitive shift and emotional recalibration for me. Subconsciously, by necessity, I started to separate the psychological trauma of what I was dealing with at work from what I allowed myself to think about and focus on after hours. I wasn't interrogating my mental processing methods with a great deal of rigour, but, as a more deeply instinctive means of self-protection, I was accepting that I couldn't afford to ruminate on all the pain, suffering, death and loss I was seeing every day, or I'd never be able to get out of bed. I can only assume that most health professionals are forced to do this to some degree, although we each have our own means of coping and carrying on. I was slowly getting the hang of being a doctor, but I hadn't entirely cleaned up my act.

*

I made it to the halfway point of my intern year and had finally found a rotation I genuinely enjoyed – the Emergency Department (ED). After being borderline broke all the way through medical school, it was also nice to be finally getting paid to hang out at the hospital all day. I'd splashed out on a motorbike, which I'd ride up the coast to my weekend skydiving course, and the novelty of having a fortnightly pay cheque was definitely to blame for the lemony tequila I could taste in the back of my mouth one fine morning as I shuffled sheepishly in to start my shift.

Unless you're hooked up to an IV line full of strong drugs and salty fluids, the ED is a terrible place to have a hangover. *You can get through this*, I told myself, trying to find some inner steel as I cursed whichever bacchanalian bartender invented the margarita. *Just keep your head down, pick up the not-so-sick patients, steer clear of any serious emergencies and try not to breathe in anyone's face.*

'McIver, get over here!' called Harvey, one of the ED consultants, as soon as he spotted me. Shit. So much for keeping a low profile. I made my way over to where the boss was beckoning, trying to look sprightly as the bile rose in my throat. What on Earth was that smell? *No, no, please God*, I prayed, willing to reconvert to Catholicism in an instant if I could only be spared this punishment, *please don't let it be my first patient* . . .

'Here's your first patient,' Harvey said, dropping the notes in my hands as he walked away briskly, exhaling with obvious relief as he left. I turned slowly towards the lady in the bed beside me.

I glanced at the name on the patient's file.

'Hi Susie, I'm Lachie,' I said with an outstretched hand.

The middle-aged, emaciated woman in the bed remained silent and still, her eyes half closed as she lay flat on her back. I squeezed her hand. It was cold and bony. No response. Liz, one of the senior ED nurses, arrived at the bedside with a box of rubber gloves.

'Morning Lachie, lucky you. I see you've met Susie. She's been responding to voice and touch and breathing on her own, but she's only said a few words and I don't think she's really aware of what's going on.'

I stifled a burp and put on a mask – better for everyone that way.

'What's the story, Liz? Do we know who brought Susie in or why she's here?'

'All I heard was that someone at her address phoned 000 to say she was unconscious. The ambulance officers found her sitting in an armchair in a pool of her own urine and faeces. There were a couple of guys in the apartment, but they disappeared when the ambulance arrived. Awful situation, apparently.'

I took a pair of gloves from the box that Liz had brought.

'Take two,' she said quietly.

'Why?' I looked up at her, puzzled.

'You'll see in a second.'

We drew the curtains and I gently explained to a still-mute Susie that we were going to examine her as carefully as we could. I fumbled with the gloves as Liz peeled back the sheet. The smell that wafted up through my flimsy mask as she did so made my eyes water. Christ almighty! I was about to sprint off to find some nausea tablets or a sink to throw up in when my brain made sense of what my eyes were seeing. Maggots. Hundreds of them. A squirming carpet of tiny grey larvae swarming around Susie's waist and disappearing under her pants. Or, no, wait, were they coming out from under there? My knees buckled slightly.

'Lachie, you okay?' Liz asked.

I mumbled back at her, transfixed. Liz tapped me on the arm with some scissors.

'You cut, I'll pull.'

I snipped at Susie's clothes and Liz put the filthy, stained pieces of fabric in a hazardous material bag on the floor. A bowl of warm, soapy water had been brought over, to which we added a bottle of antiseptic. We carefully scraped away the maggots and washed Susie's skin as we went. The heaving mass got thicker as we approached her pubic region. I was beyond nauseated and had reached some kind of transcendental state, where my hands were working, my mind wisely kept its thoughts to itself and the rest of my body was on autopilot. We were now needing both hands to scoop up the maggots, flicking them into the biohazard bag and checking to make sure none had wriggled down inside our gloves. Liz and I exchanged worried looks.

'They're coming from inside, aren't they?' I murmured.

She nodded tightly. 'Yep.'

'So, I guess we need to do an internal exam.'

'Yep. You do.'

I tracked down Harvey to explain what we'd discovered and to get his advice on how to proceed. He was tied up with a trauma case and waved at me to get on with it. Back at Susie's bedside, I inserted an IV line and started some fluids, as she was clearly badly dehydrated. While Liz drew up some morphine, I contemplated what needed to happen next. I took a deep breath and knelt down beside the bed.

'Susie, I'm not sure if you can hear me or not, but we're trying to get you clean and warm and comfortable as quickly as possible. We have to examine you down below though now, okay? Liz is with me, she's a very experienced nurse, and she'll be helping both of us.'

Liz and I switched places as she clasped Susie's hand and talked her through what was happening. I wheeled a stool over and prepared the instrument tray. This particular gynaecological problem was uncharted territory, at least for me, so my priorities were to make the procedure simple, painless and quick. Susie, who'd barely reacted up to this point, groaned softly as I slowly inserted a speculum into her vagina and more maggots poured out in a sticky river of fluid and pus. As gently as I could, I cleaned and rinsed until all the bugs were gone. We dried Susie, dressed her in a fresh hospital gown and gave her some warm blankets and IV antibiotics.

As Liz and I cleaned ourselves up, emptying another bottle of antiseptic as we scrubbed our arms raw up to the elbows, the lab called with Susie's blood test results. She was HIV positive. She'd never been seen in our hospital before and it seemed there was no record of her having this diagnosis in the past. I read the report from the ambulance officers who'd brought Susie in. It mentioned that the bottom-floor apartment in the poorer part of town where she was found had been littered with empty liquor bottles and used syringes. With no one offering any supporting information, we could only assume that Susie had been left alone, slipping in and out of consciousness for at least a few days, in unimaginable distress, being eaten alive from the inside.

She was admitted to the ICU and given the best treatment available, but a few days later, when I went upstairs to check how she was doing, I found out Susie had died. I felt deeply sorry for her. When I imagined the final weeks of her life, considering what the paramedics had reported about the toxic environment from which they'd extracted Susie, I found myself wondering if death may have come as something of a relief. I couldn't understand how the people who'd been with Susie in that apartment had neglected her to that extent. They must have had some serious problems of their own. What about her family? Surely someone, somewhere, had once cared about her. How painful it must be to be so lost to anyone who ever loved you. I'd only been a doctor for a few months, and I had an enormous amount yet to learn, but Susie taught me an important lesson that would stay with me for the rest of my career. Loneliness is a poison.

*

Every patient teaches us something, but I've always found the ED to be the most consistently stimulating learning environment, even more so when I belatedly acknowledged that I needed all of my limited brainpower when at work. I pulled my head in and started to be a bit more selective about when I hit the drink. Many of my medical colleagues seemed to be able to party hard at night and work hard the next day, but it seemed I could only do one or the other. I felt I was finally finding my groove in the ED and I didn't want to fuck it up. I relished the detective work involved in figuring out the causes for the symptoms and signs each patient presented. By the time I was approaching the end of the term, I was thinking seriously about applying to join the emergency medicine training programme. I liked the idea of specialising in being ready for anything and constantly in the action. And, as the name of the place implies, genuine emergencies were never far away . . .

'ETA five minutes, copy that.' Rick, another of the ED consultants, hung up the red ambulance phone and looked around at us. Despite his seniority, it was clear he, too, was feeling a wee bit nervous after taking that call this busy Saturday evening.

'Major trauma on the way, guys. Sharkbite. Massive blood loss. Coming in hot. Everyone know what their role is?'

I nodded. I had my assigned job to do: I was the 'Circulation Doctor', meaning my main responsibility was to get IV access and make sure that whatever the patient needed in terms of fluids, blood and drugs was going in. And I felt okay with that. I'd stuck needles in veins in patients' scalps and ankles and thumbs and groins, often in the middle of the night and sometimes half asleep, as was inevitable 30-something hours into a 48-hour on-call ward shift. But I really had no idea what to expect here. Did I just hear Rick say, 'Bitten in half'?

Poor thing was only 14. She looked exactly how most of us imagine surfers to look. She had a lean body with long, sun-bleached hair and a freckled tan that was still discernible even though her skin looked eerily pale as she was wheeled in. Her appearance was the second thing I noticed.

The first thing was the pool of blood. So much blood, so vividly red on the white fabric. *We should really reconsider the colour of the sheets we use here*, mused one half of my brain, as the other half grappled with the horror of what I was seeing.

Holy shit.

I tried not to look at what the rest of the team were doing down the other end of the bed as I mentally slapped myself into action. Concentrate, goddamn it!

The first IV cannula went in easily enough. The second was a struggle. Her body's circulatory system was so shut down through blood loss that her veins were hard to find and even harder to pierce with my needle. It didn't help that the other guys were jostling around, pushing on the patient's pelvis and bumping my elbow repeatedly in the process. After several unsuccessful pokes, I finally saw a flash of blood run back through my needle. I was in. A litre of fluid was now barrelling in through each arm and the bags of O-negative blood were on their way. We'd need to get an even bigger, three-pronged IV in shortly, probably in the patient's neck, but my two peripheral lines should be enough for now. What next? I assumed my Circulation Doctor responsibilities extended to helping control the haemorrhage, so I finally allowed myself a good look at the patient's lower body. Or what was left of it.

Jesus. Those great white sharks don't fuck about.

The horribly unfortunate young lady had suffered what is technically – and emotionlessly – termed a 'hindquarter amputation'. She'd lost not only her leg, but her right hip and half of her pelvis with it. In a single, horrifying chomp. It was incredible that she'd survived to this point. Her unbelievably brave buddies had fought off the shark and dragged her to shore, where she was given first aid on the beach and whizzed up to us in the ambulance, sirens blaring and lights ablaze. The initial rescue had all been commendably efficient, but it was now over an hour down the track, and with the litres of blood she'd already lost, every minute that passed pushed her ever closer to the precipice. All the fluid going through those IV lines was just buying time. She needed the bright lights and cold steel of the operating theatre – the trauma surgery team were prepping upstairs – and blood. Lots and lots of blood.

'Blood's here!' said Tracey, the haematology technician, as she came charging into the resus bay with the precious polystyrene box.

'Great, thanks Tracey,' replied Rick, looking up from where he was trying to tie off some of the biggest bleeding vessels amid the carnage around the patient's crotch. 'Give it to Lachie.'

Tracey popped the lid off and handed me the first bag of packed red blood cells. We checked the label together and I hooked it up to the infusion line we had ready. *Okay, here we go . . .*

'Wait!'

I looked around to find the source of the unfamiliar voice. A stocky gentleman with short-cropped grey hair pushed his way through the throng towards me.

'Stop!'

I paused, blood poised to go in. 'Why? Who are you?'

'I'm her father,' he said firmly, reaching out and grabbing my arm. 'You're not giving her any of that.'

'What do you mean? It's blood. She needs a lot of it, as quickly as possible!' I gave him a perplexed frown, still holding the line of scarlet liquid, now dripping slowly onto the floor.

'You're not giving her blood. It's against our religious beliefs.' He frowned back at me, tightening his grip on my arm.

'I'm sorry, I don't understand.' I really didn't.

'We're Jehovah's Witnesses. No blood products.'

Fuck.

'Rick!' I called out.

'What?' he replied, squinting down at where he was stitching.

'She's a Jehovah's Witness.'

'Bollocks,' he said, looking up.

'This is her father,' I told him, tilting my head towards the gentleman who still had a hold of me.

'You take over,' Rick said to the registrar beside him, handing over the suturing instruments as he stood up and snapped off his blood-covered gloves. He strode over to the sink, washed the rest of the blood off his wrists, dried them quickly and came over to the head of the bed.

'Hello, I'm Rick, the senior emergency doctor here. I'm very sorry about your daughter. She's had a terrible accident and we're doing all we can. She'll be going up to the operating theatre in a few minutes, as soon as the trauma surgeons are ready. In the meantime, she needs blood. She's lost a great deal and she needs an urgent, massive transfusion if she's to have any chance of surviving.'

'I'm Kevin, I'm her father and I appreciate all that you're doing. But you can't give her any blood. It's a sacred gift from God and transfusions prevent us from experiencing everlasting life.'

Rick's eyes widened slightly. To his great credit, he kept his cool.

'Sir,' he said (Rick was British, so he could get away with addressing him like that), 'with the greatest respect, your daughter will likely die if she doesn't receive the transfusion. Her injuries are extremely serious and her life is at risk.'

'No, you can't give it to her. She's a minor and you do not have my permission.' He let go of me and folded his arms tightly across his chest. He glanced over at the bed, where the rest of the team were still hard at work, the blood around the girl's body now darkening and hardening into clots.

35

He thrust his chin out slightly and looked back at Rick, a mixture of fear and defiance in his eyes.

Rick stared at him for a moment, then exhaled slowly. 'If you will please excuse me then, Kevin, it seems I will need to make some calls.' He paused, then looked up at the man thoughtfully. 'I believe I detect an accent; may I ask if you live here or are visiting?'

Kevin gave a curt nod. 'We're from Hawaii. Here on a family holiday. Wish we'd never come, nightmare that it's turning out to be.'

Rick laid a sympathetic hand on Kevin's shoulder briefly, then strode away. He wandered around the ED for the next hour or so with the phone welded to his ear, patiently and repeatedly explaining the situation to the various hospital administrators and legal experts who apparently resented the intrusion into their weekends, seafood and sauvignon blanc. The ethical serpent's nest that this scenario had exposed meant that no one seemed willing to take responsibility for a clear decision. Rick paused from time to time to answer questions from other members of the ED team, who were dealing with the usual tempest of strokes, drug overdoses and broken bones, and to oversee the ongoing management of our young surfer. In the ocean of chaos, Rick was an island of calm.

While Rick was still on the phone, our patient was wheeled up to the operating theatre and the trauma surgeons got to work. She'd lost so much blood and received so much IV fluid by that stage that her heart was pumping mere iron-flavoured water through her veins. The salvage efforts of Rick and the team in the ED and the subsequent superb work of the surgeons saved the girl's life, despite her never receiving any blood. She was still extremely pale two days later when I nipped up to the ICU to check on her, but she looked like she was going to pull through. The fact that she was young and fit meant that her physiology had found a way to fight through what for most people would have been a quick and violent death.

I struggled to reconcile in my mind the circumstances of the teenage surfer's near-death experience. All of the people directly involved in her care – from her surfer mates, to the ambulance officers, the ED team, the surgeons and the ICU staff – had acted swiftly and appropriately, while the health executives and lawyers had seemingly dragged their heels over the decision of whether or not to overrule her father's directive about the blood transfusion. I was brought up to respect other people's beliefs, but I'd been a teenager myself not long ago, and I found it hard to believe that, if I'd been in her situation, I would have been willing to risk losing my life for the sake of my faith. Reflecting on my own experience of abandoning my childhood religion, I wondered if this young lady had shared her father's beliefs to the same degree. I found that train of thought deeply troubling. There are certain situations in which we sometimes find ourselves where our power over others is truly terrifying. Where we have to take enormous responsibility and make the most serious of all decisions. Life and death decisions.

*

I finished my ED rotation with the idea that I might have found the best (or the least worst) fit for me in terms of specialty training, but I still had an itch that I needed to scratch. I wasn't convinced that life and work in a big city tertiary hospital was quite my jam, and I had a niggling feeling that I might get frustrated spending the rest of my career dealing with a ceaseless flow of patients *in extremis*, without doing anything about the problems that led to them ending up in the ED. In the hundreds of conversations I'd had with patients about their problems up to this point, I could clearly see it was far more common for people's health to deteriorate over time than for them to suffer a sudden, unexpected illness or injury. I was still thinking about the topics and professors who'd most inspired me in my final year of medical school – my tropical medicine rotation in Darwin, the MSF doctor's grim reports from the frontlines of international humanitarian medicine and, of course, Ray and his ability to manage just about anything, anywhere, anytime. I wondered if perhaps I should try working for a few months out in the bush. My intern mates were already lining up their second-year jobs, schmoozing with the registrars and trying their best to impress the consultants in their preferred specialties. Would it be possible for me to slip out of the tertiary system for a bit without burning all my bridges? How would I do such a thing?

One morning, during my final intern rotation in orthopaedics, my registrars had left me to tidy up the ward as they disappeared off to the operating theatre. With the most urgent of the jobs on my 'To Do' list done, I was licking brownie crumbs off my fingers in the junior doctors' common room when I saw a pamphlet on the notice board. 'Prevocational General Practice Placement Program'. No idea what that meant. I wasn't particularly keen on general practice anyway. 'Kimberley Population Health Unit'. I didn't really know what that meant either. What did it have to do with general practice? Was 'population health' like the public health subject we'd glossed over in a few weeks in med school? All I remembered from that was some boring shit about air pollution and lead levels. But now, hang on, that fine print looked interesting. I yanked down the flyer for a closer look 'Based in Broome'. I liked Broome. Great beaches. Hot weather. Cold Emu Bitters. 'Regional role with regular outreach across the Kimberley region.' Hello, adventure, my old friend! 'Accommodation and car provided.' Where do I sign?

My application was accepted (it wasn't exactly stiff competition; I believe I was the only candidate) and I prepared to move up to the Kimberley – the spectacular, sparsely populated region in Western Australia's far north, stretching from the hot, red dust of the Tanami Desert to the warm, milky blue of the Timor Sea. I was told that one of the main parts of my job as the junior public health doctor would be to monitor the notifiable infectious disease database, meaning that every case of every infection with the potential to proliferate through the communities there would come across my desk. While I was more interested in tropical diseases, especially those spread by insects and animals, a big chunk of my day-to-day work would apparently be to help track sexually transmitted infections (STIs) – syphilis, in particular. This meant that, prior to my departure from Perth, along with putting my stuff in storage and reluctantly selling my beloved Suzuki Intruder, I would spend a couple of months working in the sexual health clinic.

Up to that point, I'd considered myself a fairly open-minded, cosmopolitan kind of guy. In the decade since I'd left the family farm, I'd taken a slightly experimental approach to discovering my own sexuality. I'd eventually conceded that I was cis-het, but always respected other people's identities, preferences and practices. Nevertheless, my liberal sensibilities aside, I swear to you now, by all that is holy, the things I saw and heard as a sexual health doctor made me feel like a priest in the Playboy Mansion.

Some of it was simple stuff – anxious girls wanting to be tested after having unprotected sex, and shamefaced men with pain when they peed, who knew they needed treatment but were usually loath to do the right thing by notifying their partners. There were sex workers of every form and orientation, who'd breeze in for their regular check-ups and regale me, often in unnecessary detail, with their recent exploits. And then there were the tight-fitted T-shirted chaps who'd come in on Mondays, worn out after weekend-long binges on ecstasy and Viagra, asking me to peruse some new sore or spot. I learned a lot about life from these patients, all of whom had a different story, and I did my best to listen and attend to their concerns, even though I'm sure more than a few of them enjoyed it when their gossipy stories and teasing made me blush. Once I got over the initial strangeness of spending my days inspecting genitals, I realised what a privilege it was to be entrusted with managing not only each patient's physical ailment, but their associated emotions, from mild embarrassment about a few warts through to anxiety about potential infertility and very real fears about dying from HIV. Most people with a health problem have some kind of psychological reaction associated with it, naturally, but sexual health was like putting the practice of medicine under a psychosocial microscope.

Kimberley region, Western Australia

Once I'd finished my crash course in sexual health medicine and could confidently rattle off the required tests and treatments for all of the common STIs, I went on a farewell bender with my former-intern buddies, left them to their second year of pounding the wards and flew with my two suitcases for three hours north to Broome. I picked up the keys to my work car, settled in to my musty one-bedroom duplex and felt like I was top shit. No other junior doctors I knew had free accommodation and wheels! I didn't have much supervision – the only other doctor at the Population Health Unit was often absent and hadn't yet completed his training as a public health physician anyway, so I was largely left to my own devices. I didn't know much – the main thing internship had taught me was how to be a decent junior doctor in a big hospital, and that didn't really apply here. I also didn't really know anything about public health, so I started reading a few textbooks and discreetly quizzed the nurses, epidemiologists and health promoters about how they spent their days. The sweet, elderly nurse who led the immunisation programme taught me the basics of what I needed to know about vaccine-preventable diseases and I tagged along with one of the male health workers when he visited some remote communities to talk to young people about safe sex.

The one thing I did have at my disposal was the infectious diseases database, which was updated on a weekly basis with all the new cases of infections that met the criteria as 'notifiable diseases', meaning they had the potential to occur as epidemics and thus required prompt action and careful follow-up. I figured out how to make graphs of the trends in each disease over time and something interesting struck me. I'd arrived in Broome during the wet season, which had been even wetter than normal this year, and it seemed the numbers of cases of Ross River virus disease (also known as Ross River fever) – a very uncomfortable and potentially debilitating, albeit not life-threatening, disease spread by mosquitoes – were way above normal. Ross River fever is the most common mosquito-borne disease in Australia, particularly in the northern tropical regions, where it is endemic (that is, always present). Here in the west Kimberley, it seemed the peaks in the numbers of cases were happening in the same months each year, with the size of the peaks increasing over time.

I spent an entire day painstakingly mapping out the last ten years of Ross River fever cases, week by week, marvelling at the predictability of the epidemic curves and wondering what would happen if we could plug in some rainfall data, and maybe temperature too. Would that match up as well? I contacted the local meteorology office, who very obligingly sent me several years of monthly temperature, rainfall and humidity data. I then reached out to a medical entomologist (a scientist specialising in insects that spread disease) down in Perth, who gave me a turbo-tutorial in mosquito-borne diseases over the phone and agreed to help me look into it. I also started searching textbooks and medical journals for information about the relationships between weather conditions and outbreaks of infectious diseases. It turned out to be quite a hot topic, with public health experts from around Australia right up to the headquarters of the World Health Organization (WHO) in Switzerland pointing out the links between weather variables and disease trends and sounding the alarm about what this might mean in relation to climate change. I was enthralled and appalled at the same time. This was big news! Shouldn't all health professionals be aware of this, not to mention politicians and the general public? We'd been taught about climate change in primary school, almost twenty years earlier, but this was the first time I'd learned anything about how it might impact on our health.

My musings were cut short when a wiry mop of brown hair and a slightly manic smile appeared at my door. It was Bridget.

'Hey, Lachie, let's roll.'

I switched off the monitor and grabbed my bag. I'd befriended several of the other doctors around Broome during my early sorties out on the town, and Bridget, one of the rural GP registrars, had invited me to accompany her on one of her week-long clinics out in Balgo, a community of a few hundred people to the north of the Great Sandy Desert on the Tanami Track. We drove through the gate of Broome airport and pulled up alongside a single-prop, six-seater plane. Bridget threw her bag in the hold, along with two coolers – one full of food, the other full of medicines – and clambered aboard.

I looked around. 'Who else is coming?' I asked.

Bridget grinned again. 'No one, it's just us. Private charter. Pretty cool, hey?'

It was. I climbed in and buckled up, then we taxied out and took off south-east over the sea of red dirt. I sprawled across three seats and put my feet up.

This was rock-star doctoring.

Bridget set me up in a consulting room in the little clinic that squatted in the dust in the centre of the community. Helen, the cheerful nurse who ran the clinic, somehow managed to be relaxed and energetic at the same time as she bustled around, unpacking the medications from the cooler we'd brought, taking vital signs from the patients who meandered in and calling out instructions to the health workers, driver and her husband, Keith, who – like many other partners of remote area nurses I'd meet – was a kind of all-purpose assistant capable of doing almost any job required. I was surprised to find, next to the drug fridge that Helen was loading, another fridge labelled 'Bush Medicine', with photographs of local plants, bark, ochre and ash on the door with fantastic names like *Ngurnu ngurnu*, *Yapilynpa* and *Piltji*, alongside explanations of how to prepare them and what conditions they were useful to treat.

I busied myself seeing the patients who turned up, mostly for checks of their blood pressure and diabetes, and enjoyed the feeling of being a debutant rural doctor for a morning. When the waiting room was finally empty, I made myself a cup of tea and was absent-mindedly sipping and gazing out of a window at some lanky kids kicking a deflated football around the grassless oval when I heard a cough. A loud, harrumphing cough with a hoick and a pause and a spit at the end. I turned to see a little old lady, barefoot, with a blue bandana around her head, huffing hard and hacking up phlegm from deep in her chest as she staggered into the clinic with a walking stick. I rushed over to her.

'Are you okay, Auntie?'*

---

* It is common to use the honorifics 'Auntie' and 'Uncle' when speaking to elderly Indigenous people in many communities in Australia, depending on the context. I don't claim any expertise in such sensitive matters; this is simply what many of my health professional colleagues and I tend to do as a sign of respect.

'Asthma,' she wheezed. 'My asthma's playing up.' She could barely get the words out.

I looked around for Helen. No sign of her. I called out. No response.

'Bridget!' I shouted.

Nothing.

Shit! Where was everybody? Acute asthma was a medical emergency and one I'd definitely never dealt with by myself before.

I ushered the woman into the tiny emergency treatment bay, grabbed an oxygen mask, fastened it around her bandana and cranked it up to max flow from the tank beside the bed.

'What's your name, Auntie?'

'Daisy,' she puffed. 'Daisy Mason.'

'Daisy, I'm Lachie. I'm a doctor here doing a clinic with Bridget. I'm going to try and help you but this is my first time in Balgo so I don't know where everything is. Do you have any pain in your chest?'

'No, just short-wind.' Clearly so. I was worried.

I knew she needed salbutamol, at least, and probably steroids too, to open up her airways and keep the oxygen level in her blood from dropping. Maybe antibiotics as well, if her asthma flare-up was due to a bacterial infection. I hunted around the room but couldn't find any drugs, nor the nebuliser thingy I'd seen used in ED to give inhaled medications. I realised I'd never actually given patients medications myself before; there had always been nurses around to do that. Doctors scribbled in the medication chart and then strolled off while the nurses got the drugs, checked the drugs, double-checked for allergies and gave the medications to the patient. That was the system, at least in the big hospitals where I'd worked. Now, alone in this clinic, in the desert, with an elderly lady on the bed next to me, eyes closed and chest heaving, I felt impotent.

I left Daisy in the treatment bay and ran around the clinic, poking my head into doors, looking for people, equipment, medicines, anything. Where the hell did everyone go?

Finally, behind the kitchen, I found a door with a handwritten sign saying 'Dispensary'. Thank fuck for that. Quick jiggle of the handle – no luck, locked. I sprinted outside, wild-eyed and desperate.

'Helen!' I yelled to nowhere in particular.

'Yes, Lachie, what's up?' Helen peered around the corner from where she was sitting, having a cuppa and a biscuit with Bridget and Keith.

'Daisy Mason's having an asthma attack and I don't know where anything is!'

I must have looked pretty stressed. Helen stood up, shuffled into her sandals, swigged back her tea and led me back inside, yanking a lanyard jangling with keys out of her pocket and pausing at the dispensary as we entered. She cracked open ampoules and plucked syringes from cupboards and had them all drawn up in a jiffy. Seconds later, back at Daisy's bedside, Helen squirted salbutamol into a chamber she screwed onto the mask.

'Good job with the oxygen,' she smiled over her shoulder at me.

Before I knew it, she'd stuck in a drip and had given some steroids with a fluid chaser into Daisy's vein.

She patted Daisy gently on the arm. 'You'll feel better soon, okay Auntie?'

Daisy nodded and settled back onto the bed.

As we walked out, my heart rate slowly returning to normal, I was so relieved I gave Helen a little hug. I explained to her that I'd never been in that situation before, more or less knowing what needed to be done but having bugger-all idea how to do it. She gave me a squeeze back.

'Well, now you know, and I guess you'll never forget.'

Sitting in our corrugated-iron bungalow that evening, munching on vegetable curry as a rusty fan whirled the hot desert air above our heads, I debriefed with Bridget.

'Don't sweat, I get it,' she reassured me. 'In places like this, you don't have any of those little comforts you took for granted as a junior doctor, like having senior colleagues around to help bail you out when things go pear-shaped. You gotta shake that off and learn to become more independent out here. It's tough but it can be very rewarding, that's for sure.'

The odd thing was, I didn't feel put off by the experience. In fact, I was inspired. I thought back to Ray and his tales of adventures in Papua New Guinea, as well as my own cameos in Halls Creek and the mixed feelings I'd had when completing my internship – enjoying the emergency work but not the city hospital scene. It was becoming clearer to me the kind of doctor I wanted to be. I wanted to be like Ray and Bridget and that guy from Médecins Sans Frontières – not experts in one narrow field, but able to deal with whatever came through the door, at least up to a point. And if I could find such jobs with a bit of off-road adventure thrown in, even better! I blathered something along those lines to Bridget, who laughed and said she got that too. She explained to me the various ways in which it was possible to train as a specialist in rural and remote medicine – otherwise known as a 'rural generalist' – in Australia. I listened intently. This was all news to me. In six years of medical school in Melbourne, and in the couple of years since I'd graduated, I'd never heard anyone mention rural generalist medicine as a distinct career. How was I only hearing about this now, all the way out here?

Daisy Mason, it turned out, was a famous artist. Balgo was home to several of them, with the local art centre – Warlayirti – one of the best known in the country. I went to visit the gallery a couple of days later and found Daisy sitting on the floor, legs apart, bent over a painting of intricate dot patterns. She was feeling much better, she assured me with a semi-toothless smile. I sat with her for a while, admiring the skill required for her to paint with such pinpoint precision, building up from one corner of the canvas into an entire story of digging for yams, hunting for witchetty grubs and secret women's business, told from a bird's-eye perspective, all in different-coloured dots.

I met a few other VIPs in my brief time in Balgo. I had the privilege of doing a home visit to check on Helicopter, a community Elder, world-renowned artist and traditional healer who was now not so well himself. As a child, some sixty years earlier, he'd had a nasty accident and his astonished family had watched as a machine appeared out of the sky and thundered down into their desert camp, from which a doctor emerged to take the boy away for treatment. His parents had never seen anything like it before, but they were so impressed that by the time he got back, fully healed, their son had a new name.* I did my best to help 'Uncle Chopper' with his chronic lower back pain and he clasped my hand with his arthritic fingers warmly in thanks as I left.†

When our own little flying machine buzzed into Balgo to take us back to Broome, Bridget and I tossed our bags into the hold and were about to

---

* A couple of years later, in Papua New Guinea, I was learning how to speak Melanesian Pidgin – the *lingua franca* of PNG, Solomon Islands and Vanuatu – which forms possessives by the use of the word *blong* (belong) as a conjunction, as in *buk blong mi* (my book), *haus blong yu* (your house) etcetera. The language structure appealed to me in how it can be both very direct, e.g. *haus sik* (hospital); and roundabout, e.g. *missus blong brata blong yu* (sister-in-law). But my all-time favourite 'word', which I was tickled to discover at the time and that made me think back to Balgo, is *Mixmasta blong Jesus:* helicopter.

† I had the opportunity to reconnect with Uncle Chopper briefly over the phone while finalising this book and he told me he was doing well and still painting.

board when a dusty old station wagon squeaked and rattled its way over to the plane. A man leaned out the window.

'Hey, doc, got something for you.' He held out a cardboard cylinder. 'My auntie said to give this to you.'

When I got home that night, I opened it. It was a painting, signed by Daisy Mason. A striking piece of white dots defining waterholes and sand dunes over a yellow and ochre desert background. It's had pride of place on the walls of the various homes I've lived in ever since, as a precious reminder for me to try and be self-reliant.

Alice Springs, Northern Territory

I finished my six-month public health stint in the Kimberley with a deep affection for the region and a growing affinity for the specialty of public health, but a feeling that I couldn't do the latter full-time. I appreciated having direct contact with patients and liked the high-energy action of emergency medicine. What I enjoyed most, though, was being out in the bush. Could the rural generalist thing that Bridget mentioned be a way to combine all my main interests in one? I gave myself an ultimatum: I'd do a few more months of ED work, but in a regional hospital somewhere exotic, rather than back in another big city, and by the end of the year I'd make a decision about what to do with my medical career. With that determination in mind, off I went to the heart of Australia – the Red Centre.

Alice Springs (or Mparntwe, as it is known by the traditional owners, the Arrernte people) is the main population and administrative hub for the southernmost region of the Northern Territory. It's a flat but rather pretty smear of a desert town nestled in the gap in the MacDonnell Ranges halfway between Darwin, the NT capital, and Adelaide, the capital of

South Australia. It has two special characteristics that I have found over the years seem to be unique to a particular group of regional centres: their importance is out of proportion to their size, and they attract certain people because of their remoteness, beauty and/or lifestyle. Broome belongs in that group; Darwin and Cairns do too. 'Alice', as it is referred to by most folks, has a distinct bohemian appeal, with art centres, music festivals and events such as the Henley on Todd Regatta – an annual 'boat race' where teams dress up and stampede in various stages of inebriation down the dry bed of the Todd River carrying home-made 'boats' – revealing a surprisingly lively cultural scene.

I liked Alice immediately. I had a full-time job in the ED, got on well with my colleagues and found the work interesting. I knew that paediatrics was a major knowledge gap for me, as I'd been haphazard, to put it generously, in my attendance during that rotation in med school and I hadn't had a chance to treat any kids in Perth, as they all went directly to the children's hospital. I thus tried to see as many paediatric patients as possible in Alice Springs ED and I gradually, with help from the friendly registrars, developed the most basic but important skill in paeds: being able to recognise when a child is really unwell. It sounds simple, but they're tricksy little creatures and it takes quite a lot of experience to make a reasonably confident clinical distinction between 'sick and miserable but probably going to be fine' and 'sick and miserable and, shit, this one's a worry'.

One part of the population seemed to be shouldering far more than their fair share of the burden of ill-health. Aboriginal people make up around a quarter of Alice's population and closer to half the population of the Central Australian region, but they are sadly overrepresented in terms of serious illnesses and hospitalisations. The majority of the patients we saw in ED in any given shift were Aboriginal. The time it took for many patients to be assessed in the clinic in their community and transferred to Alice meant they were often very unwell by the time they arrived. It was unnerving to see patients with end-stage kidney disease in their forties, chronic lung disease in their thirties and heart attacks in their twenties. I recalled my brief visits to Aboriginal communities around Halls Creek and what I'd been taught by the doctors, nurses and health workers there about the importance of one's living conditions, including the basics of food, water and shelter. I'd started a Master of Public Health and Tropical Medicine degree in my spare time and I was gaining a better understanding of the role of social and environmental determinants of health. I'd had a tiny glimpse of those problems out in the communities, and now I was seeing the results here in the ED. This was a large part of the reason why the life expectancy of Indigenous Australians around this time was some nine to twelve years lower than for non-Indigenous Australians.[*]

Another problem it was impossible to ignore was that of the pernicious effects of alcohol. While the proportion of the Indigenous community who drink alcohol is less than that of the non-Indigenous population of Australia, a higher percentage of Indigenous people drink at levels that are hazardous or harmful.[†] As for any person, of any background, this can lead to terrible consequences. I lost count of the number of times I found myself stitching up a scalp wound in the ED in the middle of the night on a

---

[*] Addressing this has been a health policy priority for many years, particularly via the 'Closing the Gap' initiative, which aims to eliminate the difference in life expectancies between Indigenous and non-Indigenous Australians by 2031. While there do appear to have been some modest improvements over recent years, with the current gap estimated at 7–9 years, the 2020 report makes clear that the target is unlikely to be met: https://www.aihw.gov.au/reports/australias-health/indigenous-life-expectancy-and-deaths.

[†] https://www.health.gov.au/health-topics/alcohol/alcohol-throughout-life/alcohol-and-aboriginal-and-torres-strait-islander-peoples.

drunk patient who'd been hit over the head with a *nulla-nulla* – a catch-all term for any kind of wooden club – only to discover old suture threads from a previous injury.

I was getting quite jaded by the endless tide of emergencies and, despite the undeniable charm and beauty of the desert, I hailed from waterfall and coastal country and was suffering a little from a lack of somewhere to swim. As the end of my second year as a doctor approached, and with it my self-imposed ultimatum, I made my decision. I didn't want to spend the rest of my life in the ED, nor did I want to work purely in public health. I respected both of those specialties, representing as they did the two extremes of the spectrum – the latter mostly about trying to stop people getting sick; the former mostly about treating people at their sickest. But I wanted to be able to do a bit of both, and keep having adventures in the most interesting parts of the country. Maybe I'd even try and find work overseas someday. But in order to be at my most useful and competent, I decided I should finish some form of specialty training first. I channelled Ray's can-do spirit, took Bridget's advice, bit the bullet and applied to join the training programme of the Australian College of Rural and Remote Medicine (ACRRM). I was interviewed and accepted. I already knew where I wanted to go next. I was keen to learn about the other main population of Indigenous people in Australia and I yearned to be back in the tropics, surrounded by sea. I phoned Jack, the medical superintendent* of the hospital on Thursday Island (TI) – the administrative capital of the Torres Strait, the archipelago between the north-east tip of Australia and the coast of Papua New Guinea.

'What do I need to do to get a job on TI?' I asked him.

---

* The medical superintendent is the boss of all the doctors in a particular facility.

'Can you do a caesar?'*

'No.'

'Can you give an anaesthetic?'

'No.'

'Well, call me back when you can do at least one of those things,' he said, and hung up.

---

* A common abbreviation for caesarean section – an operation by which babies are delivered.

CHAPTER FOUR

2008–9

Far North Queensland, Australia

'There's been a knife fight on a fishing boat.'

It took a few seconds for that to sink in. I spun around to look at Sue, the nurse who'd just hung up the phone and was scribbling a note.

'What did you just say, Sue?'

'Knife fight. Fishing boat. One guy stabbed in the chest. Police and ambulance are on their way. You alright, Lachie?'

Yikes. This is what I'd signed up for. I was in my third year of postgraduate training and was officially now a registrar, working towards the specialty qualification that awaited if and when I made it to the end: Fellowship of the Australian College of Rural and Remote Medicine (FACRRM). In order to get there, I needed to spend several more years working in rural hospitals and primary care clinics. Plus, to get my dream job up on Thursday Island, I needed to do a year of sub-specialty training in either anaesthetics or obstetrics. I found obstetrics quite frightening, to be frank – yes, the miracle of childbirth is beautiful and all, but my very limited experience suggested that when things go wrong, they tend to do so rapidly and dramatically, with double the number of patients. I'd decided to try and avoid that as much as possible, so had signed up for a year of anaesthetics instead. That was 12 months down the track, though, and to get to that point I needed to survive my first year doing real rural medicine. And shit was now, indeed, getting real.

I was the on-call doctor for the little hospital in Cooktown, a rough-and-tumble coastal town on the Cape York Peninsula in Far North Queensland, where the highway peters out into rust-coloured dust and many of the locals live off the grid and deliberately out of reach of the systems that are supposed to hold society together. My initial impression was of a rugged, windy, violent place, where people drank heavily, fought hard and died young.

I swallowed hard and looked up at Sue. 'Yep. Just checking I heard right the first time. So, umm . . . I guess . . . '

She gave me a little smile. Sue was nice. All of the dozen or so nurses here were. They looked after me, knowing when to slip me a biscuit if I was hungry or find me a vacant bed on the ward if I was clearly in need of a nap.

'Shall I phone for an x-ray? Maureen's on call tonight.'

'Ah, yeah, good idea, thanks.'

I shook myself out of my stunned funk and quickly made my way over to our cramped, single-bed ED. I looked around, checking where the oxygen masks and ventilator equipment were. I hadn't seen many stabbings before. I'd seen a guy who had slipped while brandishing a samurai sword and impaled himself through the back, but he had miraculously managed to avoid penetrating anything important, so had walked away from that with nothing more than a bunch of stitches and an awesome story. I had been but a minor player in that drama, which took place in a big city hospital with multiple surgeons jostling for centre stage. This time it was just me, Sue and the other nurse we were calling in to do the x-ray.

'We have two units of O-negative blood, if we need them,' Sue said as she bustled into the ED behind me. 'And here are our chest tubes.*

---

* A chest tube, also known as a chest drain – or, more formally, an intercostal catheter – is a flexible plastic tube that is inserted through the wall of the chest, usually about a handsbreadth beneath the armpit, in order to release blood, fluid, pus or trapped air.

54

We only have these two, so take your pick. And remember we need to keep one spare, so no pressure.' She winked at me. 'I'm sure you'll be fine.'

I picked up one of the packages gingerly, as though it might explode, and stared blankly through the transparent plastic at the equipment kit. I couldn't remember ever seeing any of this stuff before. I cleared my throat.

'Umm, Sue, do you know if they come with instructions? It's just that, you know, I'm not sure if this is the same brand that I'm used to using.'

Sue looked over at me from where she was rummaging in drawers and drawing up drugs.

'Yep, it's all there inside. Don't fret, we'll figure it out.'

If her faith in me was fading, she didn't let it show.

Lights flashed outside, doors slammed, and our quiet, empty ED was suddenly very noisy and crowded.

'I can't breathe! I can't breathe!' gasped the man on the stretcher the ambulance officers were wheeling in.

He didn't look real flash. Grey's not a great colour on anyone, particularly as a shade of skin. He was wide-eyed and sweating and smelled like rum. The ambulance crew started rattling off information as they hoisted the guy over onto our bed.

'This is Geoff, forty-seven-year-old gentleman, penetrating wound to right anterior chest wall, BP one hundred over sixty, pulse one-twenty, sat's ninety-two on ten litres.'*

The grizzlier of the two policemen who'd arrived then chimed in:

---

* The most important information about a patient in an emergency situation relates to their 'vital signs', which include temperature, heart rate, blood pressure, respiratory rate and oxygen saturation (commonly abbreviated as 'sat's'). Blood glucose (sugar) level and Glasgow Coma Score (a measure of consciousness) are often also included in this list of 'vitals'.

'When we arrived at the scene, two male individuals were engaged in an altercation involving a frying pan and a filleting knife.'

'Second cannula's in,' Sue announced, as she flicked off her gloves and hooked up the warm fluids we'd prepared.

'That prick stabbed me! Shit, shit, shit, I can't breathe!'

'Good work, Sue. Let's give him ten milligrams of morphine straight up.'

I tried to calm Geoff as best I could while listening to his chest with my stethoscope. It was tricky to hear anything with all the background noise and his rapid, shallow breathing, but I was pretty sure I could only hear his lungs filling up on the left side. The right side was silent. Not good.

'Maureen's here,' Sue said, strapping an oxygen mask around Geoff's head and shooing the ambulance officers and cops out of the room.

Maureen poked her head in. 'Hi Lachie, I know you need an x-ray, but the machine's been playing up. Keeps getting stuck in one position.'

Fuck.

'Umm, I guess just do what you can, Maureen.'

This was way outside my comfort zone. I suspected Geoff had a collapsed lung, with internal bleeding, and the only way to treat that was by sticking one of those chest tubes, which looked like medieval torture instruments, through his chest wall to release the pressure, re-inflate the lung and allow the blood out. *And then what?* I wondered.

As Maureen wheeled Geoff next door for his x-ray, Sue and I put our heads together.

'So, chest tube?' she asked.

'Yep.'

'Then get the retrieval team up here to take him down to Cairns?'

'Yes. Good call. How do I do that?'

'Here's the number. Hopefully they'll have a helicopter available, or we'll be in for a long night.' She winked at me again. At least one of us was having fun.

Maureen wheeled Geoff back in a few minutes later. She looked frazzled. 'Sorry Lachie, I tried my best.'

We stuck Geoff's chest x-ray up on the lightbox on the wall and stared at it together. Bugger. The machine's dicky positioning had cut off most of the right side of the chest, so I couldn't be sure what was going on in there. But if I couldn't hear any breath sounds on that side . . . I listened again. Nothing.

I turned to Geoff where he lay on the bed, grimacing, mumbling, pale and panting.

'Okay, Geoff, this isn't going to be easy for either of us, but here's what I think we have to do.'

I explained to him that we needed to insert a chest tube, trying to give my best impression of someone who'd done it before. His consent for the procedure was an anguished, 'Just fucking get on with it, doc!'

With Maureen standing on the opposite side of the bed, holding open an emergency medicine textbook for me, I donned the sterile gown and gloves, set up the procedure trolley, drew up some local anaesthetic into a syringe, took a deep breath and, as instructed, fucking got on with it. Geoff swore in pain as I cut into the side of his chest. I put the scalpel down and injected some more local anaesthetic.

'Can you go back to the previous page?' I asked Maureen. She obliged and I peered at the diagram again through the visor on my mask, which fogged up every time I exhaled. I checked the instructions from the second chest tube kit that was open on the sterile tray beside me. The first kit was lying on the floor, where I'd dropped it.

I poked my finger gently into the hole I'd made in Geoff's chest.

'Just a little bit more now, hold tight.'

I felt a pop. Shit, was that supposed to happen? I had another quick look at the book. No mention of any popping. But maybe that meant I was in? I grasped the tube with the forceps and gave it a waggle. It was the diameter of a garden hose. Would it fit through the hole I'd just made? I pushed it in slowly, trying not to shove. How would I know when I'd found the right place?

A sudden gush of blood flowed through the tube and onto my feet. I looked down with horror.

'Well, I guess we were supposed to clamp it beforehand,' Sue said brightly. 'Do you want to connect it up now?'

With the tube and its chamber safely assembled and strapped to Geoff's chest, draining blood and starting to swing as the trapped air escaped and the lung re-expanded, I was relieved to hear breath sounds on that side when I rechecked with my stethoscope. I was then even more relieved to hear a thudding in the distance. The cavalry had arrived.

The aeromedical retrieval team strolled in – a flurry of high-visibility jumpsuits and armfuls of equipment. They looked magnificent to me. The medical officer inspected the tube and listened to Geoff's chest.

'Doesn't sound too bad.' He glanced over at the chest x-ray on the wall. 'Guess that wasn't much help. But nice job anyway. Let's hang up another unit of blood and we'll get going.'

I walked with them as they wheeled Geoff over to the chopper.

'Been up here long?' the medic asked me.

'Nah, just a few weeks so far.'

'Done many chest tubes before?'

I looked down at my blood-spattered boots. 'First one.'

He laughed. 'If you stay working up here, mate, it won't be your last.'

And with a wave, they whirred up and away.

I didn't know whether I needed a coffee or a beer. I definitely needed a bed. Sue called out down the hall as I was leaving.

'Hang on, Lachie, before you go, just one more patient to see.'

I stopped, slumped, yawned, stretched and dragged my ragged arse back to the ED.

'Who is it, Sue? Is it serious? Could they possibly wait until morning?'

She gave me another little smile and patted me on the arm.

'I'll make you a coffee. It's the other guy.'

Vanuatu

I was enjoying my job at the hospital – infectious diseases, palliative patients, midnight maritime knife fights and all – but it was hard going. By the time several months had passed in Cooktown, living in my little apartment above the GP clinic and spending all of my days either there, at the hospital, or both, I was feeling isolated, lonely and overworked. I realised I needed to take a break, have a holiday and see a familiar face. I called my buddy Will. We'd scuba-dived together in the Red Sea a few years back, and as the essential ingredients of my vague escape plan involved tropical islands and underwater action, I guessed that might be up his alley. Will was up for it, so, over the phone, we spun the globe. Sri Lanka, Mauritius, Indonesia, Philippines . . . All great options, we agreed, but we decided, in the interests of efficiency, to go somewhere a bit closer to home. Vanuatu looked the goods.

The island of Espiritu Santo is spectacular. The largest in Vanuatu, it's also home to Tabwemasana, the country's highest mountain; Champagne Beach, the most photogenic of Vanuatu's enviable collection; and the SS President Coolidge, an American troopship sunk by friendly mines in the Second World War just off the shore and now renowned the world over as a diver's dream. All of that proved the ideal antidote to the emotional slump in which I'd been wallowing. After a few days spent merrily working our way down the list of the island's highlights, Will and I decided to try and break out of the tourist traps and find a way into the interior. We asked around Luganville – the only town – for trucks and guides for hire but were met with nothing but polite declines. On the second day of this, with sinking spirits, we went looking for lunch in some little shacks we'd spotted down by the harbour. Each hut we poked our heads into was full of men clustered around tiny tables slurping down fish and rice served by dignified ladies in floral dresses who mopped their sweaty brows and flapped at flies with colourful handtowels draped across their shoulders. Feeling ever hungrier and less hopeful, we peered inside one packed shack after another until we heard a cheerful 'Please, kam!' The man waving at us with a welcoming smile jostled his lunch companions up the wooden bench to make room for us to squeeze in beside them. As our fish and rice arrived, we chatted to our new friend, who told us his name was Nixon.

'Like the president?' I asked.

'Exactly!' he beamed, nibbling on a fishbone.

As we munched and chuckled together, we told him how taken we were with his island home and how keen we were to explore more of it. Nixon, it turned out, had a friend who owned a small truck that Nixon occasionally borrowed to drive supplies around the island. Delighted, we asked if we could hire his services for a day or two of jungle touring, if it wouldn't interfere with his business. He shyly accepted, and we arranged to meet the next morning. As chance encounters go, this would prove to be the most significant of my life.

Nixon was a superb guide. He was proud of his island and very knowledgeable about its history, geography and culture, as well as fluent in at least five of the languages spoken across the archipelago. Together we trekked through the rainforest, swam in stunning limestone pools of sweet, sapphire water, and met with men and boys – some as young as four – working on the copra plantations, splitting the coconuts open with machetes to smoke the cracked flesh in metal drums over wood fires to make the oil.

On the afternoon of our third day together, Nixon invited us to visit his village. As his wife, Linda, served lunch from a pot over the open fire, Nixon explained to us that his parents had died many years ago, with the role of village chief being passed to his oldest brother. They were a very close-knit community, almost all related to each other, and we got the sense that despite not being the village's official chief, Nixon was the real leader of Bene. He oversaw farming and construction projects, consulted with the chiefs and elders from surrounding communities, and kept the teenage boys fit and mostly out of mischief as their boxing coach. Nixon was also a visionary. He could see the impacts of economic development on the island and was committed to ensuring that his family and community capitalised on that and worked together in making continuous, incremental improvements. As he told us about these plans, I couldn't help but be impressed. I was studying some elective subjects in international development as part of my master's degree, and here Nixon was describing classic development theory, not from a textbook but from his own lived experience and initiative. He and his community had a clear long-term strategy but just lacked some of the resources required to achieve it.

It was a far cry from my first encounter with international community development, several years earlier in Nepal, where I'd joined a group of earnest young Aussies on a volunteer expedition. We spent several weeks living and working in an orphanage and helping build a stormwater drain at an environmental resource centre, as well as hiking around the majestic Annapurnas in between. It was very well intentioned, but almost completely pointless. There was nothing that we were doing that couldn't be done – and done much better – by Nepalis with more knowledge and skills. It was all good fun for us, and Nepal will forever be one of my favourite places, but the most valuable aspect of the experience for me was the realisation that development work needed to be community-led, well planned, appropriately resourced and able to be sustained, not just done as ad-hoc, short-term volunteer jollies.

In the adventures and conversations that followed over the next few days, Nixon and I bonded, and when we reached the day prior to my departure, we sat together to *storian* (chat). I told him how deeply I appreciated his generosity and hospitality, how much I'd learned from him and how valuable I could see the work was that he was doing for his community. I asked how I could help. He gave me a broad smile, shook his head and assured me, graciously and respectfully, that it wasn't necessary. I said I meant it. He demurred. I insisted. He said he'd think about it.

When he came to meet me the next morning, I prodded him. 'Come on, mate, tell me, there must be something we can do before I leave.'

'Well,' Nixon replied, reluctantly, 'do you know about solar power? The diesel we buy is expensive and the generator often breaks down. I think we could use a solar panel in the village to have a little electricity in the evening, to help the women cook and the children do their homework.'

'Brilliant! That's a terrific idea! Do they sell them here? Let's go!'

An hour later, as he drove me to the airport, brand-new solar panel in the back, Nixon was in tears.

'You don't know how much this means to us,' he said, shaking his head.

We both choked up a little as we said our farewells. He took me firmly by the shoulders and fixed me with an intense look.

'You know, in my culture, this makes us brothers.'

I grinned at him, gave him a bear hug, picked up my bag and strode into the airport, where Will was waiting with a cold Tusker beer.

*

I returned to Cooktown and got back to work, where my days were once again filled with wounds, heart attacks and end-stage organ failures. As the months passed, I expected the memories of Vanuatu to fade. But I kept thinking about Nixon, his family and his plans for the village. I dug up the scrap of paper he'd given me at the airport, on which he'd carefully printed out a name and address in red pen. I handwrote a letter, addressed to Pastor Elvis, Santo Christian School, Luganville, Vanuatu, explaining who I was and that I'd like to come back to Bene and visit the following year. A reply never came, but I stuck to the plan and booked a flight back to Espiritu Santo.

When I arrived, I rented a truck and set off, excited but nervous, heading north along the only paved road. As I drove up the coast, trying to remember how to get to Bene, I wiped my sweaty palms and wondered if I was crazy. What if they hadn't received my letter? What if I couldn't find the village? Even if I got there, would they remember me?

The flash of a smile from a familiar face on the side of the road made me screech to a halt. It turned out my letter had arrived, and though the community had lacked the means of writing back to me, they'd taken my mention of returning 'next year' literally and had been waiting for my arrival since January. My attempts to apologise for the confusion were lost in the swirl of handshakes and hugs, as most of the family members I'd met last time and many faces I was pretty sure I'd never seen before surrounded me. As we caught up on the gossip and I settled into the rhythm of the village, it also became apparent that Nixon's mention of us having become brothers had been a very real commitment. I was extremely humbled to discover that a ceremony was to take place to formally adopt me into the family.

The high chief was summoned from a distant village two days' walk away, a traditional string band turned up on a rusty truck and the *nakamal* – the open-walled communal hall – was decorated with flowers in preparation for the feast. I knew I needed to take it equally seriously. After it was explained to me how the ceremony worked, I prepared a short speech in Bislama, the form of Melanesian Pidgin spoken in Vanuatu, with much patient assistance from Linda, who was sparklingly intelligent and whose mother had been a school principal. I also helped collect food, wood and kava – a root that is mixed with water and saliva to make a tongue-numbing intoxicant that looks and tastes like a puddle past its prime but has profound ritual value in Vanuatu and elsewhere in the Pacific.

That evening, in front of the assembled village, Frank, the old chief, oozing gravitas through his grey beard, grass skirt and bare chest covered in coconut oil, summoned me to join him at his side as he began to address the crowd.

Nixon sidled up to me and handed me a stout branch.

'What's that for?' I asked.

He cleared his throat softly and looked pointedly over in the direction of the small black pig that was trotting about a few feet away, snuffling exploratively under a pamplemousse tree. Nixon and I had purchased this 'tusker' – a sacred animal in Vanuatu – earlier in the day, and I had the vague notion that it was probably going to be eaten at some point. But what the fuck was this now?

I followed his gaze for a moment, then stared aghast at the heavy stick he'd just given me. 'I thought you said I didn't have to kill it!' I hissed.

Nixon gave me a wry little smile. '*Sori tumas* (I'm very sorry), brother, I thought it was better to wait to tell you.'

I hefted the club in my hand, glanced over at the pig again and grimaced. 'What if I don't do it right and he doesn't die straight away?'

The smile dropped from Nixon's face as he took a step towards me and looked me directly in the eyes. 'It will be okay,' he said, gently, 'the boys can finish the job. But it really would be better for everyone,' he paused and tilted his head slightly back towards the snuffles, 'if you get it right the first time.'

Frank finished his speech and turned to face me. He lifted a bamboo cup to his lips and took a long swig of kava, then wiped the thick brown drops from his whiskers with the back of a gnarled hand and passed the ceremonial vessel to me. I hesitated for a second, then, with an encouraging nod from the chief, gulped down the rest of the bitter liquid. I passed the cup back, bent down, picked up the branch and, accompanied only by the shrill hum of the jungle cicadas and 50 sets of eyes, walked slowly over to the pig. *I'm going to have nightmares about this for sure*, I thought, as I focused on the point at the top of the skull where I'd been assured was the best place to aim. I steeled myself, raised the club high above my head and whacked it down as hard as I could, bashing the poor little pig's brains out. Nixon gave me a proud hug, then all the rest of the village lined up to embrace me as I battled the urge to vomit.

Gory induction notwithstanding, I was now an adopted member of Bene village, East Coast Santo, Vanuatu. A fascinating new aspect of my life had just opened up, and I already knew deep down that I would be spending a lot more time in Vanuatu in the future, but for now I still had commitments back in Australia. I'd finished my first year as a rural generalist registrar and it was time for me to dive into anaesthetics. I had a 12-month job lined up to do this in Cairns, the small coastal city not far from where I grew up.

Far North Queensland, Australia

Cairns is an attractive, tropical town and the anaesthetists in my department turned out to be a fun bunch. It was interesting work, too. Anaesthetics essentially involves twiddling the dials of the human machine, adjusting physiology via pharmacology and putting a lot of tubes into people in the process. My twelve-month programme included three months working in ICU, so I was building skills in resuscitation and critical care that I could see would all be very useful when I went back out to the bush. Getting to know the staff specialists at the referral hospital was valuable too. Nothing bonds a bunch of doctors quite like having to give CPR together when a patient's heart stops beating or sticking needles into a patient's chest* while they're trying very hard to have a respiratory arrest in a CT scanner. In the meantime, I had a bachelor pad in town, biked to work and partied with my hospital pals on the weekends.

I also had the chance to catch up with Marco – my high-school friend who'd introduced me to punk music and with whom I'd played in a band. He'd moved up to Cairns to look after his sick father. Marco had also dreamed of being a doctor, but life, it seemed, had other plans for him. He'd taken way too many mind-altering substances, found Jesus, lost Jesus, lost more than a few jobs and got into quite a bit of trouble for trying to burn down a church. Throughout his tortured journey, however, he'd managed to stay the same sweet guy, and it was nice for me to be able to reconnect

---

* A technique known as needle thoracostomy is an emergency procedure that involves insertion of a needle through the front of a patient's chest. It is done when a patient is suspected to have something called a tension pneumothorax, where the lung is collapsing due to trapped air. Sometimes more than one needle is required. Insertion of a proper chest tube is usually required after that.

with someone from my teenage years, which were already seeming like a long time ago.

When I reached the halfway point of my year of anaesthetics, I was finally able to make the long-awaited phone call.

'Hey, Jack, it's Lachie McIver. We spoke a couple of years ago when I was enquiring about jobs in the Torres Strait.'

'Right, yeah, Lachie,' the Thursday Island hospital boss drawled down the phone. 'How's it going?'

'Good, thanks. Listen, I'm calling to let you know I can give an anaesthetic now.'

'Oh, yeah?'

'Yeah. I've been doing a year of it in Cairns, getting my ticket, like you said I'd need to get a gig up there. I was hoping you might have a job for me next year.'

'Okay, cool. I'll see what I can do,' he said, and hung up on me (again).

That seemed like about as much reassurance as I'd get about the next step in my career at this point, so I concentrated on preparing for the assessments I'd have to do at the end of the year to get signed off as a rural hospital anaesthetist. I was also approaching the end of my master's degree in public health and tropical medicine and was trying to make the most of the new connections and opportunities that came with that. Several of my classmates had worked abroad, and some of our subjects, such as refugee health, were quite blatant recruitment drives for MSF. *Be patient*, I told myself. *Crack on, finish your training and then you should be ready for some of that action.* It seemed that breaking into the ambiguously broad field of 'global health' involved something of a catch-22, whereby organisations like MSF, WHO or the International Committee of the Red Cross (ICRC) preferred to hire people with experience working in developing countries, which was reasonable enough, but it was tricky to get such experience without working for precisely those kind of organisations.

I wasn't quite sure how to square that circle, but I kept thinking back to Ray and his stories of working in Papua New Guinea. When I realised it was possible to do an elective in tropical paediatrics in PNG in the final part of my master's programme, I leapt at the chance. I took a few weeks of annual leave from my anaesthetics job and booked a ticket to Madang.

Papua New Guinea

Leprosy is a subtle, insidious, sneaky disease. It's an old-timey, biblical-sounding affliction that seems out of place in the twenty-first century. But here I was, sitting on the front deck of a wooden hut in the jungle on the north coast of Papua New Guinea, chatting to a lovely elderly lady who'd been living with leprosy for decades. For a young doctor like me with an interest in tropical medicine, she was a fascinating person to meet. Her cracked, wide-rimmed glasses masked the thickened eyebrows and drooping lids that were typical of long-standing leprosy and her home-made ankle brace only partly compensated for the nerve damage she'd suffered in her lower limb. Contracting leprosy requires prolonged exposure to *Mycobacterium leprae*, a cousin of the organism that causes tuberculosis (TB). Most people aren't aware they have the disease until it has already progressed to the point of attacking nerves and numbing skin. As it can be difficult to diagnose and requires many months of treatment, even where the medications are available, most leprosy patients are left with deformities and disabilities, which can lead to stigmatisation and significant psycho-emotional suffering.

The lady here in the village seemed cheerful enough, as she explained to me how to cook the yams she was preparing for lunch and shooed away the children playing too close to the fire. *It can't be easy for her*, I thought, as I watched her shuffle around on her swollen, twisted feet and peer owlishly through her lenses and the smoke to poke around in the pot she had on the boil. I admired her resilience, as I did that of many people I'd meet over the following weeks in PNG: a little girl in an antique wheelchair whose brain and spinal cord had been severely damaged by inflammation due to measles (an entirely preventable disease that should have no place in this era of vaccinations); a fit young man who'd fallen out of a coconut palm and broken both his legs, which were being treated by traction, leaving him semi-recumbent for six weeks with ropes around his ankles tied to heavy bottles of water dangling over the end of the bed; and a solemn pair of new parents who kept vigil over their baby who'd been born with a hole in her heart and was slowly dying of oxygen starvation.

A cholera outbreak was occurring in Madang at the time our little group of Aussie doctors and nurses arrived for our intensive immersion in tropical paediatrics, where we were to work alongside the staff at Madang Hospital. Cholera is yet another avoidable, anachronistic disease that still causes millions of infections and tens of thousands of deaths per year, most of them children in developing countries. It has to be one of the most pitiful ways to die – diarrhoea so severe you literally shit yourself to death. This was the worst cholera outbreak recorded in PNG in the last fifty years, so it caught quite a bit of international attention. Perhaps too much.

Eric, the Papua New Guinean doctor who ran the Madang Hospital ED, seemed a bit rattled. He was responsible for overseeing the cholera treatment centre – a special tent that had been set up next to the hospital, with a trench dug around it, chlorine tanks at the entrances and exits and buckets placed under every stretcher. Every stretcher, in turn, had a skinny, dehydrated patient in it, hooked up to IV fluids and looking desperately miserable. On top of that, Eric had to manage the various international medical emergency teams that appeared out of nowhere to assist. It was a phenomenon I'd see repeatedly over the years, whereby well-meaning individuals and organisations would take it upon themselves to show up to an epidemic or a disaster zone, often loaded with supplies that were out of date, inappropriate, illegible or otherwise useless in such resource-constrained contexts. These groups and their gear would often overwhelm the local staff and prove reluctant to coordinate with other groups or submit to leadership from other sources.

We assisted Eric and his colleagues as best we could, but when the folks from MSF and WHO showed up, setting up new protocols, hauling in their own equipment and sweating into their beers every evening at the beach bar, we realised we were no longer needed, so we decamped inland to Yagaum. I felt for Eric. He was a good doctor – the first emergency specialist to be trained in PNG – who knew his stuff and was respected by his team, but it was clear he felt conflicted. The extra help was mostly welcome, but where he should have been able to lead, he was being forced instead to follow. The MSF team made a particularly poor impression on the Madang Hospital medical staff, seeming arrogant and dismissive of the efforts made prior to their arrival. I still dreamed of working for MSF, and they've long had a legitimate claim to being the world's best in delivering medical care in humanitarian emergencies, but from the little I saw in Madang, I realised they still had quite a lot to learn.

I learned a lot myself in PNG. I saw my first cases of malaria and TB – two of the principal infectious scourges for poor people in tropical countries. We helped treat paediatric patients suffering from meningitis, diarrhoeal disease and pneumonia, which together constitute the other main killers of children in the developing world. Other patients had experienced nasty trauma – machete wounds, open fractures and even one poor bloke from whose skull we had to extract a rusty nail which had penetrated into his brain.

It was impressive to see the Papua New Guinean doctors in action. They calmly went about their business, doing the ward rounds, attending to the emergency patients and popping off to deliver a baby, take out an appendix or drain an abscess on a regular basis, all the while putting up with our presence. We peppered them with questions and excitedly pestered them to come and check out the enlarged spleens and optic nerves we were seeing when we plonked our precious ultrasound probe on malarial abdomens or meningitic eyeballs. These guys were hardcore rural doctors, very experienced in their own settings, just lacking a little by way of training opportunities and a hell of a lot by way of resources. They were every bit as inspiring to me in the present as Ray had been with his stories of working in PNG in the past. When it came to providing medical care in isolated places, I was learning to appreciate the value of making the most of what was available, rather than lamenting what was lacking. And I was developing a more nuanced understanding of the role of doctors in rural and remote areas, where nurses or clinical assistants typically do much of the work that doctors would do in the city. Anaesthetics was a prime example. I was almost qualified as a rural hospital anaesthetist in Australia, yet here in PNG, the nearest neighbouring country, most anaesthetics were given by nurses or anaesthetic technicians, with the discipline barely considered a 'medical' specialty at all. Honestly, I could see why. If you only have one or two drugs available to knock a patient out and keep them pain-free during surgery, whether you're giving those drugs into a vein or via spinal injection, it doesn't take years of medical training to be able to do it. That's not to say that specialist anaesthetists aren't a vital component of a tertiary hospital team in a developed country, where the ceiling of care is so much higher, but in the bush, particularly in a low-income setting, I was starting to see how skills and tasks shared between health professionals working as a team could, and often must, be distributed differently.

With these insights in mind and fired up by this spicy taste of tropical medicine, it was finally time to take up my long-anticipated post. Jack, the medical superintendent on Thursday Island, had proved true to his word and offered me a job as one of the Senior Medical Officers in the Torres Strait. The archipelago, which straddles the busy, watery, porous border between the north-east tip of Australia and the south coast of PNG, includes close to three hundred islands, fourteen of which are home to permanent communities of Torres Strait Islander people – Australia's other main Indigenous population. Politically, the Torres Strait is Australian but ethnically and culturally, Torres Strait Islanders are distinctly Melanesian. They have more in common with the Indigenous peoples of PNG, Solomon Islands, Vanuatu, Fiji and New Caledonia than with most of the Aboriginal communities of the gigantic, desert continent to the south. The Torres Strait represents a unique bridge. A comparison of the two countries on either side reveals some of the greatest discrepancies in socio-economic and health indicators of any countries that share a border anywhere in the world. For the next fifteen months or so, this would be my home.

CHAPTER FIVE

2010

Torres Strait Islands, Australia

I was asleep when the phone rang. A deep, delicious sleep – the kind from which you wake up delirious and disoriented and it takes several seconds to remember where you are, who you are and whether or not you're wearing any underpants. Having successfully worked my way down to the end of that mental checklist, I scrabbled for the light switch and fumbled around until I found the offending phone.

'Doctor's on-call phone, Lachie speaking,' I mumbled.

'Lachie, it's Nellie here, calling from ED. I'm sorry, did I wake you?'

'Yeah, but it's fine, Nellie.' I yawned as I struggled to prop myself up in bed and pay attention. 'What time is it?'

'It's half past nine.' Lordy. How could I have been so sound asleep at nine thirty on a Friday night? I could blame those long hours at the hospital, I supposed, or just admit I was getting older. I was yet to turn 30 but felt well on my way to becoming a grumpy old man.

'Copy that,' I replied, stifling another yawn. 'What can I do for you?'

'Could you please come down and take a look at this little boy who's just arrived? He has a high fever with abdominal pain and vomiting and seems to be in pretty bad shape.'

'No worries. Let me chuck some clothes on and I'll be there in a few minutes.'

As I picked my way down the hill to the ED, sweeping my headtorch around to avoid treading on any snakes or cane toads that might be enjoying the warmth of the concrete path on a cool island night, I pondered some of the possible scenarios that might be awaiting me. If our little patient had simple gastroenteritis, that shouldn't be a problem. Even if it was severe, we had a few spare beds on the paediatric ward and could keep him overnight, at least, to see how he progressed. If it was appendicitis, however, then things could get a lot more complicated. Only two of our medical team on Thursday Island were trained to perform appendicectomies and I didn't know if either of them was 'on island' at the moment. To make matters a damn-sight worse, several parts of the hospital had been badly damaged in the cyclone that had passed through a couple of days earlier and I wasn't sure what state the operating theatre was in.

I strode into the ED to find Nellie inserting an IV line into the arm of a typically stocky little Islander lad of about eight or nine, who was crying and clearly in pain, although whether that was from Nellie's efforts or his belly wasn't clear just yet. It became clearer 30 seconds later when I examined his abdomen, gently pressing over the key regions to see where he was most tender. He could barely tolerate me touching him at all, but my worst suspicions were confirmed when I got to the area just above his right hip and he bleated pitifully and pushed my hand away. That amount of pain, with the poor boy's high fever and vomiting – all signs pointed to appendicitis. Added to that, his high pulse rate, low blood pressure and tense abdominal wall suggested the pesky thing had probably already ruptured. Bugger. Time to summon a surgeon.

'Hi, it's Max,' is what I could just make out on the phone over the sound of wailing and warbling to music being belted out in the background.

'Max, mate, it's Lachie,' I shouted. 'Where are you?'

'I'm at the Torres, bro.'

Ah, of course. Friday was karaoke night at the Torres Hotel – Australia's most northerly pub, as they claimed, although The Grand was probably miffed that they missed out by a matter of a few hundred metres.

'How pissed are you?'

'Ah, lemme think, I've had three beers . . . '

Well, okay, obviously not ideal, I thought, but maybe we could straighten him out and steady those surgeon's hands with a couple of stiff black coffees, and then—

' . . . and about five tequila stuntmen.'

'Tequila *stuntmen*? Like snorting the salt and squeezing the lemon in your eye and all that?'

'Ha ha, yeah, man, it's been mayhem down here! We've been playing pool and drinking games with the customs and border control guys and I'm taking all their money, whoo wh—'

I hung up on him. Max was a good friend and a skilled clinician but he was pretty intense at the best of times – a competitive ultra-marathoner who spent his annual leave sloshing past penguins during week-long races in Antarctica and the like. For him, living on a small island four kilometres wide was like being a panther in a cage. He definitely needed to let off some steam every now and then.

I called Johan.

'Hello, Doctor Vandenbergh speaking,' came my colleague's low South African lilt.

'Hey, Johan, it's Lachie. Are you on the island?'

'Yes, I'm here at home. What's up?'

'I've got a kid with a red-hot appendix here in ED. Seems to be ruptured. You up for it?'

'Ah, man, I was up late last night with that guy with the stroke. Is Max around?'

'Yeah, but he's on the turps* at the Torres. Speaking of which, have you had anything to drink this evening?'

The surgical team didn't have an official roster, which was a double-edged sword – it meant they could go several nights without being called if we had no surgical emergencies but could then get punished relentlessly with few chances for breaks.

'Not yet. I was just about to open a nice bottle of Malbec.' No doubt. He was approaching retirement, old Johan, and appeared to have reached the stage in his life where he knew most things worth knowing in rural medicine and even more about red wine.

'So, are you up for it?'

He sighed. 'Okay, if you call the theatre team in, I'll be down there in fifteen minutes.'

'Great, thanks mate. See you soon.'

Nellie turned to me with a phone in her hand and a worried expression.

'Lachie, Trish says the operating theatre is out of action because of the cyclone damage.'

'Shit a brick. Let me talk to her.'

Trish, the boss of the operating theatre, could be a handful. She was a very experienced and respected nurse but could be painfully prickly at times. Nevertheless, despite her reputation as a chain-smoking doctor-killer, I had the sense she had a bit of a soft spot for me, although I hadn't the faintest idea why. Maybe she had a thing for gingery beards.

'Trish, it's Lachie. Sorry to call you so late on a Friday night.'

'Lachie, my boy,' she rasped, 'what's this I hear about you trying to

---

* Aussie slang for drinking alcohol, usually in the context of drinking quickly and/or to excess.

arrange an appendicectomy when we don't have an operating theatre to operate in?'

'I don't think we have a choice, to be honest. Looks like this little guy's ruptured his appendix, so we need to get in there ASAP.'

'Well, if our theatre's out of action, shouldn't we be shipping him down to Cairns?'

She was right. That option would normally be on the table, if we could keep our patient stable for at least the next few hours until the Flying Docs could get up here and collect him, but . . .

'But, Trish, I just heard the maintenance guys were crawling all over the helipad this afternoon and they sent a message around to say it was unsafe to land on until the cyclone damage is repaired. I can't see any option but to try and sort him out here. I think we're pretty much stuck.'

'Stuck,' she muttered (or at least I think that's what she said). 'Okay, I'm coming in.'

Johan clomped into the ED and loomed over the patient's bed, his kind, twinkling grey eyes and soft touch belying his intimidating frame and huge, knobbly hands.

'Yes, Lachie, I agree, it's probably a ruptured appendix. We're going to have to open him up.'

The eyes on the little boy's tear-stained face widened further and he started crying again, this time more from fear than pain.

'It's okay, *smol bala* (little guy),' I reassured him, squeezing his cold, chubby, sweaty little hand, 'you won't feel a thing, I promise. You'll just have a nice sleep and when you wake up, you'll be all better.'

As Nellie cracked open the morphine and started the IV fluid infusion, Johan and I conferred.

'What do you reckon, Johan? Is there any way we can use the operating theatre?'

'Nope,' barked Trish, as she heaved around the corner, wheezing. 'I just checked and there's no power or lights in there at all. Must have damaged the wiring or something.'

'Can we do a quick-fix job or get a generator hooked up in there?' I wondered out loud, the frustration adding to my concern.

'Nope, it's Friday night, Lachie. No repairs or maintenance available until Monday.'

Johan leaned back against the resuscitation trolley and pushed his scrubs cap back to scratch his silvery head pensively.

'You know, guys, back in South Africa we basically used to do these appendicectomies on a kitchen table. We just need light, an air supply, suction and oxygen for the anaesthetic machine. Just like we have over on the labour ward . . . '

The three of us stopped and slowly looked at each other in turn. Could we? Should we?

'We wouldn't be able to come close to ideal sterile conditions,' I pointed out, doubtfully.

'That's true,' Johan mused, 'but you could say this is a life-or-death situation. If we don't operate soon and take out that bit of busted bowel . . . '

We both looked at Trish. She was the only one who could make it happen.

She pursed her lips, narrowed her eyes at us briefly, then gave a firm nod.

'This is the real deal, gentlemen,' she said briskly, bustling us off towards the change rooms. 'We'll get everything ready and you two meet us in maternity. Don't dilly-dally!'

I gazed around our makeshift operating theatre with a mix of anxiety and awe. The surgical equipment was crammed in all around us, sterile drapes covering every possible surface. It was far from perfect, but it would have to be good enough. The machine behind me beeped and I updated the marks in the chart to record the anaesthetic I'd given so far. Our little patient had gone off to sleep easily enough, particularly with the previous doses of morphine on board, but the fluids and drugs he was needing now suggested he was heading into potentially fatal septic shock. I peeped over the operating drape at Johan. He was frowning, his furrowed brow glistening with sweat under the dim yellow glow of the light that was usually the first thing our Torres Strait Islander babies saw as they emerged into their noisy new world.

'How are things down your end, mate?' I asked quietly.

'I'm having a tough time, to be honest. This appendix must have been ruptured for a while. There's a lot of gangrenous tissue and his belly is full of pus. I can hardly see what I'm doing with this *kak* (shit) light in here,' came the terse reply.

I hadn't seen Johan struggle like this before. He was a careful, experienced surgeon, so if he was finding it difficult, we should all be worried.

'Do you want to use my headtorch?'

Johan paused and blinked up at me.

'Yeah, sure, that would be great. Do you have it here?'

'Yep, right here.' I fossicked in my bag and squeezed around the side of the bed to strap the torch onto Johan's sweaty head. 'Which would you prefer, the red light or the strobe?'

'Wh—?' Johan half turned and bumped into the equipment tray, nearly knocking all of our (hopefully) sterile surgical instruments onto the floor.

I chuckled and patted him on the back.

'Just kidding. Thought I should lighten the mood a little. You know, *lighten*? Sorry, I'll stop now. Here you go.' I clicked the headtorch onto the brightest setting. 'How's that?'

Johan peered into the open abdominal cavity, then looked up at me. I thought I caught him smiling before I was blinded by the light.

'That's much better. Thanks. You wanker. We should be alright now.'

Once the problematic appendix and the pools of pus were safely extracted from the boy's belly, Johan closed the wound with his typically neat sutures. I wheeled our little patient back to the ED to wait with his grateful parents while he woke up, as Trish and her colleagues got to work reconverting our one-time operating theatre back into its usual role on the labour ward.

Johan strolled through to check on things before he headed home. He handed me my headtorch with a smile and a wink. 'That'll be one for the memoirs, eh?'

*

It seemed that every day in the Torres Strait would bring some patient or problem that was new, challenging or different in some way. The context contributed to the craziness. We were so far away from our nearest referral hospital – Cairns was almost a thousand kilometres, or two hours' flying time, to the south – that we had to be able to do almost all of the diagnosing and treating ourselves. One Saturday night saw me sticking an extra-long needle in the back of a big guy who'd had a headache all day, to find his spinal fluid spurting out in a cloudy, high-pressure rush. Our lab manager, Janet, called me over to look at it under the microscope. The smattering of pink-stained, double-barrelled bacteria throughout his cerebrospinal fluid could only mean one thing: meningococcal meningitis.

Janet phoned me up frantic another weekend evening when she noticed a very alarming pattern of liver enzymes on a blood sample I'd sent over. I had to apologise. I should have told her the patient I was seeing in ED whose name, 'Harry Labrador', I'd scribbled on the pathology form, was the hospital radiographer's beloved Golden Retriever. Poor little fella had pretty severe pancreatitis, so I tried my best to figure out what he needed in terms of pain relief, fluids and antibiotics, as we had no vets in the Torres Strait.

I was particularly fond of doing aeromedical retrievals – lugging the emergency kit into the whirlybird* and thundering off at low altitude over the coral reefs, turtles and occasional dugong to the outer islands to collect an elderly lady with heart failure, a baby with severe respiratory disease or a psychotic teenager who'd chopped his own fingers off with a machete.

*

On one blustery afternoon, while I was busy in the ED, the on-call phone clipped to my belt blared into life yet again. It was Kaz, the nurse from just across the water on Horn Island. My eyes widened as she hurriedly explained what she was dealing with: a teenage girl having seizures that refused to stop.

I offered the best advice I could think of in the moment. 'If it's too difficult to get an IV line in, Kaz, then you'd better just give her another twenty milligrams of rectal diazepam. I'll be there as soon as I can.'

Shiiiiiit, I thought, as I hung up the phone. This was a tricky one. The only hospital in the Torres Strait was on Thursday Island, so any sick patients on any of the other islands needed to be transferred there, usually by helicopter. Horn Island was only a ten-minute chopper ride away, but there was no way we could fly in this wet-season wind. I brainstormed with the ambulance officers. The only option, we quickly realised, was to find a boat willing to brave the waves to take a paramedic and me over to the other side. We called George, the owner-captain of the inter-island ferry service. He was a gruff old bugger at the best of times, but he had a good heart and was perhaps our only hope.

---

* Slang for helicopter.

'Sorry, Lachie, I would help, but our boat got banged up by the waves as we were docking and the outboard's busted. I'm fixing it now, but it won't be back in action until tomorrow. You could give Wilhelm a call if you're desperate; he'd probably do it.'

Wilhelm. I wasn't sure that was a good idea. He was an eccentric German who ran deep-sea-fishing tours, roaring around the Strait with a cooler full of beers in his souped-up speedboat that had two massive outboards and needed a reinforced transom to handle the extra power. I'd been in that boat and it leapt over the water like a rabid greyhound. But George was right, Wilhelm would probably do it. And we were desperate.

'*Ja*, Lachie, no problem. I'll see you at the pier.' Wilhelm sounded excited. Hopefully he'd only had a few beers by this time in the afternoon.

I clung fiercely to the seat and rail of Wilhelm's monster-boat as we smacked through the waves, whacks of salty water spraying over us as we thumped down into each trough, with Wilhelm at the wheel, barefoot and shirtless, legs apart, teeth bared and hair billowing behind him like a four-hundred-horsepower pirate. Casey, the paramedic riding with me, had to sit on our gear bag to stop it bouncing off into the angry grey sea. This twenty-minute traverse was wild enough with just the three of us; I couldn't imagine how we'd do it in reverse with a heavily sedated patient on board. I was relieved to see Horn Island's ambulance at the dock, waiting to whisk us up to the clinic.

After we'd scrambled back up onto dry land, I had a few minutes in the back of the ambulance to think about a plan for the patient who awaited. Kaz had done a good job – giving rectal medication isn't easy, particularly with a moving target – but the girl was still convulsing when we arrived. She had two family members, plus the clinic assistant, holding her firmly in the bed so she didn't fall off. She was bleeding a little from the arm where

Kaz had tried to get an IV line in and I could see her legs were covered with infected sores. Her eyes were closed but her face looked swollen. And then the penny dropped.

'Has she ever had a fit like this before?' I asked her worried mother, who was helping hold her down.

'Never, just started this afternoon,' she replied.

'Has she had a fall or hit her head or anything?'

'Don't think so, doc.'

I turned to Kaz. 'Does she have a fever? What's her blood pressure doing?'

'Temp's thirty-eight point one, blood pressure's one-ninety over one-twenty. I assumed she was hypertensive from the seizure.'

'Might be the other way around, I reckon. With those leg lesions and the puffy face, this could be a bad case of PSGN.'

Post-streptococcal glomerulonephritis is a bizarre immune response that some people's bodies mount in the presence of certain bacterial infections, typically in the skin. The immune system goes into overdrive and the kidneys become inflamed, which causes bleeding into the urinary tract and an elevation in blood pressure. It was possible, I reasoned, that this lass's blood pressure had been high enough for long enough that her brain had become swollen and scrambled – a phenomenon called hypertensive encephalopathy. That might explain why Kaz's rectal sedatives hadn't done the trick in stopping the seizures. These were pretty much the worst possible circumstances in which to attempt what I knew had to be done. I motioned Kaz and Casey over to the side of the room for a quick conference.

'We're going to have to intubate,' I said quietly. 'Not the best setting for it, I know, but we have to stop the seizures; she can't protect her airway and we've got to get her back over to the other side safely.'

They both nodded.

'I've got the kit set up already, Lachie,' said Kaz, pointing to a trolley.

I did a quick check and gave her a thumbs-up. 'Yep, that's everything we need. Love your work, Kaz.' Remote area nurses. They're absolute legends.

We explained to the mother what we had to do. She left the room with her other daughter hugging her tightly as she sobbed softly into her shirtsleeve. Kaz carefully injected the hypnotic drugs* into the cannula I'd managed to get in one of the girl's veins, as Casey squeezed the ventilation bag at the end of the mask I held tightly over our patient's face. The seizures slowed, then stopped, and once the final twitch that came from the paralytic medication we'd given had subsided, I flipped open the metal blade on the laryngoscope† and slid it into the girl's mouth. For a moment all the little light showed me was teeth and gums and tongue and then, at last, the larynx flopped into view. I passed a plastic breathing tube through the gap between her vocal cords and into the top of the trachea. Casey used a syringe to inflate the cuff on the tube to keep it in place and gave the ventilation bag another squeeze.

'All good?' he asked, as all three of us watched her chest rise and fall.

I had a quick listen to her lungs with my stethoscope and heard breath sounds on both sides – almost always what you want to hear.

'All good. Thanks guys. Let's get the infusion pumps running and get out of here. We've got a boat to catch.'

I swear I saw Wilhelm sober up a notch or two when he saw us wheeling our unconscious, intubated patient down the dock ramp.

---

* An anaesthetic procedure involving manipulation of a patient's airway usually involves a minimum of two or three drugs: hypnotics to make the person go to sleep, then paralytics to stop them moving, typically with the addition of an analgesic to ensure they don't feel pain.

† The hand-held instrument used to visualise the vocal cords.

'Woah, okay, there's a first time for everything,' he said with a low whistle and a shake of his head. 'I guess we'll be taking it a bit easier on the way home!'

We arrived back at the dock on Thursday Island to find another ambulance waiting. All of us, patient included, were soaking wet, but we'd managed to keep her paralysed and ventilated, despite the gale and spray. When the wind died down and the helicopter could take off, she was collected by the Flying Doctor plane and flown down to the intensive care unit in Cairns.

I saw her back on the island a few weeks later, meandering down the main street, giggling with a few friends. She looked okay from a distance, but it's hard to know what long-term damage can be caused by such an insult to a teenage brain.

*

One of the wildest parts of the job as a doctor in the Torres Strait is flying out to the other, smaller, even more remote islands to do clinics. Late one stormy night, I was on Boigu, one of the northernmost islands in the Strait, from which – when it wasn't pissing down with rain – you could see the smoke and fires from the villages across the water on the southern coast of Papua New Guinea. I was staying overnight to do a two-day clinic and when Angie, the nurse, came banging on my mosquito-proofed screen door after dinner I knew it couldn't be good news.

'Got a lady in labour,' she panted, apparently having sprinted over from the clinic.

'Fuck. Not my forte, I gotta say. How's she going?'

'Not great. She's been brought over in a dinghy from a village on the other side of the ditch. They say she's been labouring for two days and now she's really fatigued. And she has a fever.'

'Double fuck. Okay, I'll come take a look.'

I slipped on some shoes and followed Angie nervously back through the dark and the rain, trying to remember the treatment for chorioamnionitis* and hoping like hell she wouldn't haemorrhage.

She did not look good. Her brown skin was pale, she was sweating and cold and she, too, was panting. I tried to reassure the lady and her partner in my best Melanesian Pidgin, then quickly inserted a couple of IV lines, started some fluids and antibiotics and got on the phone.

'Hey, Chris, it's Lachie. I'm up on Boigu with a PNG lady in labour. Think she might have chorio. Possibly septic too. I'm giving her fluids and antibiotics but I'm up against it here. What else should I be doing?'

As I'd learned on that first phone call to Jack, the med super, the docs in the Torres were all skilled in either anaesthetics or obstetrics or, for a rarefied few, both. Chris was one of those few. He had worked at a senior level across at least five different departments in tertiary hospitals in the past and nothing, it seemed, could faze him.

'Sounds like a good start, Lachie. What's her CTG† look like?'

Good question. Did we even have a cardiotocograph in this clinic? I turned around to see Angie wheeling in an ageing machine and attaching it to our patient's belly. Guess that must be it. At least we'd be able to monitor her contractions and the baby's heartbeat now.

'I'll get back to you on that. What else?'

'Is it her first baby? Is she full term?'

---

* An infection of the amniotic fluid, placenta and/or foetus that can be a serious complication of labour. It is often abbreviated as 'chorio'.

† Abbreviation for 'cardiotocograph' – a machine that is attached to a woman's abdomen to monitor uterine contractions and the heartbeat of the foetus during labour. Sometimes an electrode is also attached to the baby's scalp by inserting it through the woman's open cervix.

A quick four-way discussion took place in Pidgin.

'Yep, first bub. No idea how far along she is though.'

'Hmm, okay. Well, what you're gonna have to watch for is . . .'

The patient's sudden scream drowned out Chris's voice over the phone. I turned around to see her half sitting up in the bed, gritting her teeth, grappling at the bedrails and puffing like a steam train. And . . .

'Shit, she's crowning, Chris. I'll have to call you back.'

I hung up the phone and rushed over to where Angie – gloved, sweating and shouting instructions – was crouching like a baseball catcher between the huffing lady's legs.

I shuffled nervously from one foot to the other as Angie guided the baby's slime-covered head out and held the little body firmly as it rotated along the curve of the birth canal. It slowed in its egress, then stopped. Was it stuck? Angie and I glanced at each other anxiously.

'Come on now, love, you can do it – just one more push!' Angie cried.

With a wail and a shudder from the mother, a tiny shoulder popped out, then another and, after a few long seconds and one last maternal caterwaul, the rest of the baby slithered out in a gush. Angie bundled it up in a couple of towels and began rubbing it briskly, simultaneously cleaning, warming and trying to stimulate the wee thing to breathe. I tried to keep one eye on Angie and an ear out for a baby's cry while maintaining gentle traction on the cord still attached to the yet-to-be-delivered placenta. It was dim and humid in our clinic and I was feeling very hot and jumpy. We were stuck on a remote island with no help at hand and no prospect of rescue any time soon. The worst thing that could happen now would be . . . Bugger. Bleeding.

It started as a trickle. Barely an ooze at the edges of the birth canal. I dabbed at it with some gauze, but it kept coming. I tried not to pull too hard on the cord. *Don't panic*, I told myself, *a bit of blood loss from labour is normal.* But, as I rummaged around in my overbaked brain for what remained of my basic obstetrics training, I realised this lady was a sitting duck for a post-partum haemorrhage. First baby, prolonged labour, sick with a fever – this could go very badly, very quickly.

'Angie,' I called over to her quietly, trying not to sound alarmed.

Angie turned towards me and I could see she was worried too, as, despite her vigorous rubbing and best attempts at warming, we were yet to hear a peep from the newborn.

'What's up?'

'She's bleeding quite a bit here.' I pointed with my gauze.

We exchanged another long, tense look.

'Have you done much obstetrics?' she asked.

'The bare minimum,' I confessed. 'Have you done much midwifery?'

'Only the basics.' She jiggled the baby in her arms and bit her lip.

'Right. Umm. Okay.'

It seemed we'd all drawn the short straw that evening.

'Okay,' I said again, in a failed attempt to strike a confident tone. 'Let's do this: you keep looking after the baby and I'll try and sort out this bleeding. Don't suppose we have any blood in the fridge here?' I knew as I asked the question how stupid I sounded. Angie just stared back at me in silence. 'No, of course not,' I said, shaking my head to clear my thoughts. 'Never mind. We must have some emergency drugs though, right? Some oxytocin or ergometrine or something?'

We had both, as it turned out. I gave one as a jab in our lady's thigh and the other as a squirt in her vein, hoping that they'd make the uterine muscles contract and constrict the bleeding vessels. I hung up another bag of IV fluids, found some suture thread and sterile instruments and set it all up like I knew what I was doing. I hadn't much of a clue, though, and could barely see a bloody thing anyway. One of the clinic assistants was sent running back through the rain to my room to grab what was becoming the single most useful tool in my rural doctor's kit: my headtorch. I strapped it over my sweaty brow and squatted on a stool between the stirrups holding the lady's legs akimbo. All I could see was bleeding flesh. The placenta had emerged, at last, and to my inexpert eye, at least, it seemed to have all its bits and pieces, but in the birthing process the poor woman's genitals looked like they had been blown open by a grenade.

I hadn't even seen enough normal deliveries to be confident about what 'normal' looked like, let alone what to expect with a 'typical' post-partum haemorrhage (commonly known as PPH). But, even though I didn't know much about obstetrics, I knew there was nothing normal or typical about this scenario. I tried to kick my brain into gear. I'd given the important drugs, attempted to massage the lax uterus back into action from the outside and now had my left hand pressing on the lady's pelvis as my right hand was buried up to the wrist in the birth canal, squeezing the uterus from both directions in a manoeuvre that the textbooks blandly refer to as 'bimanual compression'. I tried that for a few minutes, but the warm, persistent trickle down my right forearm warned me I needed to move on to the next step. It was stitching time.

'How's the baby doing?' I called over my shoulder to Angie.

'Not good.'

I looked over to where Angie was hunched over the bundle of towels on the other bed, giving quick puffs of oxygen to the still-silent newborn.

'He's not doing much. Barely moving or breathing at all. Apgar scores[*] are poor.'

---

[*] This is a simple indicator of a baby's health in the minutes following delivery, based on rapid assessments of their pulse, breathing, skin colour, muscle tone and response to stimulation.

The woman on my side of the room, who'd been quiet herself for a while – *a bit too quiet*, now I thought about it – struggled to sit up, freed from the hands she'd had clamped around her pubic bone.

'Is it a boy?' she asked softly.

'Yes, a lovely baby boy.' Angie gave her a brief, tight smile. 'But his little lungs aren't working very well right now.'

The woman sank back into the bed. She'd been pale and sweaty earlier, but with the blood she was losing and the natural adrenaline of the labour subsiding, she looked even worse now. With the light from my headtorch, wielding a large, curved needle and a thick suture thread, I did my best to stitch together the most vicious of the gashes in the lady's birth canal. It was difficult to know where and what to suture that might slow the bleeding, and I couldn't help worrying that I was making things worse. I slipped and struggled through the blood and shadows, swearing under my breath and trying not to stab myself in the process.

'Lachie,' Angie called me over, 'I need your help here.'

I put down my suture kit, peeled off my blood-covered gloves, strode over to the other bed, saw what Angie was dealing with and swallowed hard. Newborn babies – healthy ones anyway – tend to be pink and warm and noisy. This one was pale and cool and quiet. Angie kept gently squeezing the tiny ventilator bag attached to the oxygen mask on the baby's face, his little chest rising and falling, but the respiratory support didn't seem to be making much difference. Both our patients were crashing on us simultaneously. This was a fucking nightmare. I got on the phone again.

'Chris, mate, it's Lachie. Our lady delivered but now she's having a PPH and the baby's flat as a pancake. Any way you can get us out of here?'

'Hang on, Lachie, let me check.' I heard muffled, urgent voices arguing at the other end as I waited, dripping sweat over the phone as it burned into my ear. Chris came back, sounding sheepish. 'I'm really sorry, mate, but the chopper can't fly at night in this storm. We'll send it up at first light in the morning, but you'll have to hold on until then. You coping okay?'

I explained to him what I'd done to try and manage the lady's haemorrhage so far and that now we were really worried about the baby.

'Shit, that's tricky,' Chris sympathised. 'Sounds like the baby needs an IV, fluids and antibiotics too. But listen, with just you and Angie there and two sick patients, you might end up having to prioritise, you know?'

Chris paused meaningfully and it took a few seconds before I realised what he was saying. If things continued to get worse, we might not be able to save both patients. In which case, we'd have to be prepared to make a horrible sacrifice. I felt my heart rate creep up, but this was no time to get emotional. We had two patients genuinely at risk of dying here.

I hung up the phone, wondering if I should share with Angie what Chris had hinted at. I decided to keep it to myself for the moment and concentrate on the jobs at hand. After a few painful, futile punctures in the baby's arm, I managed to get an IV cannula in and gave some fluids and antibiotics while Angie soldiered on with the breathing support. I then went back to check how the lady was doing. She was drowsy and still pale, with a rapid heart rate and low blood pressure – all signs of shock, from blood loss, infection or both. The bleeding from her birth canal seemed to have slowed back to a trickle, at least, after my crude attempt at suturing. There was little else we could do now but keep giving fluid, add a little bit of adrenaline, cross our fingers and wait for sunrise.

With the dawn came the welcome sound of a helicopter approaching. Angie and I wearily raised our eyes from what must have been our fifteenth cups of coffee and stared out the window into the fog. Angie looked terrible.

'You look like shit, Lachie,' she said.

'I believe you,' I replied. 'We survived though. Nice work, sister.'

We gave each other a tired hug. It had been an epic night.

Chris, good guy and great doctor that he was, had come up to do the retrieval himself. He and the paramedic didn't waste any time packaging up our two still-very-sick patients and getting airborne again.

I needed a shower, some breakfast and another strong coffee or three. My clinic started again in an hour.

I'd learn later that Chris and the rest of the team back on Thursday Island would manage to save the lady from her septic-haemorrhagic shock, but the little baby passed away. Further tests would reveal he had a rare and usually fatal genetic disorder. I had mixed feelings upon receiving that news. There was no way we could have known that when he was born and, what's more, even if we had managed to keep him alive, he almost certainly would have died when he got back to the village on the other side of the channel in Papua New Guinea. If we had, somehow, known about his condition, I wondered if that would have changed the way we tried to manage the emergency scenario at the time of his birth. Would that have made it 'easier', or less traumatic, for us to try and decide which patient we should focus our efforts on if we realised we couldn't save both? I honestly didn't know the answer, nor what I would do if faced with that same situation again. Every patient is equally important, surely. But sometimes we have to face the simple and terrible truth: we can't save everyone.

*

My tour of duty in the Torres Strait continued in more or less the same vein – wild, frontier medicine in a beautiful, equatorial region that was something of a limbo zone. The Torres Strait Islands are part of Australia, while the communities just north across the water on the coast of the mainland are in Papua New Guinea. As medical professionals, of course we didn't discriminate – any patient who came to our clinics received treatment, no matter which side of the invisible border they came from. The two populations are closely related, and although Torres Strait Islander people certainly have very significant health issues, people from PNG seem to suffer even more, and the health system in that part of the country has for a long time now been almost non-existent. As I was gaining experience, and building on my earlier work in public health, I was becoming increasingly interested in the factors that affected people's health, and the things that could be done to prevent illness in the first place. I passed my final exams, qualifying as a Fellow of the Australian College of Rural and Remote Medicine, completed my master's degree and wondered what I should do next. I was also struggling with the frustration of seeing so many sick patients, one after another on an endless treadmill, without being able to do more to address the underlying causes of their health problems.

I was dabbling a little more in research by this stage, and some of my work had caught the attention of the Australian Primary Health Care Research Institute in Canberra. They offered me some funding to spend a month at a partner institution in Washington DC, working on a project I'd designed exploring the factors that contributed to avoidable deaths, comparing remote communities across Australia. I took a few weeks' leave from my job in the Torres Strait and flew to the US, armed with tables of life expectancies and lists of social determinants of health. It was interesting research, and I felt our findings were valuable, but when I thought deeply about where it led, my heart would sink. We were mostly 'proving' with statistics what anyone with first-hand experience of remote communities already knew. These populations had, overall, a range of characteristics that contributed to poor health: higher rates of poverty; lower levels of education; fewer opportunities for employment; more children per family; more single-parent families; more overcrowded households; higher rates of smoking; less access to clean water, sanitation and hygiene; fresh food (particularly fruit and vegetables) that was limited, expensive and often of poor quality; and more traumatic injuries than urban populations. For Aboriginal and Torres Strait Islander communities who, as a proportion of the total population, increase in number with remoteness, these problems are amplified, as they suffer from the health inequities of both their ethnicity and their rural location. Where did that leave us? In order to improve health in remote communities, particularly for Indigenous Australians, we needed to work together to find ways to sort out, at a minimum, the issues of poverty, education, employment, housing, water, sanitation, hygiene and nutrition. Piece of cake.

I understood how important this was and I could see that I had the opportunity to pursue it, but I was weighed down by the feeling that this was too much for me. I couldn't find in myself the level of commitment, strength and stamina it would take to devote my professional life to trying to tackle those kinds of problems. I didn't consider myself a quitter, but I simply couldn't convince myself that this was the right fight for me. I rubbed shoulders with a few DC power-players, attended some fascinating meetings on Native American health, wrote my reports, talked at a few conferences and went back to the Torres Strait feeling like a failure.

I consoled myself for a while by diving back into clinical medicine. As always, there was plenty of it, most of it interesting. I stuck a breathing tube down the throat of a lady in the back of a moving truck after she'd been paralysed by a snakebite. We juggled complex medication regimes and worried about a malaria outbreak across the islands after an elderly gentleman brought the parasite back from PNG, swirling around in his bloodstream in a potentially killer cocktail along with his HIV and the bacteria causing his pneumonia. And we scratched our heads for days about a boy with red lumps on his skin and blood in his urine while we were simultaneously treating the leprosy and TB that had spread throughout his little body, wondering if we'd caused a drug reaction or he had post-streptococcal glomerulonephritis (in a milder form than the unfortunate girl who'd suffered seizures). Maybe both, shrugged the various specialists we consulted in paediatrics, nephrology and infectious diseases.

Of all the tropical diseases we encountered in the Torres Strait, there was one that I found particularly intriguing, albeit sinister: melioidosis. This potentially deadly infection is caused by a bacteria that lives in the soil and bubbles up when it rains to find a way in through the skin. It then migrates to almost any organ in the body, growing rapidly into abscesses and shedding off satellites to metastasise elsewhere, killing in a matter of days if untreated. The bug in question has been named *Burkholderia pseudomallei*. And it's a beast. It can infect pretty much any part of the body (TB is a similarly versatile killer), and the cases I saw included the most common forms – nasty pneumonias and bloodstream infections – as well as patients with pus built up in their prostate glands (and dripping out of their penises), bones, joints, livers, spleens and brains.

I'd first encountered melioidosis during my tropical medicine elective in Darwin during my final year of medical school. Some of my supervisors back then were world experts in the disease. So, when we noticed that melioidosis seemed to be appearing more often in the Torres, I called my old mentor, Fred. He was a tall, brisk chap who bore more than a passing resemblance to one of the members of Monty Python, which was even more impressive to me than his vast knowledge of tropical infectious diseases.

'Yes, Lachlan, I remember you. Been a while. So, some spikes in melioid over your way, hey? We're seeing the same thing here in the Top End, you know.'

'Oh, yeah?' I replied, my interest now well and truly piqued. 'What do you reckon's going on then, Fred? Is it just an increase in cases due to population growth or an immune system thing or more bugs in the soil or what?'

'Well, population growth is certainly a factor, and we're definitely getting better at diagnosing it, too. But when you think about it, it also has a lot to do with environmental exposure. Here in the Territory, conditions seem to have been gradually getting warmer and wetter, with the storms in the rainy season becoming more severe, so the bacteria are getting flushed up to the surface more often. These increases could be linked to climate change, you know – it's a curse for health all across the tropics.'

I was struck by the logic and implications of that conversation. I was reminded of what I'd learned in my earlier, amateur dallying with climate change and its impacts on health. I read up on some of the latest research findings. The key points were very clear – climate change was already having a damaging effect on the health of human populations around the world, not just due to infectious diseases, but also through heat stress, trauma, malnutrition, chronic diseases and mental illness, among other things – but a lot of the details remained murky. I worried about how Indigenous communities in the deserts and islands of our region would be affected and wondered how we could be doing more to avoid the health problems that seemed to be emerging over the horizon. At one of our weekly medical meetings on Thursday Island, I explained to my colleagues what Fred had said about melioidosis and the possible links with climate change. Another doctor buddy pointed out that we'd also been seeing more cases of Irukandji syndrome recently – patients with severe toxicity from the highly venomous stings of a tiny jellyfish. We looked into it and found that the Irukandji season was indeed lengthening, with their habitats expanding as the ocean waters warmed.

I felt I had to do something. But what could I do? The health problems related to climate change certainly seemed extremely serious, but did I have the stomach for that? I'd already chickened out of the opportunity to take my career in the direction of studying causes of avoidable death in rural communities because I thought the problem was too daunting. Was I completely soft in the head to think I should try and tackle climate change? What about MSF? Wasn't that the plan? I needed a sign.

Late one night, slumped on my tatty couch, looking out over the stormy ocean, luxuriating in not being on call and slurping on a beer, I googled 'global health jobs'. I scrolled through ads for expedition medics – they seemed fun, accompanying groups climbing Kilimanjaro and the like and read the much-less-fun descriptions of what Red Cross doctors did working with prisoners and victims of torture. Wait, what was that? I scrolled back up to the jobs listed with Australian Volunteers International.

Climate Change and Health Officer, World Health Organization, South Pacific Office.

CHAPTER SIX

2011–12
Fiji

My new boss leaned back in his office chair, stroking his beard and re-reading my résumé.

'So, you're a medical doctor, huh? We didn't really expect any actual doctors to apply for this position.'

'Oh, okay,' I replied, not really knowing how to take that news.

Paul looked up at me with a friendly smile. 'I mean, it's great to have you, we're just not used to having MDs on the team.'

I looked around the bustling headquarters of WHO in the South Pacific, as dozens of Fijian and expat staff from myriad countries muttered down telephones, strode in and out of offices and nodded soberly at each other as they clustered around meeting tables. Most of the men sported bula shirts (the Fijian version of the Hawaiian-style floral clobber) and the women swished around in figure-hugging two-piece dresses of bright colours overlaid with Pacific motifs. They all looked extremely busy and important, but if they weren't doctors, who worked for WHO?

'Okay,' I said again. What else was there to say?

I'd arrived in Suva, the humid, humming little capital of Fiji, having gate-crashed two meetings en route. The first was in Canberra, where I'd bowled into the office of Professor Tony McMichael, the most famous and distinguished figure in climate change and health research in the world, and asked if he'd be willing to supervise me if I managed to wangle myself onto a PhD programme to explore that topic in Pacific island countries while working for WHO. Tony patiently listened to my pitch, agreed to my thesis proposal, then invited me to dinner in the senior academics' refectory with a couple of his colleagues. I mumbled shyly into my wine glass, overawed by the brainpower around me, as my dinner companions earnestly discussed strategies to improve 'planetary health'. I then bought a ticket to swing through the hilariously named French Pacific territory of New Caledonia, which bears about as much resemblance to Scotland as a blancmange. A symposium of sorts was being held there between a clutch of cross-disciplinary academics and some health representatives from a number of Pacific island countries to figure out what had already been done on the topic of climate change and health in the region (essentially nothing) and what was left to be done (basically everything).

To begin with, it was clear we had to try and figure out, for each country, how the habitats and populations of climate-sensitive organisms such as mosquitoes would change, along with the patterns of transmission of the diseases they spread. We'd also have to attempt to predict and thus minimise outbreaks of water-borne bugs after floods and droughts, as well as reduce hospitalisations and deaths from heatwaves and severe storms. We'd need to find ways to ensure people had enough healthy food to eat as crops and fisheries withered. And then there was the Pandora's box of psychosocial problems that would surely appear as people lost their land and livelihoods from rising seas and altered environmental conditions. All of that then had to be pulled together into a sensible series of reasonable recommendations for what each tiny little island country's government could do to avoid the worst of those impacts.

By the time I finally sat down with Paul for my formal induction, I felt overloaded with information but had little idea of how to start doing my new job.

'I mean,' he said again, 'it'll be great to have that medical perspective in the environmental health department here. Most of us come from wash, you see.'

What the hell was he talking about? Was he telling me he and his team showered together or something? I must have looked confused enough to prompt an explanation.

'WASH, you know? Water, sanitation and hygiene. We're all scientists and engineers, out there doing the grubby stuff, testing chlorine levels, building tanks and fixing latrines, not treating patients and all that.'

I nodded, trying not to look surprised or disappointed. It sounded like my highfalutin new job with the United Nations wasn't going to be all that glamorous after all.

'Anyway,' Paul drawled on, sounding every bit the Midwestern farmer he'd been in his younger years, 'now that you're here, we can get this project going. We've got – what is it, a little over a year, Ana?' he called out to his assistant, a stylish, middle-aged Fijian lady who, I realised over the following weeks, was the one who mostly ran the show. With an affirmative wave back from Ana, Paul nodded and went on. 'Yep, a little over a year from start to finish, with a dozen different countries needing to have their climate change and health risks figured out and action plans put in place.' Paul leaned back in his chair again, clasped his hands behind his head and grinned at me. 'Got it? Great. Orientation over.'

Given I had *carte blanche* from the boss but no real clue where to begin, I spent the first few weeks reading everything I could get my hands on that seemed relevant to climate change and health. Looking up textbooks and downloading research papers was straightforward; breaking into mildew-ridden repositories in the basements of the regional universities to track down publications specific to the Pacific was more of an adventure. Eventually, once I'd surrounded myself with waist-high piles of printed papers and dusty journals – pages folded, notes inserted – and had sticky notes plastered all over the wall of my little workspace, I told Paul I thought it was time I was let loose.

'Excellent,' he said, reaching for a phone. 'I'll give Rani a call and tell her you're ready for the four plagues.'

Rani was the smart, hard-working coordinator of WHO's climate change and health project in Fiji. It's easy to forget, even for a country like Fiji, which enjoys (and deserves) a global reputation as a tropical island paradise, that around half of the population live in poverty. The health of Fijian people is exemplified by what is known as the 'epidemiological transition', where the ancient, ever-present spectre of infectious diseases is coupled with more modern problems like obesity and type 2 diabetes. The majority of the resources of the Fiji Ministry of Health (MoH) were already dedicated to trying to prevent and treat chronic diseases, so the decision had been made to focus our project on four of the most deadly infectious diseases in the country: dengue fever, typhoid fever, leptospirosis and diarrhoeal diseases. These are common problems in the tropics and occur all around the Pacific. All of these four 'plagues' were known to spike in certain weather conditions, so concern about the effects of climate change was well founded.

Rani and I spent a few months cloistered in a broom cupboard in a dim corner of the office, dredging the data from the MoH and the national meteorology service. The analysis we did in collaboration with a stats guru in New Zealand showed that each of these diseases was indeed linked to extremes of temperature, rainfall and humidity. Even more intriguingly, it appeared that the spikes in cases of those diseases could be predicted a month or two in advance based on weather conditions. This made sense. Heavy rainfall and prolonged drought increased the risk of water supplies becoming contaminated with bugs causing diarrhoea and typhoid fever.

Viruses such as dengue replicate more rapidly in humid conditions, as do the mosquitoes that spread them. And flooding brought rats into houses and caused pooling of water containing animal urine that inevitably led to cases of leptospirosis. We worked hard on our mathematical models, excited by the idea of using weather and climate information to minimise the impact of outbreaks of these diseases. We proposed a collaboration between the meteorology service and the MoH, with the meteorology service providing up-to-date weather data and seasonal forecasting that would enable health centres and clinics all over the islands of Fiji to call in reinforcements and stock up on supplies if a particular disease outbreak was expected, and batten down the hatches if the conditions suggested another severe storm was on the way.

A reality check, however, awaited as we started making forays out to the provincial hospitals and rural health centres to share these ideas with the doctors, nurses and health workers on the frontlines across Fiji. A typical conversation would go something like this:

Head nurse in clinic (let's call her Tupou): *'Io, vinaka vakalevu vuniwai,** (Okay, yes, thank you very much, doctor). What you are saying is very interesting. But we see these kinds of things already, you know?'

Me: 'What do you mean?'

Tupou: 'Well, we know that after the big storms there are usually increases of cases of diarrhoea, especially in the children, and sometimes we see outbreaks of dengue and things like that.'

Me: 'Right. But wouldn't it help if you had some warning that they were coming?'

Tupou, smiling gently: 'Vuniwai, they are always going to come.'

---

* Fijian is a beautiful language, and *vuniwai* (doctor) is one of my favourite words, not just in Fijian, but in any language. Its literal translation is 'tree of water'.

Me, rapidly losing the wind in my sails: 'Okay, sure. But wouldn't it help if you had extra time and staff and other resources to manage the epidemics and disasters when they hit?'

Tupou, still smiling: 'And where is that funding going to come from? Does your programme include a budget for more staff and supplies for us?'

Me, deflated: 'Well, no. But perhaps we could ask the MoH . . . ?'

Tupou, her smile taking on more than a hint of pity, doesn't need to say anything else at this point.

As such conversations were repeated over and over, it was clear that Fiji's health system was already so stretched by the day-to-day needs of the population that asking health workers to do more, particularly in the midst or aftermath of a natural disaster such as a severe storm or flood, was going to be a huge challenge. Even if we thought the overall benefit of pre-emptive action based on our early warning systems would be to reduce the health needs of the communities in question, the resources – people, money, equipment – simply weren't available. This paradox would haunt me throughout my years working on public health problems in developing countries.

*

Leaving Rani to deal with the politics of our findings on Fiji's four plagues, I moved on to the other countries on my hit-list. I spent the next year or so flitting around the region, helping to develop climate change and action plans for 11 more countries, from the malarial jungles of Solomon Islands to the verdant limestone nuggets of Palau. These beautiful island nations have historically been so far removed from the predominant global consciousness that they might as well be different planets. Since the turn of the twenty-first century, however, they have come into the spotlight for the saddest of reasons: they are the canaries in the coalmine of climate change.

Despite contributing the least of any countries to greenhouse gas emissions, these countries have been among the first and hardest hit. I hopped from island to island, meeting with health ministers, analysing disease data and working with a range of international experts. We found that the effects of rising temperatures, severe storms and failure of crops and fisheries would potentially cripple Pacific island communities already suffering from the highest rates of obesity, diabetes and cardiovascular disease in the world. The worst health effects would probably be linked to the region's most precious resource: water.

The Pacific is fondly referred to by many as the 'Blue Continent' and the people of the region are inextricably connected to the sea. The fact that the oceans are slowly and steadily warming, acidifying and rising presents a major long-term peril, while contamination of drinking water sources is a constant threat, made worse by droughts, floods and overcrowding. To examine this problem in detail, I was sent north to the Federated States of Micronesia.

Federated States of Micronesia

Like many Pacific islands, those of Micronesia were used as pawns in various capacities by a variety of more powerful, less considerate countries during the drawn-out agonies of the colonial era. Britain, France, the US and Japan all left their stains on the region throughout their periods of occupation, with the latter's influence most visible north of the equator and the clumsy thumbprints of more modern regional players such as Australia and New Zealand yet to come. Of all the barely believable incidents that occurred in the region in wartime, one of the most dramatic took place in the shallow waters of Chuuk lagoon. In a penultimate convulsion of the Second World War, in early 1944, the Americans discovered that what was left of the Japanese navy was attempting to remain hidden in this equatorial stronghold, ringed by fortifications on the nearby low-lying islands. Over three days of the macabrely named 'Operation Hailstone', the Americans proceeded to strafe the living daylights out of everything in sight, sinking dozens of battleships, carriers, destroyers, tankers, gunboats and submarines – as well as wiping out several hundred aeroplanes on the ground – and leaving the lagoon the largest ship cemetery on the planet. This morbid history also meant that, decades later, Chuuk would become so famous as a destination for scuba junkies that the licence plates on the islands' vehicles would unabashedly state World's Greatest Wreck Diving.

I couldn't resist.

'It's a graveyard down there, man,' said Gary, my dive guide, as we strapped on our tanks. 'Freaked me out the first few times.'

I looked Gary up and down. He didn't seem the type to get freaked out. With his beer belly, long beard and thick gold earrings, he wouldn't have looked out of place with an eye patch and a cutlass. As we waddled out along the pier to our boat, I spotted something odd.

'Hey, mate, you've still got your jeans and singlet on. Don't you want a wetsuit?'

'Nah, these are fine,' he grinned at me. 'When I'm doing cave dives in Florida and we're down there for hours, I whack on a wetsuit. Here in the tropics I just jump in with whatever I'm wearing.'

Despite his atypical dive attire, Gary was an excellent guide. His fins barely moved as he led me down into the wrecks, bubbles blibbing behind him only every ten seconds or so as he took a lackadaisical breath of compressed air. We flicked on our waterproof torches as we floated through a portal of a warship, lying on its side in the sand, fish flitting around the coral that had flourished on this artificial reef. Gary signalled to me to remember not to stir up the silt, then he disappeared down into the bowels of the boat. With my knees bent, making tiny circular kicks with the tips of my fins, I exhaled and floated slowly into the darkness. I followed Gary's faint yellow beam as my own light picked out the rusty, algae-coated metal underside. Gary's torch waggled suddenly up ahead. As I drifted towards him, I sucked in hard. Crates of bombs and guns were clumped together across the sloping floor. Gary reached down and tugged off the lid of a metal box. I tried to call on what remained of my high-school Japanese to decipher the characters written on it, then my breathing rate sped up as our torches flashed across its contents. Gas masks. Gary picked one up and held it over his face for a moment, then offered it to me. I shook my head. They were just old relics, probably never used, but it still didn't feel right. Gary shrugged, put the lid back on the box and descended head-first through an oval-shaped doorway. The broken crockery and upended tables showed us we were in the ship's galley. From there we glided through a bathroom area and into the captain's quarters. As he floated up to another portal, Gary turned to me and, shining his torch up to his head, made a slicing motion with his thumb across his throat. Now I was freaked out. I was breathing fast and we were more than thirty metres below the surface. My air consumption had gone up and I felt the slightly drunken effects of nitrogen narcosis.* I was at the limits of my diving experience and knew I should be planning my return to the surface but had no idea how to get out of the wreck and now my guide was signalling . . . What? He was going to murder me? With no option but to trust him, I followed his bubbles into the next room. He was waiting for me in a corner, his torch slowly circling something. It took a few seconds for me to focus. It was a

---

* This is an effect of breathing compressed gases at depth. It's also known, distinctly more poetically, as 'rapture of the deep', but it can be very dangerous for divers, given how it impairs mental and physical function.

pile of human bones. I counted 17 skulls before I forgot what I was doing and banged down against the bottom of the boat. I kicked up silt, obscuring our visibility, then felt a firm hand clutch my arm as Gary yanked me back up. I gave him the 'Not okay' signal and pointed to my head to indicate I felt narked. He gave me the thumbs-up sign to ascend in response. As we made our way slowly back up out of the ship, finning over antique motorbikes and rusty trucks, I felt like I'd been in the presence of ghosts. In a few days of fiery cascades all those decades ago, as death rained down from the sky, thousands of men had been swallowed up by the sea. We paused in our ascent every few minutes to blow off nitrogen and minimise the risk of decompression illness ('the bends') and, as my mind cleared, my thoughts turned to the work ahead. Ultimately, the main risk from climate change was that these low-lying islands would themselves disappear, with many more souls joining those already underwater.

*

Back on land, I grappled with the other main water-related issue at hand: faeces. Chuuk had the highest rates of diarrhoeal disease in the Federated States of Micronesia, partly due to its low elevation and relatively high population density. The environmental health officers tested and treated the water as best they could with their limited resources, but safe drinking water is a fragile thing. Whether it's 'harvested' from rainfall or pumped up from an aquifer underground, at any point from collection to consumption it is vulnerable to contamination. This means that to keep drinking water safe, it needs to be free of bugs right up to the point where it's drunk, when even a tap, cup or shit-flecked finger can spoil the process and cause gastroenteritis. For adults, most of the time these infections are uncomfortable but not life-threatening (unless we're talking about our old enemy cholera), but for children, diarrhoeal illnesses can lead to deadly dehydration. This was a problem in many communities in the Pacific. And some of their island homes are only barely above sea level at all.

Kiribati

Kiribati (pronounced *Kiri-bas**) has to be one of the most interesting countries on Earth. With the highest point on the main inhabited islands only three metres above sea level and the ocean rising by several millimetres every year, climate change is a very real and present threat for the i-Kiribati.†

It's one thing to read about something like that; it's another thing to see it. The coral atolls that constitute the entirety of the country are narrow and crescent-shaped, with the concave side encircling the calm, shallow lagoon and the convex side pushing out into the waves and dropping off into deeper water. Even at its widest, in the middle part, Kiribati's capital atoll of South Tarawa is only a few hundred metres from one side to the other, with the sea, upon which the livelihood of the people depends, slowly creeping up on both sides. Not only was this causing the obvious problems of flooding, particularly in the wake of tropical storms and the

---

* This curious, counter-intuitive pronunciation is reportedly the result of a bizarre little quirk of history, whereby the first European missionaries to spend time in the country had a single printing press with a broken *s* key. In their communications to the outside world they therefore had to come up with a way to render the pronunciation of the country without using that letter. The best they could come up with was *ti*, as in the sound in words like *invention* and *adoption*.

† The official term for people from Kiribati.

infrequent but devastating king tides;* the salt water was also intruding into the freshwater wells and the scarce topsoil used for gardens.

Over the course of several visits to Kiribati, my colleagues and I would spend our days trundling up and down the atolls in overcrowded minibuses, having our eardrums blasted by home-made but annoyingly catchy electro music, inspecting water and sanitation facilities and trying to figure out how to make Kiribati's health system more 'resilient' – the buzzword used in the field of climate change adaptation. The enthusiastic local health promotion team decided to make a video to explain the effects of climate change on health in their communities. In doing so, they interviewed several local residents about what they were already experiencing, and those stories were truly frightening. Staring out at the lapping, turquoise waters of the innocent-looking lagoon, one man explained how his family had been forced to move their house inland twice in the space of three generations due to the insidiously rising sea.

Dejected, we'd spend our evenings getting drunk on warm beers and palm wine, eating fish and rice and trying to get our heads around a country whose various presidents had, by sheer necessity, become leading voices for action against climate change on the global stage. Their government had to be the only one in the world to have an official policy encouraging 'voluntary out-migration'. One of the country's most outspoken presidents, Anote Tong, had speculated that a couple of billion dollars would be needed to build floating islands 'like oil platforms' within the country's Exclusive Economic Zone in order for the i-Kiribati to maintain their sovereignty and keep living within their country's borders, even in the

---

* 'King tides' are particularly high tides that are caused by oceanic and meteorological conditions in combination with the moon's gravitational pull. Historically, they have been reasonably regular and predictable, but – like many other climate change-related phenomena – they are becoming more frequent and severe as the sea level rises.

absence of solid ground. What must it mean for your sense of nationhood and identity – not to mention your mental health and the well-being of your family – when your own political leaders are recommending that you leave your country?

Kiribati isn't the only population in the world facing the threat of extinction from climate change. It's not even the only one in the Pacific.

*

The Republic of the Marshall Islands (RMI) and Tuvalu, Kiribati's neighbours to the west, share similar geographic characteristics, with their communities clinging like stalagmites onto their flat coral crescents as the warming equatorial waters rise. Unfortunately, that's not all the three countries have in common. These atoll nations have some of the highest burdens of TB in the Pacific region, made all the worse by widespread cigarette smoking and high rates of diabetes, as both impair the immune system, meaning the mycobacteria can more easily spread the infection. We had other clever colleagues trying to sort out that mess, however. What worried us was what was happening as families were forced to relocate repeatedly as the level of the sea continued to rise. These tiny countries had such limited land areas that there was often literally no space to build new houses. Many households in Tuvalu, RMI and Kiribati were already terribly overcrowded, and these communities had some of the region's highest fertility rates. Their populations were increasing but their land was disappearing at the same time. This cruel combination, together with climate change, meant that overcrowding in these atoll communities was likely to get much worse over time, which was perfect for diseases like diarrhoea, TB and other respiratory infections that spread from person to person.

The feeling that we were shining a light on problems that were largely political and probably intractable was slowly growing inside me. I was increasingly convinced that we were doing little more than completing a project, ticking a box, making a donor happy and writing a document that few people would know about and about which I doubted many would really care. In the eyes of most of the Ministers of Health, who nodded gravely as we presented our findings, I saw the same weary acceptance that the recommendations we were making had little chance of being implemented by their governments, given all their competing priorities and resource constraints.

'What do you mean by "enhanced" surveillance system?' they would ask.

'We should "ensure food security", is that right?'

'Our health facilities should be "climate-resilient", as it says here?'

Most of these ministerial meetings ended with a solemn handshake and something along the lines of: 'Well, thank you for this very impressive report. We shall be sure to consider it carefully.'

My initial enthusiasm was waning and my usually positive outlook was starting to turn distinctly cynical. Then I arrived in Nauru.

Nauru

The Republic of Nauru (RoN), or 'Ron' as it's cheerily referred to by many of its citizens, as if it were a favourite uncle or a moustachioed cigarette salesman from the 1970s, is pretty close to unique in every way. It's one of the smallest countries on Earth, by both population and land area, with the entirety of its eleven thousand residents scattered around the perimeter of one tiny, isolated, potato-shaped piece of rock. For thousands of years, life on Nauru revolved around fishing, coconuts, pandanus fruit and the usual human occupations of making love and war. The latter became decidedly feistier after trade with European whaling ships in the early 1800s led to the introduction of alcohol and firearms, but far more harm was to come from what lay beneath the islanders' feet. Of all the things to bring about a country's downfall, for poor Nauru, it just had to be bird shit.

Right at the turn of the twentieth century, a visiting Australian prospector recognised that the top layer of rock covering Nauru's surface was phosphate – a build-up from millennia of deposits from migratory seabirds. Large-scale mining commenced almost immediately, with the valuable shipments being exported for fertiliser production. Within a few decades, and after major squabbles over ownership of the faecal assets, this resource boom enabled Nauru to declare independence. By 1970, it was officially the second-richest country in the world by gross domestic product, behind the United Arab Emirates, who were revelling in an enthusiastic extraction industry of their own. The RoN government purchased expensive property all over the world, along with a fleet of aeroplanes, parochially and ambiguously named Our Airline. Ridiculous amounts of money were splashed around on international travel (particularly for 'official business' such as golfing trips in the Bahamas) and for a brief period Mercedes Benzes were commonly seen puttering along the dusty road that ringed the rock. Few Nauruans needed to work for a living, as their collective future seemed secure through the phosphate-revenue-funded government trust.

Then, a truly nation-shattering quadruple whammy happened. The advent of synthetic fertiliser manufacture led to a crash in the price of phosphate, at roughly the same time that Nauru's natural reserves ran out. And those investments? Pissed away through a combination of poor planning and corruption. In under a hundred years, the island had been transformed. Eighty per cent of the land area had been strip-mined, with the scalloping out of the phosphate leaving only a narrow strip of inhabitable land abutting the beach and a Martian landscape across the middle of the island. Nauru had cannibalised itself, and now it was bankrupt too.

The effects on the health of Nauru's people, in hindsight at least, were predictable. Within a generation, the combination of wealth and leisure had made obesity rates soar (another reason Nauru has been nicknamed 'the Kuwait of the Pacific'), with diabetes, heart disease, stroke, cancer and most other chronic diseases rising with it. There was hardly any arable land left for agriculture, and in any case most such knowledge had been lost, along with much of the skill and inclination for fishing.

Nauru's only other significant income in recent years has come from hosting an Australian prison for refugees. The existence of this ghastly facility (referred to euphemistically as an 'asylum-seeker processing centre') violates international conventions against torture, is categorised as a humanitarian emergency, has led to widespread protests, burned roughly ten billion Australian dollars and brought incalculable shame on both countries for the two decades it has been operational. Several thousand Australian doctors signed a petition in 2018 for the federal government to allow care to be provided for the refugees being held against their will. Of most concern were the children. The representative of the paediatrician members of the Australian Medical Association described it as ' ... the only situation I've come across where it is deliberate government policy which is causing the pain and suffering of these children'.

The former Prime Minister of Australia,* about whom the kindest thing it can be said is that the intellectual demands of the job clearly exceeded his capacity to perform it, oversaw the programme during his hectoring tenure as Immigration Minister. His message has been

---

* I'm referring here to Scott Morrison, the incumbent at the time of writing, in early 2022, keeping in mind that Australia appoints and deposes PMs like it's a national sport.

consistent, if nonsensical: 'I will not put at risk any element of Australia's border protection policy.'* Despite the assertion of the International Criminal Court that such detention is 'cruel, inhuman or degrading treatment' and the irreversible damage being inflicted, the programme was still operational in 2022, with over one hundred detainees – the majority of them legally recognised refugees – being held against their will, at a cost to the taxpayer of over four million Australian dollars per year for every single one of them.†

As I squatted in a dusty corner in the basement of the national hospital, poring through the decades of health data provided by Nauruan colleagues I was working with, I realised something else horrifying. Based on its own government's official statistics, the population of Nauru had experienced a substantial decrease in life expectancy, it having dropped by approximately five years within the space of a generation. The only plausible explanation for this was the catastrophic rise in chronic diseases. That meant, as far as I could tell, Nauru would be the sole, or at least the first, example of life expectancy trending downwards for any country in modern human history untouched by war or HIV.‡

---

* https://www.theguardian.com/australia-news/2018/sep/20/scott-morrison-rejects-ama-plea-to-bring-children-from-nauru-to-australia.

† https://www.theguardian.com/world/2022/jan/24/nauru-offshore-regime-to-cost-australian-taxpayers-nearly-220m-over-next-six-months?CMP=Share_iOSApp_Other.

‡ Six years later, in 2018, a study published in the *British Medical Journal* reported a detected decrease in life expectancy in a dozen different rich countries, whose populations' lifespans had been reduced, on average, by an estimated 0.2 years. The explanations proposed for this finding included people dying at younger ages from cardiovascular and respiratory diseases, as well as deaths due to increased use of and overdose with opioid medications.

I struggled with this knowledge as my new Nauruan friends and I inspected water supplies, checked the air quality – which wasn't great, given most of the country was now dust – and ate Chinese food every night. Climate change was going to be a big problem in Nauru, for sure, but they had more immediate problems to deal with. I helped draft their national action plan for climate change and health, including a table outlining the awful truth about their plummeting life expectancies, but I knew it was all but impossible that anything could be done to address any of those issues any time soon.

Fiji

Back in Fiji, several unsettling things were happening in my life around the same time. First of all, Paul, my boss at WHO, was moved on to his next placement in South-East Asia. Despite the fact that this had been on the cards for many months, it seemed to take everyone else by surprise. The WHO Director summoned me into his office, and following 15 bewildering minutes in which he asked about my previous experience, patted me on the shoulder and cheerily mentioned 'learning by doing' about five times, I was appointed the acting head of emergency humanitarian action and environmental health for WHO in the South Pacific region. With this unexpected promotion (which was possibly illegal, given I was still on a volunteer contract), I suddenly found myself responsible for shipping emergency medical equipment to disaster zones and overseeing million-dollar WASH projects.

I decided to try to use my new-found influence to convince the higher-ups at WHO to publish an official report on climate change and health in Pacific island countries. I was worried that no one would ever read the national action plans we'd written, and there was even less chance of anyone ever reading my PhD thesis, if I ever got around to finishing the mongrel thing. If this information was going to be useful, I realised, we had to get the message out through more formal channels. It worried me that so few people seemed to really understand what was going on. The science was clear and unambiguous. The idea of debating whether climate change was real or not was a complete waste of time, and a luxury only available to people in wealthy countries with the resources to feed themselves, find water, and hide in air-conditioned comfort while hundreds of thousands of their fellow global citizens starve, overheat or die in natural disasters and epidemics. This shit was keeping me awake at night.

My PhD supervisors and academic colleagues, who understood the science perfectly well, agreed it was a nightmarish scenario when I summoned the courage to share my worries with them, but I couldn't help feeling that, even among such experts, there were more than a few who were a bit too detached from the action to truly comprehend the existential nature of the threat. Occasionally I'd encounter someone in the field who obviously got it. You could see it in their eyes. It was a silent stare that said: *Yep, if only everyone else knew what we knew . . .*

Partly as a way to deal with such existential quivers, but also because Fiji was a fun place to live, I caroused like an ancient Roman after hours. The expat lifestyle, with all the accompanying booze, weed and casual sex, reminded me of the months I'd spent backpacking around the world while still in medical school. This time, however, I had responsibilities. It was a strange double life – attending serious meetings with UN, government and non-government organisation (NGO) representatives and then going home to dress up as a schoolgirl/zombie/pineapple for yet another costume party at someone's house, most likely after the host returned from their own serious day of meetings. I was introduced to the diplomatic corps, who turned out to be another bunch of high-functioning alcoholics, and even bought a cheap guitar and started a garage band with a few friends to play at embassy events.

Then suddenly, out of the blur of hard work and partying, came some very bad news. I got a call from my high-school sweetheart, Megan. She needed to tell me about Marco.

As I listened to her words, I felt the blood drain from my face.

'Fuck off!' I blurted.

'He did, Lach,' Megan sobbed back through the phone. 'I thought I should be the one to tell you.'

Our kind, funny, messed-up mate, who'd lost his way through addiction and religion, had died. Suicide. It had seemed like he'd finally got his shit together when he moved back home to care for his dad. The compassionate nature he'd always had made him ideal for the job. He'd even started training as a personal care attendant. We knew he was still doing drugs. He and I had been on more than a few benders together back in the day, from snorting speed in his bedroom when we were teenagers to taking pills at jungle raves during the hedonistic uni years. Marco had always been inclined to take things too far, too often, and he'd been through a bunch of interventions and a couple of rounds of rehab. What we hadn't realised, but we should have at least considered, was that Marco also suffered from depression. The thought of his suicide bored into my mind. How could one of my friends, with whom I'd shared so much, have reached a point in his life so dark and desperate that death seemed like the best – or only – option?

I flew home for Marco's funeral, after which my high-school buddies and I hugged and cried and got drunk together, reminiscing about the gigs our little punk band played in Marco's parents' garage; the time Kenny jumped off the roof of Marco's house and left his own tooth implanted in his thigh; and the time we went camping and Marco made us all play 'Centurion' (where you drink a shot of beer every minute for one hundred minutes, which is a lot more difficult than it sounds) and Jo vomited her nose ring into the bonfire.

We raised countless toasts and speculated about what went so wrong in the life of our friend. Through the sadness and the haze of alcohol, I had a revelation.

'Purposhleshnesh,' I declared, slurring and spilling my beer over myself as I unwisely waved it around for emphasis.

'What are you trying to say, you pissed idiot?' asked one of the blurred figures at the table.

I cleared my throat and tried again.

'Purposelessness,' I said, slowly and more carefully this time. 'That's what happened to him, I reckon. He was coming good when he was looking after his old man. Then when his dad died, he lost the plot. Had nothing left to live for.' I slipped back into my dismal, drunken stupor as a few of the others mumbled their agreement.

*

My WHO contract was coming to an end and I was preparing to leave Fiji and return to Australia while I figured out my next move. I'd reached a kind of professional crossroads. If I wanted to continue working in international public health as a full-time career, it might mean I'd need to give up clinical practice. I'd embarked on a second round of specialty training as a public health physician, but I didn't feel ready to hang up the stethoscope, as almost all of my doctor colleagues working for WHO (there turned out to be quite a few in other departments) had done. At least not yet. Following Marco's death, I found myself preoccupied with the question of what – if anything – was my own real purpose in life.

I needed to find an equilibrium between tackling the big-picture, complex issues like climate change, for which there was little prospect of any signs of improvement in the short term, and offsetting that with the more immediate rewards of working with patients. I girded my loins in preparation for an attempt to straddle the divide between public health and clinical practice and reflected on what I'd learned over my two years with WHO in the Pacific. Even though I'd been largely concentrating on disasters, climate change and environmental health, I'd also had the opportunity to see how healthcare was provided in a dozen different Pacific island countries. Again and again, I'd observed that health professionals, particularly doctors, were concentrated in the urban centres, despite the fact that the majority of the population of the Pacific region lived in rural areas, which was also where the most significant health challenges were to be found. The problem was similar to what had happened in Australia a few decades earlier, when the lack of doctors in rural communities had reached such a crisis point that a new specialty college – the Australian College of Rural and Remote Medicine (ACRRM) – had been established with the specific mandate to train rural doctors. Two years earlier, I had served a term as a director on the Board of ACRRM, and had the opportunity to peek behind the curtain at how such training programmes were run. Now, in my final weeks with WHO in the Pacific, I started wondering out loud to a few of my senior health colleagues. Was there anything from the Australian model that could be adapted to the needs of Pacific communities in order to bring better-quality primary healthcare to more people across the islands of the region?

*

'That's exactly what we need,' Steve said, nodding enthusiastically.

Dr Steve Homasi was a bear of a man who was Tuvalu's Director of Health and the country's only surgeon. He still did shifts in the ED and outpatient clinics and helped out with ward rounds, as a true generalist himself and one of only ten doctors in the entire country at the time. I had enormous respect for Steve and had enjoyed working with him and his colleagues in Tuvalu. We were having coffee in my office in Suva, debriefing prior to my departure. We'd finished chatting about their climate change and health strategy and I was sharing with him my musings about the rural generalist approach to medical training.

'We definitely need more jack-of-all-trades doctors in the Pacific,' he affirmed. 'If you could help us set up something like that, it would make a really big difference to our health workforce and enable us to provide better care to rural communities, especially the people living on the outer islands.'

I was fired up, but it wasn't to last long. More tragedy awaited, as within a few months Steve, too, was dead. He'd had a fall and broken his neck. Tuvalu lost a brilliant doctor and the Pacific region lost a great leader in the field. His words, however, stayed with me as I packed up once again and moved on.

CHAPTER SEVEN

2013–14
Central Australia

It gets cold in the desert at night. Bone-rattling cold. Not a problem if you have somewhere warm to sleep, but if your bed is by a fire in a camp out of town and you're old and tired and falling-down drunk, then all you can feel is the sharp teeth of the air on your skin.

The old lady shuffled up to the hospital entrance. In fact, she wasn't really that old – in her mid-fifties, at most – but a life of desert living, hard drinking and violent men seemed to have stolen 20 years from her. She pushed the after-hours emergency buzzer and squinted up, swaying slightly, at the camera overhead.

'What's your emergency?' crackled the intercom from the brightly lit interior.

'I'm sick,' she rasped into the videophone.

'Sick in what way?' asked the voice.

'I'm sick and I'm cold and I need a sleep,' she answered back.

'Deidre, my dear, you know we can't let you in just because you're cold and want somewhere to sleep,' the nurse in the Emergency Department replied, not unkindly.

'Yeah, but I'm sick!' the lady insisted.

'If you can't tell us what's wrong, exactly, we can't open the door.' The response was prim now, with a hint of impatience.

The lady turned away, muttering to herself, and staggered about outside the ED entrance for a few moments, searching around the ground. She bent down, picked something up and tottered back towards the light. She looked up at the camera, raised the broken beer bottle in her right hand and sliced it across her throat.

'What about now?' she gurgled, a flicker of triumph in her eyes as the doors slid open and she collapsed to the ground, blood gushing through her fingers from the gash in her neck.

The on-call phone buzzed into life beside me. I sighed, muted the cricket match I was watching on TV and tried not to sound tired or grumpy as I picked up. 'Hi, it's Lachie, doctor on call.'

'Hey mate, it's Dave. Sorry to bother you but I really need you to come in.'

He sounded nervous. Not a good sign. Dave was a capable, confident young doctor, so if he was worried, it was probably for a bloody good reason.

'Sure, I'll throw some clothes on and be there in five. What's going on?'

'It's Deidre. She's slit her throat.'

'She *what*?'

'Slit her throat. With a broken beer bottle. Just outside ED. It looks bad, man, bleeding a lot, not sure if she's penetrated her trachea but it's anterior neck, so . . . Definitely in the danger zone, you know?'*

'Okay, get the airway gear ready, I'm on my way.'

I pulled some trousers and boots on and strode quickly over to the hospital through the chilly night air. I'd met Deidre before. We all had. She was a smart, stoic woman of the local Warumungu people, as well as a talented artist. She'd raised seven children of her own, despite her

---

* The front of the neck is home to several important parts of our anatomy, including the trachea (windpipe), larynx (voicebox) and carotid arteries, which supply blood to our brains.

abusive, alcoholic husband disappearing many years earlier, and usually had several grandchildren running around under her care. She was often in the ED, either bringing in a sick child, unwell herself with a chest or bladder infection, or bruised and bleeding after a drunken brawl. On better days, she was there with some paintings to sell – vibrant, captivating images of life in Australia's Red Centre, of which her people have been the proud custodians for tens of thousands of years. She'd had a tough life, but this was an unusually desperate move on her part. If Deidre had cut through a carotid artery, she'd probably be dead by the time I arrived. If she'd pranged one of the nerves supplying her vocal cords, she might never be able to speak again, even if she survived the injury. My main worry, though, was that her airway was damaged and she'd soon be unable to breathe.

I hustled into the ED to find Dave checking the lights on the laryngoscope and opening up packets of equipment on the crash cart. Beside him, Sandy, one of the nurses, was drawing up emergency sedation drugs and Jim, another nurse, had both gloved hands pressing a blood-soaked dressing over Deidre's neck.

'Is she conscious?' I asked, as I snapped on gloves and strapped on a plastic gown.

'She was GCS* eleven when we got her in here,' Dave replied over his shoulder.

I took Deidre's hand. It was cold.

----

* The Glasgow Coma Scale (GCS) is an indicator of a person's level of consciousness. It is divided into three components: motor (how they move), voice (how they speak) and eyes (whether they are open on their own, only open to speech or painful stimuli or do not open at all). Someone who is fully conscious scores 15 out of 15. Usually once someone's GCS drops to around 8 it means the person is close to the point where they won't be able to breathe on their own and will require support to do so. Oddly, the lowest you can score is 3, even if you're dead, which one might well think should score a 0.

'Deidre, it's Lachie. Squeeze my hand if you can hear me.' No response. I pinched her earlobe firmly between my thumb and forefinger.

'Deidre, open your eyes, I need to know if you can hear me.' Nothing.

As a last resort, I rubbed her sternum with my knuckles, painfully hard. Her eyes flickered open, she raised her arms and head briefly and she coughed, dribbling pink-stained saliva from her mouth and spraying specks of blood out from the hideous wound at the front of her neck, then sank listlessly back onto the bed again.

'Shit, guys, her GCS is more like six now. It's tube time. You got the gear ready to go there, Dave?'

'Yep,' said Dave, as he wheeled the crash cart over to the head of the bed.

'Okay, so we'll need to do a rapid sequence intubation, going easy on the induction drugs, given she's already drunk, her GCS is dropping and she's losing blood. Sandy, you can help me with the drugs and fluids, please. Jim, you stay where you are, keep that pressure on her neck with one hand and help Dave with the intubation with your other hand.'

Dave stopped with a jolt and looked up at me. His pupils were huge.

'Wait, what did you just say, Lach? Don't you think you should do the tube?'

'No, I need to keep my hands free. You concentrate on that and I'll deal with the other stuff. I'll have a scalpel and a second tube ready if we need it.'

The fact that I was now the senior doctor in these situations still did my head in at times. It didn't seem so long ago that I was surrounded by more experienced colleagues; now I was the one with the responsibility for making the tricky decisions and teaching the registrars, helping them develop their own skills and getting the practice they needed to be able to cope on their own. In this scenario, I knew I had to keep sight of the big picture and trust Dave and the nurses to carry out their respective tasks. If Deidre proved too difficult for Dave to intubate, given her pharynx and trachea were filling up fast with froth and blood, I might have a brief opportunity to try and do it myself, but if that didn't work, I had to be ready to insert a smaller tube directly through the front of her neck, using a scalpel to widen and deepen the incision she'd already made. I'd been trained to do this in simulations, but many plastic mannequins do not a real patient make. My own heart galloped like a herd of wildebeest.

I took a deep breath and gave Deidre's hand another squeeze.

'Deidre, we're going to drift you off to sleep now, okay?'

I injected the sedation drugs slowly from the syringes that Sandy handed me, one eye on Deidre and the other on the monitor that beeped and flashed her vital signs at us, as Dave tried his best to keep her oxygen levels up with a manual ventilator bag and mask. She twitched a little, then went still. I nodded at Dave.

'Off you go. Use plenty of suction and tell me what you see.'

The plastic suction wand slurped and gurgled, and the wall-mounted vacuum bottle filled up with blood and saliva as Dave struggled to find a clear view to Deidre's vocal cords. The seconds ticked by as the steadily lowering pitch of the beep on the monitor told us her oxygen level was dropping.

'Anything?' I asked, trying not to sound nervous or make Dave feel more pressured.

'Not yet,' he said, hunched over, grimacing and squinting into Deidre's mouth.

I looked around. We'd tried to put Deidre in the best possible position, but was there anything else we could do to improve Dave's view? I noticed something.

'Hey Jim, maybe just ease off with that pressure on her neck for a second and move your hand over to the left a little.'

'Yep, stop, that's it! I've got a view,' Dave exclaimed. He slid the tube down, connected it to the ventilator bag and gave it a few puffs. Deidre's chest moved up and down and Dave gave a thumbs-up as he listened with his stethoscope. 'It's in.'

'Nice work, mate. Good job, Jim. Thanks, Sandy. Now, Dave, you see what you can do about that neck wound while I get on the phone to the aeromedical retrieval team and get her the fuck out of here.'

*

Tennant Creek – also commonly known simply as 'Tennant' – where this action was taking place, is a semi-lawless, ochre sprawl five hundred kilometres north of Alice Springs. I was there on a fly-in/fly-out (FIFO) basis. The modern Australian economy has been dependent on FIFO workers in the mining, gas and construction industries for many years. More recently, health service managers have been catching on to the fact that there are some places that are so remote and/or so disadvantaged, particularly in terms of essential services such as schools, that very few doctors – particularly those with families – would be prepared to live there long term, no matter how much you paid them. Tennant Creek was one such town. Its hospital had just barely been limping along, surviving on a revolving-door supply of locums (short-term doctors) of wildly varying levels of experience and commitment. Not all of them had the training to deal with situations like we'd just had with Deidre, as the hospital's mortality statistics showed. The consultants from the various specialty departments in Alice Springs Hospital had long ago lost faith in the ability of the medical staff in Tennant Creek to care for sick patients, particularly children, so it was now simply assumed that patients with any significant illnesses or injuries would be shipped out of Tennant Creek to the higher-level care that 'Alice' provided. It would take inspired leadership skills, and big balls, to find a way to breathe life back into Tennant Creek Hospital. And my mate Frankie had both.

Frankie and I had met several years earlier when we were both junior doctors in Alice Springs. He was posted to the paediatric ward and would often turn up in ED to admit the sickest of the little patients I'd been seeing. He was a funny, energetic guy who looked like a country music singer and who charmed the graduate nurses, surly old consultants and admin staff in equal measure. When I finished my few months there and moved on, Frankie stayed put. We'd kept in touch over the years since then, during which he'd risen rapidly through the ranks, and he was now the director of medical services for the entire region. We'd caught up for beers a few months earlier at the annual rural medicine conference in Fremantle, a blustery, arty beach town south of Perth.

'I've got a proposition for you, Lach,' he announced as we clinked our pint glasses and plonked ourselves down at a wooden table in the sun-drenched beer garden.

'Oh yeah?' I took a long sip and smirked at him. 'And what would that be?'

'Tennant Fucking Creek. The hospital there has been a bloody disaster for years now. They've had too few doctors, not many of them much chop and hardly any of them have been willing to stick around. The community deserves to have a decent, functional facility, and it's my job now to try and sort it out. So I've got a plan.'

I took another swig and waited for him to continue, mildly intrigued. I was well aware of Tennant Creek's reputation and was more than a little curious to see what Frankie had in mind. He paused for dramatic effect, hoping for a response, but I knew him too well for that. After a few seconds, he couldn't help himself.

'Job-sharing!' He grinned, leaned back, put his boots up on the bench and basked in the afternoon rays like a Cheshire cat in aviator shades.

Over the course of a couple more pints, Frankie explained the model he'd set up. He'd somehow managed to convince the bean-counters to cough up a budget that would allow him to employ five senior rural generalists to share two full-time contracts. They would each spend a fortnight at a time in the town as the senior doctor responsible for both the hospital and the primary healthcare clinic. They'd be on call day and night for the entire period and get paid double-time for their trouble. It not only allowed the town to have a consistent senior medical presence, 24 hours a day, but was more sustainable by allowing the senior docs to escape and recover after each intensive two-week stint. In the longer term, it also enabled the hospital and its clinic to be accredited as training sites for junior doctors, making it more appealing for the younger guys to live and work there as well. It was kind of genius in its simplicity. I had no idea how Frankie could have known that I was looking for a part-time job, or whether it was just a lucky hunch on his part. I was fresh back from Fiji and hanging out in Melbourne, putting the finishing touches to my PhD thesis (at long last) and bashing away at the report I'd finally managed to convince WHO to publish on climate change and health in the Pacific. When I wasn't chained to the desk or getting reacquainted with old friends and punk shows, I was contemplating my next steps, so Frankie's invitation for me to join the inaugural Tennant Fucking Creek fivesome came at the perfect time. By the time we staggered out of the brewery several hours later, we'd shaken on it.

*

I carried on with the job-sharing role in Tennant Creek over the next year or so, proud to see the difference we were making as a team. We were admitting more patients to our hospital – a sign of renewed confidence from our specialist colleagues in Alice Springs – and flying fewer emergency cases out. With the more experienced and reliable team of seniors present, even if only on a rotating basis, we now had a growing number of registrars signing up to do their training in this once notoriously terrible facility, which we were collectively and only half ironically attempting to have rebranded from TFC (Tennant Fucking Creek) to TCCCE (Tennant Creek Centre of Clinical Excellence).

Despite these improvements, we couldn't completely avoid the occasional catastrophe. The hospital didn't have a birthing service, for one thing, so the rule was that when pregnant ladies reached the eight-month mark they had to be sent down to Alice Springs for their 'confinements' – in both senses of the word.* I assume that most expectant mothers anywhere in the world would be reluctant to be separated from their homes and families for several weeks, particularly at the pointy end of their pregnancy! This was yet another poignant example of a well-intended policy being at odds with fundamental socio-cultural considerations. The result of that paradox was that some ladies would choose to hide at home for those last few weeks and then turn up to our ED in labour. This was doubly dangerous, because they'd missed out on antenatal care for the latter stages of their pregnancy and now risked delivering their babies in a hospital that lacked specialised staff and dedicated facilities. One night saw me, both of the registrars and the hospital's only midwife struggling for hours to keep control of one lady with severe pre-eclampsia – a placental disorder that causes high blood pressure and protein leakage and can

---

* 'Confinement' is an old-fashioned term for giving birth. I'm also using it here to refer to the experience of these ladies having to move away from home and stay with relatives or in a hostel for the last month of their pregnancy, in order to be close to a hospital with obstetric services.

lead to seizures that are potentially fatal to both mother and baby. In a bigger hospital, she would have been managed in the intensive care unit. The baby slipped out in a rush of blood and we were so distracted with trying to control the mother's post-partum haemorrhage that we were late to realise that the baby's temperature and blood sugar were dropping to dangerously low levels. This mother and baby both survived, but we were shaken and chastened by the experience, with emergency obstetrics and neonatal resuscitation techniques featuring heavily in the clinical education meetings over the next few weeks. We simply couldn't afford to have any major chinks in our armour in a busy rural hospital like Tennant Creek.

On another evening, all had been quiet – a taboo word in every hospital where I've ever worked – and I was strolling back to the asbestos-filled, rat-eaten shack I called home in Tennant Creek when my phone buzzed in my pocket.

'Lachie, it's Hendrick. Sorry mate, I know you just left ED, but the police rang to say there's been an MVA with multi-trauma. The ambulances will be arriving soon.'

Motor vehicle accidents were common in this vast, mostly empty part of the country. There had, until recently, been 'open' (that is, unlimited) speed limits in the Northern Territory, and the long stretches of straight highway still proved too tempting for some. Crashes often occurred when over-ambitious drivers attempted to overtake the road trains – heavy-duty trucks pulling multiple trailers that could reach over fifty metres in length – and got caught out by an approaching vehicle or unexpected bend. Although the high-velocity, high-impact nature of these accidents led to a high fatality rate, travelling in this region was a lonely business and there usually weren't too many people involved. But then Hendrick had just said multi-trauma . . .

'Do we know how many injured?' I asked, turning and striding back towards the hospital.

'The cops said something about a minivan.'

'Shit. Okay, I'll be there in a minute.'

I marched into the ED, dumped my bag in a corner, wiped my sweaty hands on my trousers and looked around. Hendrick, the night-shift registrar, was checking instruments and drugs on the crash cart with Jim, who was our nurse in charge this evening. Hendrick was a burly South African former surgical registrar who'd seen more than his fair share of trauma, and Jim was a trainer for remote area nurses. No worries there. Who else did we have? Lisa, a graduate nurse, was restocking the pharmacy; Jadav, an intern, was typing up notes, apparently oblivious; and Emily, a medical student, was heading out the door.

'Guys!' I called out. 'Quick team meeting. Yep, you too Emily. The shit's about to hit the fan.'

We huddled in the resus bay. My mind whirred.

'Listen, we don't know how many injured patients are about to turn up, but if it's a minivan, we have to be prepared for up to ten or so. Jim, can you call in an extra nurse or two, or pull one from the ward?'

'I'll try, Lach,' Jim said, pulling his phone from his pocket.

'Hendrick, you take whoever looks to be the most seriously injured, okay?'

'You got it, boss.'

'Lisa, we need you to do a rapid assessment, check everyone's vitals, look for signs of head and neck injuries and figure out the triage categories as best you can. Jadav, you'll look after the limb injuries and walking wounded.'

Lisa paled. Jadav gave me a nervous nod.

'Emily, you're with m—'

The doors of the ambulance bay crashed open and our tranquil little

133

ED was transformed into a late night at Burning Man. The lights of three ambulances flashed outside (I didn't know we had that many in town), with two police cars wailing alongside them. Stretcher after stretcher was pushed in, each with a huge, tattooed Polynesian atop it. As I directed traffic, one of the cops gave a brisk report.

'We were called to the scene of a single-vehicle MVA. Toyota Tarago overturned at high speed forty kilometres north on the Stuart Highway. Seven passengers, all seasonal workers from Tonga. None ejected from vehicle. Unknown if wearing restraints. Some appear to not speak English.'

I signalled to Jim and Hendrick to move the two quietest, bloodiest patients into the resus bays as I walked quickly along the row of the remaining five, trying to determine the order of treatment priority at a glance and see if any could wait in wheelchairs. We didn't have enough beds for all seven. The senior paramedic rubbed a dusty sleeve across his brow as he did his handover.

'We haven't had a chance to do proper assessments, sorry, Lachie. With this many patients and only three ambulances, it was a real scoop-and-run situation. The four with the collars on have possible C-spine* injuries, with those two at the end also having signs of head trauma. That guy over there shouting at us seems okay apart from his dislocated ankle. I'm worried about the fella in Resus Two. He has bruising across his torso and abdomen. I think he was the driver.'

'Fucking hell,' I thought out loud. 'Okay, thanks Phil. Hey, can you guys stick around and help for a bit?'

'Yep, we'll just go grab some water and we'll be right back. Hot night out there.'

I patted him on the shoulder, beckoned Emily over and got to work.

---

* The cervical spine, usually abbreviated to 'C-spine', refers to the vertebrae in the neck.

As Lisa checked each patient's vital signs, Emily asked them where they had pain and whether they had any important medical conditions – not easily communicated over a language barrier. I listened as best I could while I popped in IV cannulas and did a quick visual inspection for injuries. I made my way up the line until I got to the resus bays, where Jim and Hendrick were gowned, gloved and goggled.

'How are you guys getting on?'

'This chap's in pretty bad shape,' Hendrick said, without turning around. 'Fluctuating GCS, nasty wound on his scalp . . . ' – he paused as he prodded gently – 'and I'm pretty sure I can feel fractured skull in there.'

'What about you, Jim?'

'This guy's not great either. Not communicating much but clearly in a lot of pain. And check this out.' Jim pulled back the sheet, exposing the savage bruising and abrasions across the man's chest.

'Okay, so we'll need to intubate your patient, Hendrick, and maybe yours as well, Jim. The guy with the chest trauma might have major internal injuries. Let's get a bag of fluid into him for now, then we'll run some blood. We'll need to give 'em all antibiotics and tetanus shots and assume these four have fractured C-spines. The immobilisation will make intubating tricky. At some stage we'll have to reduce the dislocation of that other guy's ankle, but we'll deal with these two first. I'll call the retrieval team now to get some planes up here and give the surgeons in Alice a heads-up about what's coming their way. Jim, are we getting some more nurses in? We need all hands on deck here.'

'Preethi's coming over from the ward and Jackie's on her way in.'

'Good-o. Sing out when you need a hand.'

I phoned the on-call aeromedical retrieval coordinator down in Alice Springs. We were used to working together; hardly a day went by without us needing to ship someone out. My mate Drew was on call.

'Fucking hell,' said Drew when I told him what was happening.

'That's what I said. How soon can you get a plane* up here? We'll need two, at least, and an extra doctor, if you've got one.'

'Should be right to scramble one team immediately, Lach. We'll aim to be up there within a couple of hours. Not sure about a second plane. I'll let you know.'

'Roger that,' I said. 'Keep me posted.'

I poked my head into the resus bays. 'Retrieval team ETA two hours. I'll be back in a minute to help you guys.'

Adrenaline charged through my veins and my brain fizzed with activity. This was extreme. Not only was I the senior doctor responsible for every patient in the department, meaning I had to keep track of all their injuries and what treatments they needed, but I had to manage our scarce resources as effectively as possible. Fortunately, the two extra nurses had turned up and were busy injecting drugs and cleaning wounds. I started again from the end of the line of patients, which we'd tried to rearrange in order of severity.

'You okay with these two, Jad?'

Jadav gave me a quick thumbs-up from where he was suturing wounds and preparing plaster. His plastic apron was already covered in specks of blood and splatters of plaster but he seemed to be coping. He might have lacked a little in situational awareness, young Jadav, but that was common at his stage of training and would improve with experience. He worked hard and was pretty sharp for an intern. He'd get a good supervisor report from me when he left.

---

* The key factors determining why we use helicopters for some retrievals and aeroplanes for others include the availability of pilots, aircraft and airstrips, the needs of the patient(s), the environmental conditions and the respective ranges of rotary aircraft (i.e. helicopters), which are usually only able to fly up to 500km or so versus fixed-wing aircraft (i.e. planes), which are the only option for longer distances.

'We'll do that ankle in half an hour or so, okay? Preethi, Jackie, all good here?'

'Yeah, Lachie, mostly superficial injuries so far,' said Jackie, another senior ED nurse. 'If we find anything interesting, we'll let you know.'

I whisked the curtain open in the next bay. 'How are you getting on, Em?'

'I don't know what this guy's trying to tell me,' she said with a quiver in her voice. 'He just keeps yelling at me and doesn't seem to speak English.'

'Here, take my phone, call this number for the after-hours interpreter service, give them this code and ask for someone who speaks Tongan. Keep it together, you're doing a good job.'

'Lachie, tube time,' Hendrick called out.

I hustled back into Resus One, where Hendrick was poised over the patient's head, laryngoscope flicked open and lit. Jim passed me a kidney dish of drawn-up drugs and then shuffled in next to Hendrick to hold the patient's head with his forearms while his hands tucked in beneath the broad, brown shoulders.

'You guys ready?' I asked, as I screwed onto the IV line a large syringe filled with thick white liquid magic.*

Two terse nods in response.

I pushed slowly down on the plunger. Thirty seconds later, our semi-conscious patient was unconscious. After a red syringe of paralysis medication and another 30 seconds, his twitching ceased.

'Okay, mate, fire away,' I said.

Hendrick slid the laryngoscope into the patient's mouth while Jim

---

* Propofol, one of the most commonly used medications to put people to sleep, has the colour and consistency of milk.

kept the man's head still. A minute after that, his breathing was being done by a machine.

'Nice shooting,' I said, slapping Hendrick on his muscle-clad back. 'Now come give me a hand next door, hey?'

We left Jim to twiddle with the settings on the ventilator while we stepped into Resus Two. The patient on this bed had barely said a word since he rolled in. His vital signs on the monitor were reassuring – he didn't appear to be in shock; at least not yet – but his chest looked like it'd been run over by a tractor. Hendrick adjusted the oxygen mask around the man's head and inspected his scalp for bumps and bleeding. I listened carefully to his breathing and pressed gently over his ribs, abdomen and hips. He seemed to have breath sounds on both sides of his chest, but his wincing at my prodding made me pause.

'Lisa, can you give this gentleman some more morphine, please?' I asked, then turned back to the man on the bed. 'Where does it hurt most, mate?'

He lifted a sausage finger with an oxygen probe clamped on it and pointed gingerly down the right side of his ribcage. 'It hurt a lot here, doc. Not easy to breathe.'

'What about here, does that hurt?' I asked, pushing lightly down the right side of his flank.

He sucked in sharply through his teeth and his eyes closed tight with pain.

I unplugged our ultrasound machine from the wall, trundled it over, squirted gel on a probe and ran it across the man's abdominal wall. He was a big unit. I adjusted the depth settings and peered at the monochrome images moving on the screen. Couple of rib fractures, just as expected. I passed a flash of black, scanned back and zoomed in again.

'Hey, Hendrick, what do you reckon that is?'

Hendrick glanced up from his scalp inspection and followed my pointing finger to the screen.

'Blood around the liver. Probably ruptured it, hey?'

'Yeah, I think so too. Can you get a big line in and start running some O-negative blood? Femoral line if you can, and an art line in the wrist while you're at it.* I'll leave the ultrasound here.'

'Copy that.'

Gloves off, gown off, wash hands, gown on, gloves on.

I swished through the curtain into the adjacent cubicle.

'You ready to relocate this ankle, Jadav?'

'Yes, sir, I'm ready,' he said, gesturing at the sedation drugs and plaster trolley.

Where did he pick up that 'sir' stuff, I wondered, *and how can I get him to stop?*

'Good work. And it's just "Lachie", remember?'

'Yes, sir, Lachie, very good, thank you.'

'Emily, Jackie, can you come help us for a minute, please?' I called out.

The two of them appeared next to Jadav and I looked doubtfully at their three slender figures and the tree trunk of a lower limb we had to manipulate.

'Okay, here's the plan. Emily, you're giving the drugs. Don't stress,' I said, as I saw her eyes widen. 'I'll tell you exactly how many millilitres to inject

---

* A femoral line is a type of central venous catheter – a large-bore cannula with multiple branches for injection that can be used to give fluids, blood and drugs simultaneously and/or rapidly. An arterial line is used to monitor blood pressure constantly (rather than intermittently, as with a cuff on the arm) and take samples of arterial blood to measure levels of things like acids, gases and electrolytes.

from each syringe. Jackie, if you could please hook up the bag valve mask*
and get ready to support his breathing if we need to, that'd be great. And
Jadav, I hope you're feeling strong. You're going to have to lean back and
pull hard on this guy's knee while I try and manoeuvre that ankle back into
position.' I looked around. 'Everybody ready?'

Two nods and one 'Yes, sir.' Goddamn it.

Two more syringes, one snoring patient, two sweating doctors, a
little help from a brawny ambulance officer and, eventually, a satisfying
ka-thunk later, the ankle looked straight again. I checked for pulses. All
present and correct. Jackie hoisted the patient's leg up onto her shoulder
like a side of beef and Jadav cracked on with the plastering.

'Emily, how did you go with the Tongan interpreter? Did you find out
why the guy in Bay Four keeps yelling at us?'

'Oh yeah, I almost forgot,' she said, handing me back my phone. 'The
interpreter was really friendly and helpful. It took us a while to figure out
the problem, but it seems he's just worried that they're going to have to stay
here and miss work tomorrow.'

'Conscientious lot,' I muttered as I went to splash cold water over my
face. My phone buzzed in my pocket again.

'Lachie, Drew here, on the sat phone.† We've just started our descent
into Tennant. Wheels down in ten, should be in ED ten or fifteen minutes
after that.'

'Thank fuck for that. Can you take two Tongans, one tubed and the
other with multiple rib fractures, internal bleeding and blood running?
We'll have to ship out a couple more, but they can wait for the next plane.'

---

* A bag valve mask allows a mix of air and oxygen to be delivered through a mask on a
patient's face, with higher volumes given when the bag is squeezed by hand.

† Slang for 'satellite phone' – usually the only option to communicate from a plane
at altitude.

'I guess we'll have to. Never a dull moment in TFC, hey?'
'That's TCCCE to you, you cheeky shit. See you shortly.'

*

Out of boredom, desperation or a mild case of workaholism – perhaps a little of each – I took up another part-time job as a District Medical Officer for Central Australia. This role involved being on call to provide medical advice to the remote clinics, Indigenous communities, mining sites and cattle stations where there were no doctors, perhaps a nurse, sometimes a health worker and often only an employee trained in first aid. The job, which I could do from my desk at home in Melbourne, also required me to coordinate the aeromedical retrievals for urgent cases with the Royal Flying Doctor Service and the referral hospitals in Alice Springs and Adelaide. I'd find myself faxing an ECG* of a patient with chest pain to a cardiologist, while on the phone to a jackaroo (the Aussie version of a cowboy) about a co-worker who'd fallen off a horse and had a suspected spinal injury. We'd be trying to figure out how to transport them safely to the airstrip using a four-wheel motorbike and a barn door, when the other phone would ring to request urgent retrieval of an elderly Indigenous lady who'd missed her kidney dialysis appointment and was now in acute heart failure in a clinic with no nurse. The latter situation was common and another example of a cultural disconnect. We, as clinicians, had a hard time understanding why someone whose life depended on being hooked up to a dialysis machine every couple of days would choose to skip that in favour of disappearing for a week into the desert to attend a funeral. Those patients, on the other hand, couldn't imagine such priorities in reverse.

* ECG stands for electrocardiogram - a common procedure whereby several seconds of the heart's electrical activity is recorded by placing electrodes on the chest and limbs.

Most of the communities in this vast region, covering half a million square kilometres, had two names – an Indigenous name and an English one – so I had to stick a map up on my wall with names, distances, weather information and notes about which planes could land at what times of day and night. While my brain often felt scrambled with the logistics, important lessons slowly sunk in: triage, resource management, the importance of communication and what it means to compromise while still endeavouring to provide the best possible quality of care.

Shuttling between the hipster cafés of Melbourne and the health facilities of the Central Australian desert was an interesting mix, which I mostly enjoyed, but I was almost always on the move. I was renting an apartment in the city but spending the majority of my time working in remote locations. When I was 'home', I was usually hunched over at my desk, either on call or hammering away at my PhD thesis. I rarely saw any of my non-medical friends and my love life was a pile of smoking debris. I wasn't unhappy, exactly, but I knew what I was doing wasn't sustainable in the long term. And I could feel that the mercurial lifestyle was maybe, slowly, driving me a tiny bit mad.

CHAPTER EIGHT

2015
Vanuatu

I needed to take some time out and get my head straight, so I listened to my heart and booked a ticket back to Santo. The relationship with Nixon and the community in Bene was well established by now, with even my relatives in Australia referring to them as 'family'. I had met far more members of the Bene side than they had met of the mob from my home town of Millaa Millaa, so this time, when I travelled back to the village, I took my darling ma.

'Our ma,' Nixon gently corrected me with a big grin once the first round of welcome hugs was done.

'Ma', then, as all the village called her, was treated like royalty. I hadn't realised, and Ma was embarrassed in the extreme to see, that Nixon and his little army of workers had been busily preparing for her arrival for some months. Nixon and Linda's house sported two extensions, including a bedroom with brick walls, a concrete floor, mosquito-screened windows and two brand-new mattresses, immaculately made up with crisp sheets and fresh pillows. Even more impressive was the bathroom. Gone was the stick-and-tarpaulin enclosure out the back, where we'd stand on pebbles and tip a bucket of water hauled up from the well over our heads. Gone, too, was the hole into which nature's calls had been deposited, with soil kicked over upon completion. In their place was a large, brick and concrete room with a spacious, lowered area for bathing, complete with drain, and a toilet with not only a seat but a button flush. The bucket system was unchanged. If it ain't broke, I suppose . . .

Once we'd finished feasting on lap-lap (fish, pork and root vegetables wrapped with fresh coconut in banana leaves and baked on fire-heated rocks in a hole in the ground) and we were curled up on the floor of the new guest room in pocket-sprung comfort, I was feeling pretty pleased with myself. It took me by surprise to receive a scolding.

'We should be doing more for our family here!' Ma whispered, peering around the room with the headtorch I'd bought her and poking me in the arm to make sure I was paying attention.

I pointed out that I'd been doing as much as I could. Nixon and I had cooked up quite a few schemes over the years to help the community. Under his leadership, we'd bought a number of new solar panels, dug some wells, built rainwater tanks and set up a roadside stall to sell snacks and gasoline to the drivers who passed by the village with increasing frequency, as the once-dirt road had been recently sealed as a 'gesture of friendship' by the Chinese government. We'd even set up a trust account to pay for the children's school fees.

'Yes,' Ma conceded, 'but we're all in this together now, so it shouldn't be just you. And what about your medical skills? Are you using them here?'

I had to confess that the idea had honestly never occurred to me, despite the fact that I'd been visiting the village for several years by then. I knew there was a small, run-down clinic a short walk away, staffed by Auntie Mary, an elderly relative who was a trained nurse. She hadn't been paid by the Vanuatu Ministry of Health for ten years, but she dragged herself back out of retirement whenever a sick family member banged on the door.

'Alright, well, that settles it. We'll ask Auntie Mary if we can do a clinic with her before we leave. You set it up and I'll assist.'

Mothers. They can be pains in the arse, but they're usually right.

Auntie Mary shyly accepted our proposal and graciously agreed to come out of retirement one more time. Children were summoned to clear branches and cut the grass around the clinic with machetes, while a couple of teenage boys tended a wood fire topped with a pot of boiling water full of surgical instruments. The rusty truck I'd bought for the village was despatched with messengers to the surrounding communities to let them know the clinic would be open the following day with, for the first time since anyone could remember, a doctor present for consultations. It all seemed like a good idea, but when Ma and I arrived after an early breakfast the next morning to see the immaculate clinic grounds packed with people, I realised we might have bitten off a lot more than we could chew. Everyone I saw that day, including Nixon, Linda, all the adults in Bene and most of the children, as well as folks I'd never met but who greeted me as if they'd known me for ages, was very patient and obviously grateful for our time and effort. The main problem was that – as we should have foreseen – trying to treat patients in a clinic that had essentially been abandoned meant that options for medications and follow-up care were scant, at best. I diagnosed Nixon and two of his brothers with gastro-oesophageal reflux disease, but the best I could offer them were handwritten prescriptions for a heartburn medication they'd have to try and find in a pharmacy in Luganville, the island's only town, an hour's drive south.

I saw a teenage girl who evidently had heart failure, most likely from rheumatic heart disease,* who would need lifelong treatment with tablets to remove fluid from her lungs and antibiotics to prevent deadly infections.

---

* An immune system response to the same bacteria that causes post-streptococcal glomerulonephritis, but that attacks the heart muscle and its valves, rather than the kidneys.

When I asked Auntie Mary if the clinic had those two medications, she clambered up on a chair, shuffled some boxes around in the dust on the top shelf and proudly passed me down a couple of plastic bottles. But when I explained that these would need to be dispensed in equal quantities every month, she shook her head sorrowfully. These were the last she had.

I was alarmed to discover that another teenage girl – a distant relative from an even more distant village who'd been staying in Bene for several months – almost certainly had TB, meaning she'd been unknowingly breathing the bug over most other members of the family the entire time. I wrote a letter to the hospital in Luganville and sent her off, sitting forlornly in the back of the truck. With the tropical sun already set, our outdoor waiting area almost empty and the mosquitoes in full attack mode, Ma came into the dim little consultation room where I was sweating into my plastic seat and scribbling notes. As a retired midwife, Ma had made herself more than useful taking each new patient's vital signs and helping Auntie Mary weighing babies, dispensing drugs and dressing wounds. It had been a long day, but we'd done our best, and I looked up at Ma with a weary grin.

She frowned, then put her hand on my shoulder.

'I don't know what's wrong with this last little boy,' she said quietly, 'but you need to try and help him.'

Two young parents shuffled in, the mother carrying a toddler wrapped in a calico cloth. As she lifted the fabric from the little boy's head, the mother gave me a sad smile. The poor child's face was severely deformed. His eyes were too close together and looked in opposite directions, while his nose was small and flat, with a large purple lesion in the middle of it. His forehead tapered into a point and he clearly lacked the strength in his neck to hold his head up. In soft Bislama, his parents explained to me that since he was born, over three years ago, their son had suffered almost constant seizures. They'd taken him to the hospital in Luganville, where they'd been told there was nothing that could be done and he was going to die. They lived in a village two hours' walk up into the jungle but when they'd heard there was a doctor doing a clinic in Bene they decided to carry him in for a second opinion. It was clear that the boy had a severe genetic disorder, most likely a rare syndrome with a fancy name unbeknown to me. I hunted around in the junk-filled storeroom for any medicines that might be effective in controlling his epilepsy. I found a bottle of pills with a label that said Phenytoin and a date of expiry from two years earlier. This drug was dangerous in overdose and we would have no way to measure blood levels to check for toxicity. I also wasn't sure if the medication would even be active, or safe, given it was so far past its use-by date. I explained all this to the parents, along with my overall, inexpert impression that the advice from the Luganville doctors, despite seeming harsh, was probably correct. They nodded, thanked me, took the bottle and the script I'd given them to try and find a better, safer seizure medication in town and walked out into the sound of the cicadas.

'I'm proud of you,' Ma said with a squeeze of my hand as we boarded the plane out of Santo the next morning.

'It was all your idea,' I said as I hugged her back, 'and you've still got it, old girl.'

We arrived in Brisbane later that day and said our goodbyes at the airport. I didn't want to worry Ma, but I wasn't feeling too well. My stomach was playing up, with painful rumblings (technically known as 'borborygmi' – my grandmother's favourite word from her years as a surgical nurse) and increasingly violent diarrhoea. As I stumbled out of the bathroom to the airport's baggage carousel, I felt feverish and woozy.

I fumbled with my phone as I waited for my backpack to appear and called a doctor friend in Brisbane who was a specialist in travel medicine.

'Hey, Nicole, it's Lachie. I've just stepped off the plane from Vanuatu and I feel like shit. Fever, diarrhoea, aches and pains. There's still a bit of malaria and a bunch of other stuff over there. Can I come and see you?'

'Sure, I'm in the clinic all afternoon, come right away.' Nicole sounded excited. Travel doctors do a lot of writing scripts for vaccinations for healthy people going on holiday, so a patient returning from a tropical destination with a fever gets them fired up.

I was bordering on delirious by the time the taxi deposited me at Nicole's clinic. She tut-tutted at me as she took my temperature and prodded all over my abdomen, took several little tubes of blood to be tested for different bacteria and parasites, sent me off for stool and urine samples and loaded me up with some broad-spectrum antibiotics.

'Keep your phone nearby for when I call you with the results,' she said sternly as she showed me out.

Nicole called me a few days later, as I was convalescing in Melbourne, to tell me the lab results showed I had shigella – a dysenteric disease somewhat like salmonella but with more bleeding from the bowel. I recovered quickly enough on the heavy-duty bug-killers she'd given me, but I realised I needed to be more careful with how I ate, drank and kept myself clean in environments like Bene, where such infections are common and can often be serious. My tropical medicine 'expertise' still had a few gaps in it, apparently. Nevertheless, I somehow managed to score an appointment as adjunct Associate Professor of Tropical Medicine at the university where I'd done my master's. I had also received a call out of the blue from the head of an organisation whose main role was placing doctors in areas of extreme need around the Pacific region. They had been asked by the Vanuatu Ministry of Health to find someone to help redesign Vanuatu's junior doctor training programme. It seems my name had been mentioned over the 'coconut telephone' (the Pacific's version of the bush telegraph) as someone who was familiar with Vanuatu and interested in medical education. The colleague who was calling me was a figure so well respected in the region he was widely considered the chief of all the doctors in the Pacific, and it seemed like a unique, incredible opportunity, so even though I couldn't see just how the pixelated fuck I was going to do all this stuff at once, I simply couldn't say 'no'.

But something definitely had to give.

I phoned Frankie and told him the time had come for me to step aside from Tennant Creek. He teased me for my lack of stamina but assured me he understood. We were both proud of what our team had accomplished over the previous couple of years, and we were confident that Hendrick, Dave and the other guys would finish their training shortly and be able to step up to fill the senior shoes. We promised to catch up for beers again soon, and he signed off with a cheery 'Later, dickhead.'

*

As I was trying to figure out how to divide my time between Townsville, where I'd be teaching at the university, and Port Vila, where I'd be helping train the new medical graduates, a true disaster struck.

Tropical Cyclone Pam coalesced to the east of Solomon Islands on 6 March 2015 and steadily increased in intensity as it roared southwards. By the time it tore into Vanuatu, seven days later, it had strengthened into a Category 5 cyclone (the most extreme form) and displaced almost half of Tuvalu's population en route. Its impact devastated Vanuatu, with 250-kilometre-per-hour winds, severe rains and flying debris damaging some 90 per cent of the country's infrastructure and causing at least sixteen deaths. It was the second most intense cyclone recorded in the history of the Pacific region and one of the worst natural disasters to have ever occurred in Vanuatu. And the country is no stranger to disasters. It is the long-term occupant of the number one position in the UN's Disaster Risk Index.

Not only is it prone to hydrometeorological (and therefore climate-related) disasters such as cyclones, floods and droughts, but it is also home to several active volcanoes and is intermittently rattled and pounded by earthquakes and tsunamis. In a television interview broadcast across the world from a high-level meeting on disaster risk reduction in Japan, which he happened to be attending at the time, Vanuatu's President Baldwin Lonsdale broke down in tears as he described what was happening as Pam wreaked havoc back home.

I followed with horror as the devastation was revealed on TV and online over the next few days. I attempted repeatedly, but in vain, to reach Nixon on the phone, and waited impatiently to book a ticket on the first plane to be able to land on Vanuatu's battered airstrips. I knew the emergency humanitarian organisations and disaster junkies would be descending on little Vanuatu in droves and I was conscious of what I'd seen in PNG during the cholera epidemic, when the local health system had been overwhelmed with people and stuff that they couldn't put to good use. But since I had both an adopted family and a new role specifically supporting the Ministry of Health, I felt I had more of a right to be there than most of the expats who'd be currently trying to book flights into the disaster zone.

I gathered my gear. First into the pack went my trusty headtorch – I'd upgraded to a waterproof one by now. Along with that went my Swiss Army knife, inflatable mattress, mosquito net and several cans of mosquito repellent so strong it peeled paint. I carefully assembled a medical kit, with enough supplies to cover me for the first day or two if I got sick again, plus some extra for whatever I might encounter in Bene, and stocked up on water-purification tablets. I threw in my toughest boots, my most water-resistant rain jacket, some packet noodles, tins of tuna, gaffer tape (because you can never have enough of that stuff) and a length of rope (because you never know when that may come in handy). Then, at the last minute, when

I realised I'd be trying to be in two places at once, checking on my family in Bene while likely also being needed in the ED of the main hospital in the capital city of Port Vila, I called for reinforcements.

I phoned my buddy Tom.

'Mate, any chance you'd be free to come with me to Vanuatu for a week or so to help with the cyclone response?'

Tom was a doctor colleague from the Torres Strait; a big, gap-toothed, grinning ball of eternally positive energy. We'd both arrived on Thursday Island at the same time, hit it off immediately and remained firm friends ever since. He'd worked with MSF amid the civil war in Sudan and had spent months as a volunteer doctor in rural Botswana, so I figured he probably wouldn't be too fazed in a disaster zone. There was just the small matter of his full-time job, wife and two small children.

'Shit, wow, I'd love to, yes!' he said, followed by a brief pause – during which I could almost hear the wheels turning as I imagined him contemplating his fate – and then: 'Wait, hang on, I'd better check with the boss.'

I wasn't sure whether he was consulting his lovely (and very tolerant) wife, or the medical superintendent, or both, but whoever it was he managed to convince them pretty quickly – the bloke is nothing if not charming – as 15 minutes later he phoned me back.

'Green light! Let's do it.'

*

The view from the air as our plane descended into Port Vila brought tears to my eyes. Most buildings had their roofs buckled up or completely torn off and many had been reduced to rubble, or whatever the equivalent word is for homes that were built from corrugated iron, timber and tarpaulin. There was no running water anywhere and the only electricity available was in the few fancier hotels that had generators and were now housing the hundreds of UN staff and aid workers who'd hit town in their own storm of muddy boots, quick-dry pants, solar-powered laptop chargers and pen-filled vests. We weaved around the overflowing potholes and logo-emblazoned Land Cruisers that suddenly filled Port Vila's usually sleepy streets and made our way up to the national referral hospital. Through my Ministry of Health contacts, I'd managed to wangle Tom a short-term contract that would see him paid a small stipend to spend a couple of weeks working in the ED. While Vila Central Hospital was home to the country's largest collection of medical specialists – a dozen or so surgeons, paediatricians, general physicians, anaesthetists and obstetrician/ gynaecologists – there was no such thing as an emergency specialist in Vanuatu. The ni-Vanuatu* doctor appointed to be in charge of the ED during the cyclone response was a friendly fellow who had the unfortunate reputation of being scared of blood and unable to read an ECG, so he was a fleeting figure in the department whose muddy, slippery, unlit waiting room was overflowing with patients. Many clutched wounds caused by falling debris or injuries from the clean-up efforts, all of which were susceptible to tetanus and other types of infection. Most of the patients who'd suffered more serious head, chest and abdominal injuries were already dead. Others had respiratory problems, due to the fires burning around the town, and an increasing number of children were turning up with diarrhoea from contaminated water supplies and widespread lack of hygiene. Tom and I nodded along as the weary medical superintendent went through the emergency triage protocols, pointed out where the hospital was most badly damaged and warned us how dengue fever and leptospirosis outbreaks would probably follow.

---

* People from Vanuatu are known as ni-Vanuatu, commonly abbreviated to 'ni-Van'.

I finally managed to get hold of Nixon on the phone.

'Yes, brother, don't worry, we are all fine,' came the faint crackle. 'Well, except for our brother Moses. He had a bad accident and is in hospital now because he can't walk.'

The phone connection dropped out. I went to find Tom.

'You'll be fine here, mate. Just do whatever needs doing. I've gotta go.'

I caught the next flight to Luganville, Santo's only town, and made my way up to Northern Provincial Hospital – a squat, sprawling, colonial-era building with mud-stained white and blue paint peeling off cracked concrete walls. There was no electricity, of course. I wandered through the wards, peering into dim corners, through mosquito nets, to find where Moses was convalescing. He broke into a broad smile and tried to prop himself up on his elbows as I approached, grunting with the effort. Flies circled over his bed, casually evading the swats from the towel being wielded by his wife, Anne. Moses had a brightly patterned cloth wrapped around his waist like a sarong, reaching down to his ankles, and I gulped as I imagined what might lie mangled underneath. I hugged him gently, made him lie back down again and squatted next to where Anne was sitting on an upturned metal bucket beside the bed.

'Brother, what happened to you? Did the roof of your house fall down? Is everyone else okay?'

'Ah, no, brother Lachie. The house is fine. Everyone is fine. This is not from the cyclone.'

'What? Oh, okay, I just thought, when Nixon said you'd had an accident . . . ' I tailed off and looked at him with eyebrows raised.

'Ah, well, you see, what happened was . . . ' Moses paused and gave a little cough. 'I was driving back to the village very late Friday night and I fell asleep and crashed the car.'

Out of the corner of my eye I thought I saw Anne turn her head and wipe away a silent tear.

'I'm very sorry to hear that.' I suddenly remembered something Nixon had told me a while ago. 'Had you been drinking?'

He gave me a sheepish smile and said nothing. Anne stood up from her bucket and left the room, sniffling and dabbing at her eyes with the fly-swatting towel.

I thought about telling Moses he was an idiot, but I guessed he probably didn't need that from me. Through my mind flashed the times as a uni student when I'd woken up at home in bed with a sore head and not remembered how I'd got there, only to find my car parked askew in the driveway. I swallowed my hypocrisy and went off to find his x-rays. Fortunately, the hospital generator was still working, so the x-ray machine could be cranked up to take the occasional snap. I held Moses' x-rays up to a window and let the sunlight show me where his pelvis was fractured in three places.

'You're an idiot,' I told him when I went back. I was so relieved he still had both legs and wasn't paralysed it just slipped out. 'But you're going to be okay. You'll have to lie here for a few more weeks and then the recovery process will be slow and painful. But you should be walking again in a few months.'

'*Hemi gud tumas* (That's good),' Moses sighed as he settled back in bed. 'Thank you for coming to see me, brother Lachie.'

I gave him another sweaty hug and went off to find the medical superintendent. This was a unique opportunity for me to get a good look at this facility – the second-largest hospital in Vanuatu and the only one apart from Vila Central that was permanently staffed with doctors. Northern Provincial Hospital provided care to the northern half of the archipelago, servicing a population of close to one hundred thousand, and it was quaintly referred to as 'the other tertiary hospital', although I'd soon see that was a significant overstatement.

The place didn't suffer from a lack of good leadership, at least. I tracked down Dr Leo, the medical superintendent, in his small, dark, dusty office and introduced myself. He was a short, slender fellow with a salt-and-pepper beard and a kind smile, wearing flip-flops and a traditional ni-Vanuatu 'basket' (a small bag made of woven palm leaves) slung around his neck next to his stethoscope. Leo was pleased to see me – he'd heard someone was coming to assist with training the junior doctors – and offered to give me a tour. He led me around the dilapidated rabbit warren, tracking muddy footprints from the adult medical ward, where 40 sets of febrile eyes followed us quietly; through the paediatric ward full of whining mosquitoes and skinny, listless kids; and on to the much noisier maternity ward, where a couple of dozen new mothers shared beds and plates of lap-lap while their babies suckled and squawked. I bit my lip at the overcrowding and shuddered at the lack of hygiene but could see that Leo and his colleagues were doing their best with the resources they had. As he showed me the blueprints for a renovation of the Emergency Department and pointed out where he hoped to extend the hospital accommodation for the new graduate doctors, it was clear to me that Leo – like Nixon – was a man with a plan. It was just that the plan required money and the Ministry of Health had next to none.

Despite the privations, I was strangely excited by what I saw. I could see that there might be some opportunities to put into practice what I'd discussed several years earlier with Dr Steve Homasi – the former Director of Health in Tuvalu – before he'd died suddenly and tragically from his accident. The new medical graduates were arriving soon, and I was being given some responsibility for helping design the first phases of their postgraduate training. Maybe there was a way we could tailor that to provide those young doctors with the skills they needed to work safely and competently in the rural hospitals, thus improving the availability and quality of medical care across the islands of Vanuatu. Maybe.

*

After a few days in Santo, I got back to Port Vila, where Tom had been doing a top-notch job in the ED. We debriefed over tinned tuna and a warm baguette, washed down with an even warmer bottle of French red. Prior to independence, Vanuatu had been known as the New Hebrides. The eighteenth-century European obsession of naming tropical islands in the South Pacific after windswept lumps of cold rock in the North Sea surely suggests that those explorers drank too much seawater or were homesick to the point of delusion. Ridiculous nomenclature notwithstanding, Britain and France had 'shared' rule over the territory for three-quarters of a century in an arrangement officially known as a 'condominium'. This absurd paternalistic enterprise quickly became known locally as the 'pandemonium', a far more accurate term that has persisted to this day. One of the many confusing legacies of that period, including two parallel systems of education and law, is that Port Vila has the finest bakeries and best-stocked liquor stores of any Pacific capital city.

Given I was about to replace Tom as the senior – and effectively the only – doctor in the ED of the country's largest hospital, I probed him for details of what had been happening. He told me how he and the nurses had been forced to cut up plastic bottles to use for asthmatic patients needing inhaled medications, as there wasn't enough oxygen being pumped from the hospital supply and the pharmacies had run out of the standard hand-held devices. Vila Central Hospital's few 'intensive care' beds had been rapidly overwhelmed and the operating theatre was running non-stop to deal with the traumatic injuries from the cyclone damage and the early efforts to clean up and rebuild. Children were turning up with abdominal pain and pooping out writhing balls of intestinal worms the size of grapefruits. Revolting as it sounds, this was a good thing; at least these weren't exploding inside their little bellies. And there were efforts underway to educate the community and distribute rubber boots to reduce the risk of diseases such as tetanus and leptospirosis from cuts in the skin and bare feet stomping around in the mud.

Tom was knackered. I felt guilty that I'd been away in Santo checking on a single injured relative and making grandiose plans for Vanuatu's rural medical workforce while Tom had been working sixteen-hour shifts every day in ED. He had done great work, not just in treating patients and in supporting the nurses through the first phase of the humanitarian emergency, but in demonstrating what a rural generalist could do. The Director-General of the Ministry of Health and our specialist colleagues at the national referral hospital were suitably impressed. For now, though, Tom needed to get home, where his patient wife and the patients of the Torres Strait waited. His short, hard stint keeping the ED running was done. We exchanged a smelly hug at the airport, I waved him off, drove back to the hospital and got to work.

CHAPTER NINE

2015–16
Vanuatu

I re-counted the flower necklaces and checked the number and positions of the chairs. The tent seemed big enough to seat the dignitaries, at least, but there would be standing room only for the hospital staff. The microphones and sound systems were working. A table under a large tree groaned with the weight of the lunchtime feast, which was covered with plastic wrap and guarded by watchful kitchen staff waving paper plates to keep the flies at bay. A reporter and photographer from the national newspaper, the Vanuatu Daily Post, had been busily taking names and pictures and now waited in the shade, fanning themselves with the printed programmes. I'd never organised a welcome ceremony before and I couldn't deny I was feeling a wee bit nervous.

'Newly graduate doctors return from Cuba' sputtered today's headline. This was a highly anticipated event. As a result of an opaque arrangement made between the two governments almost a decade earlier, around thirty young ni-Vanuatu students had been sent to train as doctors at *La Escuela Latinoamericana de Medicina* (ELAM – the Latin American School of Medicine) in Cuba. ELAM is by far the largest medical school in the world. Established in 1999, it hosts students from over one hundred countries, most of them on full scholarships, and each year pumps out graduate doctors in their thousands. In terms of its impact on the medical workforce in developing countries, ELAM has been nothing short of a global health revolution. Despite its questionable politics and ossified economy, Cuba has long had the reputation of punching way above its weight when it comes to the quality of its health system and the overall health of its population. Cuba's citizens have tended to live longer lives, with better access to medical care, than the populations of many wealthy, developed countries, including – as is frequently and gleefully pointed out – the US.

Cuban doctors are the country's best-known and most valued export. Tens of thousands of them have been part of the 'Cuban medical brigade', providing vital medical care in dozens of countries over the last 20 years. Over the same period, many of those host countries have been sending their own students, in increasing numbers, to train as doctors in Cuba. For free! For politicians in a tiny country like Vanuatu, it's a no-brainer.

Prior to 2015, there were approximately thirty doctors in Vanuatu, serving a population of over two hundred and fifty thousand. Only ten of those were specialists, all of whom worked in the two largest hospitals, with the rest either trainees or 'GPs' – the term used to refer to those with no formal postgraduate training, who either worked in private practices in Port Vila or who languished in the outer-island hospitals with no supervision or prospects of further professional development. The return of the new ni-Vanuatu graduates from Cuba, therefore, generated an understandable degree of excitement, both from the Ministry of Health and from the public, all of whom were desperate for the new arrivals to be sent out to the chronically doctorless provinces as soon as possible. This political imperative was made clear to me in my initial briefings.

In the flurry of activity following the cyclone and in preparing for the arrival of the new graduates, it took a few weeks before I began to suspect that I'd been handed something of a poisoned chalice. There were rumours that other Pacific island countries who'd taken up the offer of sending students to train as doctors in Cuba were encountering some major problems with the new medical graduates when they returned home. One of the first stumbling blocks, for which no one seemed to have been prepared, was that these young doctors had been trained exclusively in Spanish. They'd spent seven years of their lives away from home, with the first year entirely devoted to Spanish classes, followed by six years of medical school *en español*.

Vanuatu is one of the most linguistically diverse countries on the planet, with over one hundred different languages spoken across the archipelago, of which an average ni-Vanuatu would speak at least a couple, in addition to, depending on their level of education and which colonial system they were schooled in, Bislama, English, French, or all three.

The ni-Vanuatu students sent to Cuba came back fluent in Spanish as well, but it seemed that little thought had been given to how they might be integrated into medical practice in their home country, where Spanish was hardly spoken by anyone at all. The stories I was hearing from Solomon Islands and Kiribati suggested that their new graduates had significant gaps in their knowledge and after six years of medical school in Cuba some of them still had no idea – so the whispers went – of how to use a stethoscope. There were reports of discrimination by senior medical staff in those countries, as they refused to consider the new graduates equivalent to those from the Pacific's main medical schools in Fiji and PNG. With growing concern at the challenge ahead of me and a sinking feeling about why the Vanuatu Ministry of Health had wanted external support for this position, I tracked down my counterparts in the other Pacific island countries with Cuban-trained graduates. We started sharing information and resources, under the radar, worried about what the implications would be – for them, their patients, the community, the political leaders and even for us – if the new cohort of doctors did indeed prove to be inadequately trained and unsafe to practise. I felt I'd done my homework and was determined not to pre-judge the returning graduates. I was going to be responsible for coordinating the first year of their postgraduate training and I was as keen as anyone to see that these bright young people received a warm welcome home. The number of doctors in Vanuatu had literally doubled overnight.

This was a big fucking deal.

Once the flower wreaths had been bequeathed, the hands shaken, the photos taken and the feasting finished, we got down to it. The first order of business was to try to get an objective sense of where the new graduates were at in terms of their medical knowledge. Acknowledging it was a shitty thing to ask them to do, given they'd just finished medical school and probably thought it safe to assume they wouldn't need to sit another exam for a while, the day after their welcome ceremony I made them all complete a multiple-choice paper on basic medical science and clinical topics, written in both English and Spanish. This same test had been used for the returning doctors in Kiribati and Solomon Islands, so the idea was that we would at least be able to compare the performances between the Cuban-trained graduates in these three Pacific island countries. The results turned out to be similar between the three countries, but they weren't good news. Only two of the new ni-Vanuatu doctors got more than half the answers correct. The average score was 42 per cent. It seemed most of them were doing little better than guessing the answers. I compared their individual results to the grades they'd been awarded by their university in Cuba. Almost all of them were supposedly A or B students. I started to have my doubts about the quality of medical training they'd received in Cuba, but I swore to myself I'd do all I could to try and bring them up to the necessary standard as quickly as possible. In doing so, accepting that we couldn't simply put this cohort directly to work in the hospital as interns, we went straight to Plan B.

I'd spent the previous couple of months designing a bridging programme, whereby the new grads would spend three months rotating around the five main departments in the national referral hospital, getting a taste of the clinical work and the requirements of a junior doctor in each job, while progressing through a series of further evaluations of their relevant knowledge and skills. At the end of this 'trainee internship', as we opted to call it, a final set of clinical assessments would be conducted to determine if they were ready to be interns.

I felt I had an obligation not only to assist each of the new graduates, but to get to know them, understand their individual backgrounds and learning needs, help them grow professionally and personally and support them in their career development. This turned out to be the highlight of the job. Over the next year or so, when I wasn't back in Australia for my university commitments, we'd meet together as a group every week for an afternoon of teaching on different topics, practising essential skills and discussing interesting cases. I managed to sweet-talk the hospital kitchen staff into providing lunch for these sessions, as I knew from my own experience as an overworked, cash-strapped and hungry junior doctor that an offer of free food would usually guarantee attendance. As the weeks went by, I realised that these sessions – and the lunches – were more valuable than I had initially assumed.

'Come in, guys, grab a plate and take your seats. Quickly now, we've got a big session ahead of us this afternoon. It's called "It's 2am and the phone rings". Any guesses what we're going to be discussing?'

'Booty calls!' yipped Brian from the back of the room through a mouthful of fish and rice.

Once the tittering died down and I'd suppressed my smile, I went on.

'Thanks for explaining why you're always looking for a spare phone charger, B-ri. No, today we're going to talk about how to manage being on call. And, as it happens . . . ' – I plugged my laptop into the ancient projector and my PowerPoint presentation gradually came into view on the cream-coloured wall – 'the first thing to keep in mind is that you need to make sure your phones have plenty of battery and they're not on silent when you're on call. A junior doctor who doesn't answer their phone is going to have a very short career indeed.'

'The bosses don't always answer their phones when we need them,' muttered Jackson, to a rumble of agreement and nodding of heads around the room.

I sighed. 'Yeah, look, you can learn a lot from your senior colleagues, and it's not always going to be positive. It's just as useful to observe bad practices as it is to see good ones. You guys should be aiming to become not just the best clinicians you can be, but the best supervisors and mentors. I know it doesn't feel like it now, but before you know it, you'll be teaching junior doctors yourselves. So, let's say you're the surgical intern, and you're on call. You're in your dorm, in bed, asleep, it's 2am and the phone rings . . .'

Sarah interrupted, like always. 'What if we miss the call and we try and call back but we don't have any credit?'

More murmurs of concurrence rippled across the room.

'Well, that's part of being prepared, isn't it? Phone charged, not on silent, credit topped up.'

'What if we don't have enough money to buy credit?' Sarah insisted.

'It's only two hundred vatu* for a top-up card,' I pointed out.

The grumbles now suggested the room was turning against me.

Carl, the top of the class and unofficial leader of the pack, piped up. 'Doctor Lachie, you know we haven't been paid, right?'

'What, you mean this month?'

---

* Vanuatu's currency is the vatu. Two hundred vatu is about two US dollars.

More titters.

Carl smiled patiently. 'No, at all.'

I stared around the room at the weary faces of the young doctors I'd been working with for months. I noticed, not for the first time, that many were wearing the same clothes they'd worn the day before. In fact, now I thought about it, they hardly ever wore different clothes.

'Are you serious? You haven't received a salary since you started work?'

They shook their heads.

'I'm really sorry, guys. I had no idea that was the case. Let me chase it up and I'll get back to you.'

After a few enquiries, to my bitter surprise, I learned that the Ministry of Health had decided not to pay the new graduates, on the basis that they hadn't yet been registered as practising doctors. This meant that, although these dedicated young people had graduated from medical school and were turning up to the hospital every day, working long hours and training on the job, they had no money to buy food or clothes. The hospital did, at least, offer them small rooms in which to sleep on the hospital grounds, but when it came to meals, they were reliant on the generosity of friends and family around town, and no funds were made available even for essentials like phone credits.

As we became more comfortable with each other, they also began sharing with me some of the other difficulties they were experiencing. The saddest thing to hear was that the rumours from other Pacific island countries were being borne out here, too. Many of the graduates were being criticised and belittled by some of the senior medical staff, who told them they were 'not real doctors'. This was heartbreaking for them, as they'd been so excited to finish medical school and return home. They told me their stories of the previous seven years in Cuba, during which they'd had no money and slept with all their possessions in bunk beds in dormitories packed with hundreds of students. They had struggled to understand the first few years of their lectures in Spanish. There were so many medical students that they often couldn't even physically see the patients that were the subjects of the teaching rounds on the hospital wards. Then, when it came time to practise core skills like taking histories or examining patients, an unwritten rule gave priority to the Cuban students, then students from other countries in Latin America and the Caribbean, followed by a free-for-all for the remaining trainees if time and the patients allowed. Inevitably, the pushier students – particularly the Americans who enrolled in ELAM in surprising numbers – made sure they got to see and examine the patients and the quieter, gentler Pacific islanders often missed out.

I asked them to explain how the university's exams worked. I tried to be as tactful as possible in pointing out that they'd all graduated with good grades – and suspiciously similar scores – from ELAM but had some significant gaps in their knowledge and skills. They couldn't explain how they were graded, but I was helped to understand that the model was that of high turnover and low accountability. The most important outcome for the university, and the political deals behind it, appeared to be the number of doctors being churned out each year, not the quality of medical education being provided. It was assumed that if a developing country like Vanuatu was getting free doctors, they shouldn't be complaining.

As our weekly lunchtime sessions went on, I saw that this group of young doctors were all intelligent, committed professionals; they just hadn't yet had enough opportunities to learn how to be decent clinicians. They cared about their patients, were willing to work hard to improve their skills, and, I gradually came to appreciate, they had an attitude towards medicine that was subtly but distinctly different from a typical 'Western' graduate. Historically, surveys of medical students in countries like Australia have usually shown that most of them want to specialise in specific, narrow fields. They often make these decisions at very early stages in their career, but their choices rarely reflect with any accuracy what is actually needed in the community. I was curious to see how the young ni-Vanuatu doctors felt they were progressing, and I was keen to give them an opportunity to provide anonymous feedback about their supervisors and training experiences, so I gave them a questionnaire to complete. When I read their answers to simple questions about their career aspirations, I was surprised to see that over 60 per cent wrote something along the lines of 'I'll do whatever my country needs me to do.' Whatever one may think of Cuba's *modus operandi*, it seemed they had, to their credit, been teaching the world's medical students something useful after all.

In addition to observing how they participated in the teaching sessions and performed on the wards, I also got to know the trainee interns through regular one-on-one catch-ups in the stifling little box I'd been offered as an office. It was adjacent to the paediatric outpatient clinic, so several times a day I'd have to run the gauntlet of mothers in floral dresses fanning their feverish, squealing children in the waiting room, and smile politely whenever a head poked through my door looking for a nurse or a toilet. Despite the pedestal fan I'd bought for the office being on full blast, my skin would adhere to my plastic chair as I'd listen sympathetically to my young colleagues telling me how they were suffering from being bullied on the wards, or leaving lovers back in Cuba, or drowning their problems in drink. Despite all these issues, they kept calm and carried on. I was impressed by their dedication, and the results of the evaluations showed that most of them were improving quickly. I was optimistic that by the end of the bridging programme, the majority of them would be ready to progress to internship. We just had to find a way to squeeze some salaries out of the perennially penniless Ministry of Health.

*

When I wasn't teaching and testing the trainee interns, I continued to help out in ED. I was the only doctor working there, once again, so my emergency skills were being put to good use and I made sure the weekly trainee education sessions were loaded with emergency topics, as the plan was – despite my warnings against it – to make the junior doctors work in ED once they'd started their internships. I could see the logic behind the Ministry's attitude that 'any doctor in ED is better than no doctor', but I worried that the interns would be way out of their depth managing emergency cases on their own, particularly at night with no one else around. Vila Central Hospital ED had an abysmal reputation at the best of times. The nurses who worked there were a motley crew. Some worked efficiently managing patients with asthma attacks, minor wounds and simple infections; others apparently either didn't know what they were doing, didn't care, or both, preferring to ignore the patients scattered around the department and listen to music or watch porn on their mobile phones behind the glass window in the triage-cum-tea-room. There were no systems of triage, documentation, handover, referrals or even basic hygiene and prevention of infection. I would often arrive in the morning to find patients with conditions requiring urgent care, such as sepsis (bloodstream infections), displaced fractures or probable appendicitis, curled up on sheetless trolleys with concerned relatives around them but no nurse to be found, with the on-call physician or surgeon down on the ward, or relaxing at home, unaware of what awaited them in ED.

Little by little, I worked with the nurses to improve the systems of assessing patients and putting in place safe, appropriate management plans. But it was a slow, frustrating process and the responsibility weighed heavily on my shoulders. Port Vila is a small town, with most of the expats known to each other, so when my mates who worked for the privately funded ambulance service had a patient they were bringing in to the ED whom they were worried about, they'd often call me to see if I was there and, if not, if I could come in. I was never officially on call, but I trusted my ambulance buddies' judgement and knew they only called me when they thought I really needed to be there. By this stage I'd become so attached to Vanuatu I'd bought a timber villa with a little pool overlooking the bay on the road out of town. So, when these requests from the ambulance guys came in, usually at night, if I was at home and hadn't yet cracked open a cold Tusker beer, I'd jump in my truck and wind my way along the dirt roads, dodging the potholes and the dark shapes emerging from roadside kava bars, for the 20-minute trip to the hospital to check things out.

The clinical work was interesting, I felt I was making myself useful and I was proud of how the trainee interns were progressing, but from time to time I needed to let off a little steam.

Port Vila is pretty good for that; the rest of Vanuatu is perfect. Not only is it home to the best beaches and some of the most spectacular scuba diving in the world, but you can hike up and peer down into active volcanoes (surely the closest humans can get to a vision of hell on earth), swim in stunning blue-green limestone pools, snorkel with dolphins and turtles and camp out on uninhabited islands. There are restaurants in trees and bars on the sand. You may cross paths with an elderly cannibal – mostly reformed, they'll tell you with a wink as they pick their teeth – and be swept up in the intoxicating whirl of fire-dancing dervishes. The craziest guys in Vanuatu, though, are the land-divers.

A tradition thankfully confined to communities on the southern part of Pentecost Island, land-diving allegedly has its origins in a woman escaping an abusive husband by running away, climbing a tree, tying vines around her ankles and jumping off. Her husband then proceeded to leap off the branch in pursuit, *sans* the safety lines. While these days the trees have been replaced by specially constructed timber towers, and the diving part is practised exclusively by males, the rest of the process remains unchanged. Over a few weeks each year, each village's menfolk will settle their disputes, make peace with their wives and gods, strip down to their loincloths and, spurred on by hair-raising war cries from their fellow tribesmen and the chanting of the bare-breasted women stomping rhythmically below, launch themselves off the towers to crash head-first into the dirt slope, pulled up by the vines just short of maximum impact in a violent, ankle-snapping jerk . . . if things go well.

A few friends and I had the honour of being special guests at one such ceremony, which are highly sought-after experiences for the more intrepid of Vanuatu's perplexingly few visitors. It turned out that one of my trainee interns was the nephew of the chief of the village that was hosting us, so we were welcomed as VIPs and I was asked to join the chief in giving a speech to inspire the line-up of proud, unflinching lads before they leapt to their fate. I didn't know quite what to say as I gazed up in awe at the ceremonial towers and down at the unforgiving ground. *Extremely rickety* was one phrase that came to mind. *Spinal fracture* was another. In my best Bislama, I wished them all the very, *very* best of luck and had a quick, urgent, whispered conference with my friends about what we'd need to do if there was a serious injury while we were there. Fortunately, all the divers we witnessed survived, from the six-year-olds who climbed manfully up and lobbed themselves like little lemmings off their ten-metre-high planks, to the virile warriors in their twenties and thirties who shimmied up to the crow's nest, disappearing into tiny specks in the sun, before uttering a final, defiant, high-pitched holler and plunging down to torpedo into the dirt.*

*

---

* It was this ancient ni-Vanuatu ritual that inspired an entrepreneurial New Zealand adventurer by the name of Allan (better known as 'A.J.') Hackett to commercialise the sport of bungee jumping.

After I'd worked with the new graduates for the first 12 months since their return, most of them had successfully made the transition to interns, even the class clowns like Brian and Jackson, who I'd worried would find the temptations of kava, booze, weed and Port Vila's two tiny nightclubs too much to resist. My teaching schedule was thus a little lighter, with the group leaders like Carl and Sarah starting to organise their own self-directed learning sessions, and I had the time and opportunity to reflect on how else I could make myself useful. I'd started to consider more deeply what motivated the junior doctors and what training opportunities would be available for them once they'd finished their internship. There had been an unwritten policy at the time they had been sent to Cuba that, upon their return, the new graduates would be sent to work in the provinces. This requirement went some way beyond the mandatory rural rotations for Vanuatu's previous new graduate doctors.

The ever-so-naïve expectation on the part of the Ministry of Health was that these young doctors, having trained on the other side of the world, in another language, in another system extremely different from that of their home country, would be despatched to the outer islands indefinitely, thus miraculously solving the problems of inequity of health access and inequality of health outcomes, with everyone living happily ever after. No thought had been given to how to provide them with the postgraduate training that would be essential to enable them to continue to build the knowledge and skills required to practise in those rural facilities safely and unsupervised.

In fact, I was shocked to discover, apart from an elite rural medical specialty programme a friend of mine had set up in PNG, no postgraduate training for rural hospital or family medicine seemed to be available anywhere in the Pacific. This deeply offended my generalist sensibilities. Throughout the Pacific region (and the rest of the developing world), most of the population live in rural areas and the health needs of rural communities are, generally speaking, greater than those of their urban counterparts. Surely Fiji, as the other regional powerhouse for medical training at both undergraduate and postgraduate levels, should be offering something along those lines.

I reached out to the Dean of Medicine at Fiji National University (FNU), who confirmed that, regrettably, they had no such programme at present, but he was delighted to learn of my interest. He explained that his hand was being forced by a recent decree issued by the government of Fiji. This declared that all doctors working as general practitioners must have a postgraduate specialty qualification in a relevant discipline, despite the fact that no such thing existed in Fiji. That being a tricky circle to square for both the doctors and the Dean, there was a lot of 'enthusiasm' (if that's an accurate way to describe avoiding fines and staying out of jail) in Fiji to get such a programme up and running. The Dean invited me to come over, check things out and see if I could come up with some recommendations as to how to proceed. I reached out to a couple of senior colleagues from my time on the Board of the Australian College of Rural and Remote Medicine (ACRRM) to see if they'd be up for a little jaunt over to Fiji.

It wasn't a tough sell.

Fiji

A few weeks later, I touched back down on my old stomping ground of Suva to meet up with Doug, an affable former president of ACRRM, and Graham, a tireless terrier of a man who'd almost single-handedly set up a national programme for embedding doctors to live, work and train within rural communities around Australia, known as the Remote Vocational Training Scheme. We spent a week being whisked around hospitals and health centres of all sizes and descriptions, from snappy private GP clinics in the centre of town to district hospitals staffed by overworked doctors in the middle of their careers, desperate for opportunities to advance their skills and achieve specialist recognition in their field. All of those we spoke to were extremely supportive of the idea of establishing a postgraduate generalist training programme, including the Dean himself, a cheerful chap with a goatee and a beer belly, who assured us he would seriously consider all of the recommendations included in our report.

Our final day in Suva started early, with coffees spiked with rum at the Anzac Day dawn service at the Australian High Commission, as guests of my diplomat mate Raphael, who'd played drums in our garage band during my final year in Fiji and had since risen to the post of First Secretary. We ended the day much, much later, with too many celebratory cocktails in a seedy karaoke bar.

'We did well!' Graham yelled in my ear as the 'Hotel California' guitar solo twangled on. 'This could really go somewhere. We have to have a name for this thing.'

Between the next round of beers and an eardrum-bursting version of 'Hey Jude', we sketched out an acronym on a gin-soaked serviette. Remote Opportunities for Clinical Knowledge, Education, Training and Support for Health In the Pacific. ROCKETSHIP. We doubled over in hysterics, slapped each other on the back and gleefully toasted our own genius with some flaming Sambucas and a three-way warbling of 'Rocket Man'.

'With a name like that, it's definitely going somewhere,' Doug cackled.

'Shit! We've gotta go somewhere!' I shouted back, as my drunken attempts to focus on my wristwatch suddenly succeeded and I bundled them out of the door and into a taxi back to the airport.

It went nowhere.

Vanuatu

Soon after I got home to Vanuatu, I heard that the Dean of FNU had moved on. We were back to square one. Deflated by our wasted efforts, despondent at the lack of prospects for Pacific island doctors to train in such a fundamental specialty and despairing at the thought of rural communities around the region having no access to decent medical care, I decided there was nothing for it but to go and spend some time working in Vanuatu's doctor-free provincial hospitals myself. I spent a happy couple of days mapping out a schedule that would see me working in each province for a few weeks at a time on a rotating basis, returning periodically to Australia for my university role and then back to Port Vila to catch up on my intern teaching and ED work in between. In my mind's eye, I would swan around the beautiful islands of the archipelago, getting to experience and understand so much more about my beloved adopted country, while living the adventure- and adrenaline-filled dream of a rural generalist providing vital care to communities with no doctor. I marched confidently down to the Ministry of Health office to present my proposal to the Director-General, Roger.

Roger was a veteran operator. From relatively humble beginnings as a lab technician, he'd managed to climb the oiled-up coconut palm of the country's health hierarchy and perch atop it for a record length of time.

'This is a very good proposal, Doctor Lachie,' he mused, peering at my island-hopping itinerary through his thick glasses and glancing up at a map on his wall with Vanuatu's half-dozen hospitals hand-marked with red crosses. 'But you know, the interns, they still need a lot of support and I think we need you to stay here in Port Vila.'

I sighed. 'Okay, boss. Thank you for your time. *Naes dai blong yu.* (Have a nice day.)'

I got up to go.

'Wait a moment, Doctor Lachie,' he called after me. 'The provincial hospitals, they also need a lot more support. And doctors, of course. They all need doctors. Do you know anyone else who could come and help do what you are proposing here? What about your friend, the big fellow, the funny one who came and worked here after the cyclone?'

'Ah, you mean Tom? The rural generalist?'

'*Hemianao.* (That's the one.)'

'Ermm, I'm not sure, Roger. I think Tom is pretty busy with his regular job. And, you know, his wife and kids. But I can ask him.'

'Okay, *tankyu tumas.* (Thank you very much.)' He turned back to his desk and picked up the phone.

I recalled a gin-soaked serviette and an idea trickled into my brain.

'Roger, would you like me to ask around my friends and networks of colleagues to see if any other rural generalists would be available to come and help? If I had an official letter of request from you, there are hundreds of colleagues I could reach.'

Roger put the phone down and gazed at me for a moment, nibbling at the arm of his glasses. I could see the cogs turning in the wily old manager's head.

'You know there's no extra budget to pay them a salary,' he said, narrowing his eyes.

'That's okay, I don't think these guys would be doing it for the money. They'd probably be happy to help and would volunteer their time, at least on a short-term basis.'

'Okay then,' he beamed. 'How should I address the letter? To you?'

'Rocketship,' I blurted out. 'Make it out to Rocketship.'

Roger's eyebrows rose, then he shrugged, nodded and waved me out of the room.

As promised, Roger sent a letter, addressed to Rocketship, requesting assistance in finding rural generalists to work in the four hospitals in Vanuatu that had no permanent doctors. Given Rocketship had only ever existed as a scribble on a filthy napkin, this request prompted a series of hastily arranged teleconferences between Doug, Graham, Tom (still fired up by his post-cyclone cameo) and me. We called in favours from several colleagues working in non-profit legal and communications firms and suddenly found ourselves directors of a newly established international health charity. There were just a few minor wrinkles to be ironed out, such as a complete lack of funds and staff. Undeterred, we opened a bank account, chipped in a couple of thousand bucks each for the kitty, launched a website and proudly announced ourselves to the world. A few enthusiastic friends jumped on board, injecting some much-needed expertise in nursing and health policy, and we were up and running.

As word got around that the Pacific island paradise of Vanuatu was looking for rural generalists, friends and colleagues came out of the woodwork to express their interest and sign up to volunteer with us for periods ranging from a few weeks to a few months each. I now had quite a busy schedule in Vanuatu, where I'd spend Monday to Friday in Port Vila, working in the ED and carrying on with the intern teaching, then on weekends I'd catch one of the little six- or eight-seater planes to visit the outer islands where Rocketship's first volunteers – 'Rocketeers', as we proudly referred to them – were working.

The Director-General preened, the nursing staff were relieved, and the communities were evidently grateful to have doctors back on their islands. Rocketship ahoy!

Then things got complicated.

*

'Shit. She's blue.'

'Yep.'

'And a bit yellow, too, don't you reckon?'

'Yeah, I agree.'

I looked around, wondering what we could possibly do for this tiny newborn baby. Not much, apparently. Not only were we stranded on this volcanic island in the south of Vanuatu for at least a few days until the next plane arrived, but our busy little hospital on the hill had no electricity. We were on our own, with no power and no help arriving any time soon, or realistically at all.

'Is that a battery-powered oxygen concentrator over there in the corner?' I asked Jen, our new Rocketeer, with a flush of misplaced optimism.

'Yep.'

'Great! Does it work?'

'Nope.'

'Shit. So. She's going to die . . . '

'Yep.'

In the end, we decided to move the baby and her mother over to the window in the sun, in the hope that the light might at least help treat the jaundice causing her yellow skin – a feeble attempt on our part to mimic a standard technique known as phototherapy. It wasn't enough. She'd been born too early, with her lungs not fully formed and incapable of sucking in enough oxygen with each rapid, shallow, rattly breath. Her mother, only a teenager herself, smiled sadly at us each time we checked on our fragile little patient, then went back to sobbing discreetly and dabbing her eyes with the flowery towel/fly swat I now knew to be a standard accessory (and occasional weapon) for most ni-Vanuatu women.

When the baby died, late the following afternoon, her mother wrapped her in a brightly coloured cloth and carried her precious cargo back along the rocky dirt paths over the mountain range to the other side of the island to be buried in the cemetery next to their small, orderly village.

Jen had arrived a week earlier to begin a three-month stint as the only doctor for this community of around thirty thousand people, scattered across the villages and islands of a province considered the most difficult, unhealthy and dangerous in the country.

I'd flown down from Port Vila to spend the weekend with Jen and discuss some complicated cases. She introduced me to an epileptic woman who'd fallen into a fire while having a seizure and sustained some nasty burns to her arms and legs – a tragically common occurrence for people with epilepsy in developing countries. Jen pointed out, quite rightly, that the lady needed skin grafts and physiotherapy to avoid painful scarring and debilitating stiffening of her joints. Neither of those services was likely to be available, I apologised, promising I'd see what I could do when I got back to Port Vila but knowing it would probably be futile. I showed the lady some exercises she could do instead, which I remembered the rural doctors in PNG demonstrating to their burns patients. Jen then described how she'd done her best to manage a middle-aged man who'd almost certainly had a heart attack, despite not having the ECG machine to prove it, nor the clot-dissolving drugs to treat it.

As we finished the ward round and searched for some soap to wash our hands, Jen pulled me aside.

'Lachie, I'm really sorry to do this, but I'm going to have to leave.'

I stopped and turned to her, lathered up to the wrists and dripping water on the floor.

'Shit, no! Why? You're doing a tremendous job! What's going on? Are you okay?'

She blinked hard and shook her head, strawberry blonde hair tumbling down to cover her eyes. She took a deep breath, dried her hands briskly, straightened up and looked at me, her eyes red but her jaw set.

'Let's go for a cuppa. There are some things you need to know.'

Over a hot milky tea back in the tumbledown doctor's house, perched atop the hill overlooking the black-rock beach, Jen explained that, since she arrived, she'd become increasingly concerned for her safety. The Rocketeer colleague whom she'd replaced had warned her of the region's violent reputation, and although Jen had yet to see much evidence of that herself, she'd been hearing plenty of stories. When another single female traveller Jen met at a guesthouse told her how she'd narrowly escaped being assaulted by a man with a machete on the beach one evening, Jen decided she'd had enough. She was by herself, working day and night, sleeping only fitfully in an unlockable house, feeling lonely, isolated, unsupported and unsafe.

'I feel awful about leaving, Lachie,' she said with a troubled frown, 'but I can't stay here, not like this.'

I felt absolutely terrible. This was my fault. I'd set up this programme. The welfare of these volunteers – most of them friends of mine – was my responsibility.

'We'll get you out of here on the next flight, Jen,' I promised. 'I'm so sorry we put you in this position. You've done excellent work. I'll debrief with you as much as you want, and if you think it would help to speak to a psychologist or a counsellor, just let me know.'

The next day, Graham, Doug, Tom and I held an emergency teleconference with Kylie, a nurse friend who'd taken on the *pro-bono* role of Rocketship's Operations Manager. I told them about Jen's reasons for leaving.

'That's it, we're shutting down this whole fucking volunteer thing,' said Kylie. 'We're not ready, we don't have the resources and we don't know what we're doing. We don't even really know why we're doing it.'

I put up a half-hearted defence of the idea of supplying doctors to hospitals in Vanuatu where there were none, but I had to concede that Kylie was right. We'd over-reached and it had almost ended in disaster. Despite our good intentions, we were putting the safety and well-being of our volunteers at risk.

'It's true guys, we're not MSF,' Tom reflected.

Médecins Sans Frontières, I thought wistfully, *that ship has sailed for me, for sure.*

Graham's voice crackling over the phone brought me back to the urgent matter at hand. 'So, are we agreed? We're pulling our volunteers out of Vanuatu?'

We agreed.

It was a difficult process, and more than a little humiliating for me. I had to inform Roger, the Director-General, that we were suspending our volunteer programme less than a year after we'd started, and I had to track down the Rocketeer doctors and nurses on several far-flung islands to tell them they had to wrap things up. One nurse, an adventurous Kiwi called Tara, had been living and working in Bene for several months, staying in the guest room in Nixon and Linda's house. She'd managed to get Auntie Mary's clinic officially reopened for the first time in years and was busy doing nutrition checks on the local schoolchildren and surveying adults all around the district for chronic diseases.

'But I'm fine!' Tara objected. 'Why the flippin' heck would you want me to leave?'

I explained to her that we'd recognised we needed to thoroughly evaluate all the risks involved in our volunteer programme. I pointed to the rusty bucket of a truck I'd bought for the village, in which she'd been happily rattling around for the last few months.

'What if you have an accident? Or someone falls out of the back?'

Tara finished up her expedition early and left Bene in a flurry of tears and hugs.

When I next visited the village a few months later, and Nixon showed me the clinic, once again shut and overgrown with weeds, I didn't have the heart to report that back to Tara. Being a man with a plan, Nixon had come up with an idea since Tara's departure. Would Rocketship like to take over the Bene clinic and run it as a charitable entity, independent of the Ministry of Health? I dolefully explained to him that we didn't have any money and all the work the organisation had done so far was based on volunteers donating their time. Nixon nodded. He understood. He always did.

Australia

On the sidelines of the annual rural doctors' conference back in Australia a few months later, Team Rocketship held its first annual general meeting. It was an insalubrious affair. We couldn't afford to hire a venue, so we bunched up in the bowels of an office supplies warehouse that offered free meeting rooms if you bought more than a hundred bucks' worth of stuff. Hemmed in by our brand-new flip charts, clustered around a table covered in marker pens, sticky notes and piles of candy (Kylie was a feeder with a sweet tooth), we spent hours debating strategy for our newborn organisation that was not looking likely to survive beyond infancy. We dissected our early endeavours, autopsied our narrow escapes and eventually agreed that we were missing something fundamental. There was a blind spot in the vision and mission of the organisation, we just couldn't quite figure out what it was. So we got mind-shatteringly drunk instead.

The next morning, as we sat together, holding back bile, breathing rum fumes over each other and bumping knees in our economy seats flying back east, Graham and I attempted a semi-delirious debrief.

'Watch is the wheelie that you think us to do with the rocking ship now?' Graham burped.

I looked back at him unsteadily, wishing he'd stop levitating and stay in focus.

'What?' was all I could manage.

He tried again. 'What is it that you really think we should do with Rocketship now?'

I let the question soak into my alcohol-saturated grey matter.

'Well,' I said slowly, not sure if there were any coherent syllables lined up to follow, 'I guess maybe something like your thing. You know.'

Graham nodded thoughtfully, then turned back to me.

'What?'

I took a deep breath, which was a mistake, as it made my brain crush painfully into the top of my skull.

'Your thing. The Remote Vocational Training Scheme. Training doctors in rural communities for rural communities. Rocketship could be like that, but for the Pacific. We could help train doctors over there so they can stay living and working on their own islands, rather than having to leave for years to do their training overseas. Then eventually they become the trainers and we're no longer needed. You get what I mean?'

I slumped back in my straight-backed seat, exhausted from the effort and wondering how my tongue came to be covered in mouldy carpet.

'Right, gotcha,' he said. 'Hey, does your tongue feel like carpet?'

CHAPTER TEN

2016

Switzerland

Words can be powerful things. Spoken, whispered, shouted, sung, artfully arranged into the finest poetry, or plonked together in nondescript digital bits, they can be potent little buggers. In the space of less than a year, I received three brief messages that each changed my life.

The first was from Terry, an Aussie emergency physician colleague who'd spent the past couple of years in Timor-Leste doing a similar job to mine in Vanuatu, helping set up postgraduate training for the new Timorese doctors who were pouring out of the Cuban system.

At the time of Timor-Leste's independence, in 2002, there were fewer than fifty Timorese doctors in the country. Thirteen years later, there were close to one thousand, with almost all of the additions being products of ELAM. In an eerie preview for other countries in the Pacific, the previous year had seen the Timorese government proudly announcing a 'Doctors for the Districts' initiative and promptly packing the majority of the new graduates off to work in rural hospitals and community clinics. Within twelve months, they were all back in the capital city of Dili. After repeated disasters, many of them broadcast on social media, the government was forced to concede what the districts had told them from the get-go: the new doctors couldn't do much of anything. The Timorese government then turned to the other organisation that had been supporting their medical workforce since independence: the Royal Australasian College of

Surgeons (RACS). RACS had been sending Australian specialists to work in Timor-Leste and help set up postgraduate training programmes for so long that they had their own spacious set of offices and several full-time staff ensconced in the heart of the national referral hospital. From there, Terry sent me an email describing how RACS's attempts to set up a family medicine training programme, at the government's request, had ground to a halt, as they belatedly recognised they had no family medicine specialists available to guide the process.

> *So, mate, we're thinking the addition of a generalist with the right background could be very beneficial. Would you be interested in that?*
> *If not, do you know anyone that you could recommend to us?*
> *Cheers.*

A month later, I was in Dili. A month after that, Graham, as Chair of the Rocketship Board of Directors, signed a contract with RACS to help design and deliver the inaugural Diploma of Family Medicine programme in Timor-Leste. Our soul-searching, liver-bruising, strategic self-reflection had led us as a team to realise that Rocketship's ideal role was to support the training of family, community and rural medical professionals in Pacific island countries. We'd still use volunteers, but rather than sending them to be cannon fodder as clinicians in areas of extreme workforce shortage, which is what we'd mainly been doing in Vanuatu, this time we'd focus on recruiting experienced rural generalists who were also qualified and enthusiastic medical educators. They would work alongside our colleagues in Pacific island countries to pass on the knowledge and skills required to provide competent, quality, sustainable care to rural communities. This volunteer model, we hoped, would reduce the risk of burnout from overwork as well as avoid the kind of personal welfare and security hazards we'd learned about the hard way through Jen.

We'd finally found our niche and now we had an ideal opportunity in Timor-Leste, plus some desperately needed funding, thanks to RACS and the Australian government who paid them, to show what we could do. Once again, we put the shout out through our networks and, once again, the Aussie rural generalist community came through. We assembled a team of three trainers: Howard, a professor of rural medical education; Simon, another member of the inaugural Tennant Fucking Creek awesome fivesome; and Rex, the jovial founder of Queensland's Rural Generalist Pathway, who'd worked in Timor-Leste before. The three-man team did a terrific job, flying back and forth from their respective homes in Australia up to Dili every couple of months, working with the young Timorese doctors in their clinics, teaching them how to practise safely and independently and preparing them to be Timor-Leste's first-ever family doctors.

The majority of them graduated two years later, with great pride and relief for all involved. So did the next cohort, and the one after that. Rocketship was in business.

I hope this finds you well.

Although we don't have anything in writing yet, we may need some support for at least five months here in Geneva. Kindly let me know if you would be interested in such an offer and I can elaborate more.

Thanks.

This second email came, apropos of absolutely nothing, from Teresa, a colleague in the climate change and health department at WHO

Headquarters in Switzerland. I read those few lines over and over on my phone before getting out of bed that morning, wondering if I was being pranked. Even if the offer was genuine, I wasn't sure I wanted it. I was living in a tropical island paradise, dividing my time between supporting the interns, working in ED and doing outreach clinics in Vanuatu, and returning to Australia on a regular basis to teach at the university and catch up on my rural hospital work. Rocketship, which I was helping run on the side, was really taking off. I didn't have a plan, but I was pretty happy with what I was doing. What would be the point of going to Geneva?

After a few days of prevaricating, I accepted the offer of a temporary posting to WHO HQ. Opportunities like that didn't fall from the sky very often, after all, and it wouldn't matter too much if the double life I was leading between Vanuatu and Australia was put on hold for a few months. I handed over the intern teaching schedule to one of the ni-Vanuatu consultants, requested leave from my university, packed my battered backpack and arrived in Switzerland at the height of summer. I barely knew a soul and didn't have much money, so I spent the first few weeks renting a fold-out couch in the one-bedroom apartment of a young Italian couple, re-orienting myself within the labyrinthine bureaucracy of WHO by day and drinking beers with a bunch of Aussie expats by night.

My job at WHO HQ proved to be interesting enough, although I was starting to get a little concerned that if I did this for too long I might end up so focused on climate change and health that I'd have no choice but to work on that topic for the rest of my life. Still, there was a definite thrill to being so deep inside the belly of the beast. I would get a little surge of pride every morning when I'd arrive at the Soviet-looking monolith of a building. I'd stride through the glass doors inscribed with the WHO logo and motto in a dozen different languages, then swipe through security and negotiate the maze of offices to the one I shared with a highly strung German air pollution expert who spent most of the day shouting down the phone. Just next door was Lawrence, the global head of climate change and health, a cerebral, gangly cycling enthusiast with an endearingly corny sense of humour. After a few weeks of intensive orientation to the projects I was taking over, I was given my first 'duty travel' assignment.

Tanzania

A cholera epidemic was raging across the country when I touched down in Dar es Salaam, Tanzania's largest city. My visit wasn't part of the official WHO outbreak response, but the topic was central to the national climate change project I was to help the Ministry of Health complete. The thousands of cases and hundreds of deaths from cholera had been linked to contaminated water supplies, with a handful of underground wells thought to be the source of the initial cluster of infections.

Bernard, the stocky, one-eyed Tanzanian environmental health officer at the WHO country office, took me to see a few of the cholera hotspots in the shanty towns outside the city. After hours spent beetling forward in dense traffic, as we jumped down from the Land Cruiser, stretched our legs and donned our WHO vests, I reflected on the irony of me having become one of those wankers I'd seen in the past. The well-meaning but often obnoxious international humanitarian types, the disaster junkies, with their white four-wheel drives and muddy boots, descending on disaster zones with their spreadsheets and geo-locators, sampling and interviewing and meeting and reporting, covered in mosquito repellent and revelling in the adventure.

Don't be a dick, I told myself firmly, as I followed Bernard into the narrow, puddle-filled lanes. We navigated the hodgepodge of corrugated-iron and timber lean-tos, dodging the children playing, men on motorbikes and women swaying through the streets with cargoes on their heads.

'Most people have to buy their water,' Bernard explained. 'The government can't afford to send trucks out here to the informal settlements, so private water-sellers drill the wells and build the tanks you see on stilts. It's big business.'

He pointed out a group of women, elegantly dressed in bright patterns, waiting patiently in the sun with their jerrycans. A man in a singlet held a hose running from a tank perched precariously on a wooden frame, filling the containers and pocketing the crumpled notes handed to him by each lady as she left.

'It doesn't rain often here, so the tanks are running dry,' Bernard went on. 'We have to monitor the situation closely to ensure that the water-sellers aren't filling them up by pumping from the wells, as that's where we've found the highest concentration of cholera.'

'Can't you treat the tank water with chlorine?' I wondered out loud.

'We do, but the water-sellers don't like it, as they say the taste of it affects their business. It's the same with chlorine tablets. A lot of people don't like using them because of the taste. There are also false rumours spread by some community leaders, saying the chlorine tablets are a way for the government to control population growth, claiming they cause sterility. The preachers are often the worst influence,' he said, shaking his head sadly.

'How do you stop people drawing water from the wells?' I asked.

Bernard led me out into a dusty open area where some kids were tearing around after a half-inflated soccer ball.

'You see that small slab of fresh concrete in the corner? There's a well under there, but the government has ordered them all to be closed up.'

'Wow, it's kind of like London in the nineteenth century,' I said.

Bernard turned to me quizzically.

As we walked back to the Land Cruiser, I told him the story of John Snow – the English physician considered the 'father of epidemiology' – who in the 1850s had developed a theory about a cholera outbreak in London being caused by contaminated water. In an era before microorganisms such as bacteria, viruses and parasites had been identified, and diseases were thought to be spread by bad air (the reason *mal-aria* is called exactly that), Snow's hypothesis seemed pretty far-fetched. Undaunted, he carefully mapped out all the addresses of the cholera cases in Soho and linked them to a water pump on Broad Street. His arguments convinced the council to remove the handle of the pump. The cholera cases plummeted and the modern study of disease transmission and control was born.

'That's very interesting,' said Bernard politely.

I realised I was being a dick.

Back in Dar es Salaam, we spent the next week working with the Ministry of Health, the university and the main NGO involved in the project, modelling the future impacts of climate change on cholera and malaria and pulling all our data and recommendations together into something resembling a sensible climate change and health action plan. After handshakes all round and an official thanks from the director, we trooped off for beers on the waterfront to celebrate. Many hours, several fun parties, a blur of bad dancing and far too many whiskies later, a couple of my new NGO buddies sped recklessly through the streets in their own logo-emblazoned Land Cruiser to drop me back at my hotel.

This gig isn't so bad, I thought, as I squinted blearily at my hungover reflection in the mirror the next morning, swallowed some paracetamol and dragged my tired body and my backpack down to the swarming street to find a taxi to the airport for my return flight to Geneva.

Switzerland

I found myself getting homesick for Vanuatu. I was also getting cross with myself for not getting to know Geneva better, so I decided to branch out a bit and joined a dating app. *At the very least*, I told myself, *I'd get to see a little bit of the city*. I didn't speak much French and was shy about going to bars and concerts by myself. Better to have some company, preferably someone interesting and intelligent, and as the unofficial capital of the world, Geneva did seem to have potential in those departments. My expectations were modest, however, and I knew that any limited appeal I might have to the opposite sex would be lowered further by the short-term nature of my stay. Still, with little to lose, I put myself out there. It did not prove particularly fruitful. The women with whom I was matched on the app were mostly pretty and pleasant, and I ventured out for an *apéro* or two, but no sparks flew.

Then, just at the point where I was about to give it all up and accept my new life of sleeping on the couch and exploring Switzerland on my lonesome, along came Viri. The initial text messages we'd exchanged showed her to be witty and open-minded, so I wasted no time in asking her if she'd like to meet in person. Her casual, confident reply caught me off-guard.

Hola!

Sure, let's say 7pm at Cottage Café. It's a nice place just behind the monument in the park. Take your swimsuit in case we can't stand the heat and we want to go for a quick dip in the lake.

See you later.

With no idea what to expect, I did as instructed. I packed my bathers, spruced myself up in my least filthy T-shirt and best (okay, only) pair of flip-flops and arrived, a few minutes ahead of schedule, to scope out the venue in the late afternoon sun. It was an enchanting little place that looked like it could have been made out of gingerbread and be home to a witch. It was also heaving with people, spilling out on the large outdoor terrace, sipping rosé and dipping their feet in the fountain. With not a free chair in sight, I wandered over to the monument in the park to shelter in some shade and text Viri to see if she wanted to try somewhere else. Then I glanced up, and she was there.

She had smooth, bronze skin and long, lush brown hair. Her light dress spilled down over her curves. Her full, red lips framed straight, white teeth in a wide smile that made me weak at the knees.

'Hi,' she said. Her voice was like honey.

'Ergghhhh,' I gurgled, then cleared my throat. 'Hi.'

She took off her sunglasses and a pair of golden eyes gleamed at me from between thick lashes.

'Shall we go sit down?'

'Umm, yeah, I already checked and it seems they're full. I was just about to text you.'

'Oh, it should be fine.' She smiled again. 'I made a reservation.'

Shit, she's beautiful and classy, I thought, as I followed her back across the lawn, trying to restore my power of speech and radically lift my game. We were shown to a table in a discreet corner, where we seated ourselves and grinned at each other. After a couple of urgent swigs of the cold beer that arrived swiftly, thankfully, I felt my mojo coming back.

'So, tell me about yourself!' I invited. Not the most original opening line, I admit.

She was from Mexico City, her parents hard-working, middle-class folk who'd done everything they could to give her and her brother the chance to get a good education and make their own ways in life. For Viri, that had meant studying hard at school, then even harder at university, and getting a scholarship to move abroad for further studies. She'd been offered a place on a Master of Communications and Media programme at the University of Geneva on the condition that she became fluent in French by the time the course started. She'd done exactly that, practising with a French tutor for hours every morning before attending classes all day and working as a waitress in a Mexican restaurant late into the evening. She'd worked her way up to become the global digital communications manager of a large Swiss corporation. She was smart, successful, multilingual, gorgeous and bloody intimidating. But there was something about her that also made me feel completely at ease. I leaned forward, soaking up every detail of her story, unable to believe my luck.

When my turn came, I sketched out my journey to her, realising as I did so what an unusual life I'd been leading – doing a lot of stuff but without a clear or consistent plan behind it all. Up to this point, that hadn't really mattered to me, but suddenly now, in this moment, staring across the table at a captivating stranger, I wanted my life to at least appear to have purpose.

One drink turned into two, then a bottle of wine, then dinner. As we perused the menus, her phone dinged.

'Please excuse me for just a moment, it's my best friend,' she apologised as she rummaged in her handbag.

How would she know that without seeing her phone? I wondered idly, trying not to stare at the way the evening rays made her neck and shoulders glow. A buzz in my pocket broke my reverie. It was a message from my buddy Seamus letting me know he'd brought a spare bicycle down to the lake for me to borrow. I'd arranged the pickup with him expecting this semi-blind date to be long over by now. I glanced up to find Viri smirking at me.

'Do you have somewhere else you need to be?' she asked innocently.

'Ah no, not at all,' I stammered. 'It's just a mate texting about a bike he's going to lend me. He's at a bar down by the lake.'

'Do you mean you had a Plan B for this evening?' she enquired, still smiling slyly.

'Well, no, not exactly,' I squirmed.

She burst out laughing.

'Why? What's funny?' I asked, not sure if I should be embarrassed or relieved.

'My friend was texting me to see if I was okay and if I needed an excuse to escape,' she giggled. 'We were pretty sure you'd turn out to be a psychopath and I didn't want to end the night unconscious in a bathtub full of ice cubes with one of my kidneys missing, so we arranged for her to check in on me around now. She's also down by the lake, salsa dancing.'

One bottle of rosé later, we'd agreed that the only thing for it was to combine forces. We finished our olives and quesadillas and promenaded our way along Lac Léman, warm pinks and oranges glinting off the clear turquoise water. Seamus winked at me as he handed over the bike. As we rounded a bend, the lights of a party on a hill in the distance, Latin music getting louder, Viri paused.

'We don't have to go up there, you know. They're celebrating Colombia's national holiday so it could all be getting pretty crazy. We can go for a quiet drink somewhere else if you'd prefer.'

'What? No way! It's a lakeside Colombian fiesta on a balmy summer evening in Switzerland. I wouldn't miss it. Let's do this!'

She smiled and shrugged in a don't-say-I-didn't-warn-you kind of way, then took me by the arm and led me up the hill. We stashed the bike and plunged into the pulsing mass of happy, sweaty humans. Salsa is a special kind of dance. It doesn't matter who's dancing; whether they're girls or guys, young or old, good-looking to everyone or only to their mothers – if you're dancing salsa, you look sexy.

Being Australian, and a white male at that, means that I was born with two left feet and zero sense of rhythm. Fortunately, I'd had a brief opportunity to overcome that a little over a decade earlier, when I'd been co-captain of the Australian delegation on a life-changing international youth ambassador programme run by the Japanese government called the Ship for World Youth. When we weren't meeting princes and presidents and learning how the UN worked, we could partake in a wide range of cultural activities, and I had a whack at salsa dancing. I wasn't a good dancer, by any means, but neither was I completely hopeless, and it seemed the half-dozen hours I'd spent twirling Venezuelans and Costa Ricans across the parquet floor of the ship's ballroom were about to come in handy.

I manoeuvred through the throng, clutching a plastic cup of beer in each hand and another between my teeth, back to where Viri and her friend Ruby were waiting, shimmying away in a corner. We clunked our glasses, admired the party for a few moments, then I braced myself, downed my beer and turned to Viri.

'¿Quieres bailar? (Do you want to dance?)'

The two girls gaped at me.

'What the hell? You speak Spanish? And you dance salsa?' Viri asked in disbelief.

I realised I'd come out of the blocks way too strong. Setting her expectations this high, this early, would be a major tactical error.

'Ah, well,' I backtracked quickly, '*solo hablo un poquito* (I only speak a little). And I only know a few steps of salsa. But I'm game if you are.'

Viri laughed and finished her beer in a couple of gulps. '*¡Vamos!* (Let's go!)'

'*¡Bravo, chicos!*' (Well done, guys!) Ruby clapped and cheered as we three-stepped into the fray.

The next couple of hours disappeared in a haze of sinuous, noisy fun. Viri was, naturally, a fantastic dancer, her petite body responding gracefully to my every awkward, halting move. As she smiled up at me, her hair swaying in the opposite direction to her hips, I fell in love. I leaned down to kiss her. She pulled back.

'Not so fast, naughty boy,' she chided me softly.

I tried not to appear too disappointed. I was all out of dance moves and the heat was getting to me anyway. 'It's pretty steamy in here! How about that swim?' I suggested.

She laughed. 'I'd love to, but it's late and I should be getting home. Would you like to walk with me back to the station?'

After the frenetic tangle of the Colombian fiesta, the breeze off the lake was deliciously cool as we strolled back the way we'd come. I was wheeling the bike with one hand when I felt a warm little hand take the other. I looked over at her and my heart sped up as she smiled back. When we got to the bridge we stopped. I leaned the bike against the stone wall, took Viri in my arms and then, at last, we kissed. It was long, slow, passionate and by far the best kiss of my life. Suddenly everything made sense. It was like I was dying and seeing my life flash before my eyes. All the things I'd done and the choices I'd made, without a plan, just going with my gut and seeing what happened next, had all seemed so random at the time. Not now.

This was why I was here. I had needed to come to Geneva to meet Viri. My life just took on a whole new, unexpected purpose. She was it. I wanted to be with this woman for the rest of my life. For an instant, as our bodies finally separated, I thought about telling her everything that had just gone through my mind. My subconscious came to the rescue. *Take it easy*, it murmured at me, *you don't want to scare her off. Give it time, see where it goes and if she feels the same way, it might work out. Just be yourself. And don't fuck it up.*

Viri boarded her tram, I waved her off and I stood there in the middle of the tracks with my bicycle for a few moments like someone who's gone into their kitchen to get something and then forgotten what it was. I was at a loss for words at what I'd experienced that evening, but I wanted Viri to have some sense of how special it had been for me. I scrolled back through our previous messages, which now seemed like they belonged to another era. Her last text, suggesting our rendezvous at Cottage Café that evening, stared back at me on my phone. I didn't know how I could possibly explain how meeting her had made me feel, so in the end I sent her a single word.

Wow!

*

Viri brought meaning and magic to my life. Her cultural background, language skills, professional life and familiarity with Geneva all opened windows for me to new, intriguing worlds. The city has a reputation for being somewhat sterile and hermetic. Its role hosting the headquarters of multiple UN agencies, as well as those of MSF and the International Committee of the Red Cross, made it a very significant place for me, but juxtaposed against that was the incredible, nauseating wealth, both visible and implied, and the complete detachment of many of its residents from the reality of the rest of humanity. Fortunately, Viri and her friends were lots of fun and mostly very down-to-earth. Translators, watchmakers, financiers, artists, even a shaman or two – they seemed to me an exotic, eclectic lot. Despite my embarrassing mostly-monolingualism, they welcomed me into their various circles, invited me to overpriced restaurants and surprisingly lively house parties, and shepherded me up and down the Alps for the various outdoor activities that changed dramatically with the seasons. I was very grateful to have been so swiftly plugged into a social scene in a city renowned to be tough for short-termers. As the copper-coloured leaves coated the ground and the evenings chilled and shortened, I became painfully aware of the clock ticking on my own contract.

I wasn't thrilled at the prospect of working exclusively on climate change and health, but I needed to stay in Switzerland to be with Viri and WHO seemed to be my only hope.

A few weeks before my six months was up, I debriefed with Lawrence in his office.

'Sounds like you did a great job in Tanzania,' he said. 'And the guys in Ethiopia and Bhutan were very grateful for those training packages you put together for them. Their workshops went really well, apparently. We'll send you to Bangladesh next – need to finish up that project before you leave us.'

'Thanks, boss,' I said. 'Hey, about that. I hate to ask, but would there be any chance of me staying on here after the end of my contract? I know Teresa's coming back from maternity leave, but with all these different projects rolling out around the place I thought maybe you could use an extra pair of hands.'

Lawrence winced. He leaned back in his chair and crossed his arms.

'You're right, we could use the help. And I've been looking for a way to find an extra salary in the budget to keep you on. But you know how the bloody donors are. They're only interested in paying for projects, not people, and with our funding this tight, I really don't think we can manage it. Perhaps we could wait until the end of the year and see where things are at?'

I thanked Lawrence and wandered back to my office next door. As my desk neighbour gave her colleagues on a conference call a bollocking, I pondered my options. I had very little time left on my WHO contract and money was getting extremely tight. Geneva is a ridiculously expensive city and my short-term consultant salary was proving barely enough to live on. I was still sending money to Nixon for the children's school fees in Bene and to help support their community development projects, but I was struggling to make the payments on the mortgage on my own house back in Vanuatu. If I was to stay in Switzerland and make a go of it, I'd need a long-term contract with a reliable income. I believed Lawrence when he said he'd try and find a way to keep me on, but by now I knew how WHO worked. The majority of salaries were attached to specific projects, so it was common, even for mid-level staff, to lurch from short-term contract to short-term contract, hauling their families around the world for months at a time with no guarantees of jobs to follow.

I have great respect for WHO, the people who work there and the role they play supporting healthcare in all the countries of the world, but it seemed I'd now reached the end of the road. I needed a new job. Urgently.

CHAPTER ELEVEN

2017–18
Switzerland

'You know MSF's a fucking cult, right?' Mike asked.

He shuffled to get comfortable on his bar stool, took a sip of his pint, raised the glass up to inspect it, wiped the sleeve of his faded yellow hooded sweater across his lips and looked back at me enquiringly.

This wasn't what I expected. He wasn't what I expected.

The path I'd taken to look for other jobs in Geneva had been an extremely short one. I'd gone straight to the 'Positions Available – Headquarters' section of the Médecins Sans Frontières website and applied for the only one listed for which I thought I might possibly have a shot. I'd recently finished my second round of specialty training as a public health physician and the job title sounded right up my alley – Medical Advisor for Infectious Diseases, Epidemic Response and Antimicrobial Resistance – but I'd never heard of the department of MSF that was recruiting for it: the Access Campaign. I submitted my application anyway and did some homework while I waited to hear back from them.

The history of the Access Campaign was pretty interesting. They claim it all started when MSF won the Nobel Peace Prize in 1999, 'in recognition of the organization's pioneering humanitarian work'. I was well aware of that bit – I'd been reading books by MSF presidents and volunteer doctors from my earliest years in medical school, inspired by their adventures and dreaming of doing something like that one day. What I didn't know was that MSF had decided they should do something innovative and useful with the Nobel prize money so, after much consultation and debate, they'd decided to set up a separate department to fight for access to essential medicines. At the time, HIV was exploding all over the developing world, decimating and impoverishing entire countries, particularly in Africa. The antiretroviral drugs required to treat it were rare and expensive, with patents jealously and fiercely protected by a handful of pharmaceutical companies. With strong support from MSF, the governments of a few low- and middle-income countries, including India and Brazil, decided the human rights imperative outweighed the rights of the pharmaceutical companies to protect their intellectual property, so they ignored the patents and proceeded to manufacture large quantities of generic antiretrovirals. This surge in production brought the price of treatments down to an affordable level and blew the doors open for patients even in the world's poorest countries to access the life-saving medications. Buoyed by that triumph, over the next couple of decades, MSF's Access Campaign went on to help do the same for several important vaccines, drugs for resistant TB, combination therapies for malaria, experimental treatments for Ebola and safer antivenoms for snakebite. The Access Campaign's main foot-soldiers were lawyers, policy wonks and health advocacy experts, but they needed a couple of doctors to help provide the clinical context to the wars they waged against pharmaceutical companies, government regulators and the rest. I'd been fortunate enough to make the shortlist for the position and had bluffed my way through an hour-long, three-person pummelling in the telephone interview. That had been a week ago. Then yesterday I'd received an email from Mike, the Access Campaign's Medical Director, to see if I'd be available to get together in person. I suggested coffee; he proposed beer. Thus, I found myself teetering on a barstool in the pub at the bottom of the building that was home to MSF headquarters in Geneva, elbows wet from stale ale, nursing a pint and wondering how to respond to his opening salvo.

'Yeah, I guess I'd heard something along those lines,' I said. 'Got a few friends who are MSFers.'

Mike seemed like a straight shooter, so there was no point me pretending otherwise. In addition to my own brief experiences of interacting with MSFers in the field – particularly the arrogant displays of their cholera response team in PNG – I'd developed the impression from my various readings and conversations over the years that MSF had their own way of doing things, and you were either with them or against them. Still, it was a surprise for me to hear it put so bluntly by someone so senior within the organisation.

Mike grunted and twiddled absently with his earring.

'Ah, so you're already acquainted with the cult. That might help.' He took a pull of his pint and looked back at me thoughtfully. 'Tell me more about this climate change stuff you've been working on.'

I gave him a brisk overview of my work with WHO, from the early days in the Pacific to my recent trip to Tanzania, making sure to mention my work in infectious diseases and epidemics.

'The WHO Director-General called it the greatest global health challenge of the twenty-first century,' I concluded. 'I guess you knew that already.'

'Yeah, I'd heard,' Mike murmured, peering down at his half-empty pint. 'At least it used to be, until this other shit of a thing came along. Climate change was bad enough, and now we've got drug-resistant infections to deal with,' he said, with a sad shake of his head. 'Seems like things are getting pretty fucking apocalyptic these days, you know what I mean?'

I knew what he meant.

The description of the job for which I'd applied at the Access Campaign had been very clear that a key focus – half the work – would be on antimicrobial resistance (AMR). This is another grave problem worldwide, about which the level of public awareness is dangerously low. It's the phenomenon whereby disease-causing pathogens (particularly bacteria, but also viruses, fungi and parasites such as malaria) evolve to develop resistance to the antimicrobials (of which the best known are antibiotics, also known as antibacterials) used to treat them. Most bacterial infections can be treated by a number of different antibiotics, but as antibiotic use has increased exponentially over the last few decades, the evolution of the pathogens has been turbo-charged to the point where now some bacteria are totally resistant to all known antibiotics.

This is seriously scary shit.

Climate change is officially estimated by WHO to be causing approximately a quarter of a million extra deaths around the world each year. That figure is a deliberate underestimate, as it only accounts for a small number of climate-sensitive health risks, including malnutrition, malaria, diarrhoeal diseases and extreme heat. The real number of deaths is undoubtedly far higher, but is difficult to calculate, given the complex relationships between the causes and effects of climate change. Air pollution is one important example of this complexity. It is a direct consequence of fossil fuel use, also contributes to global heating and is responsible for around eight million deaths every year. *Eight million!* At the same time, AMR is estimated to be causing more than a million deaths per year, because some of our most precious, life-saving medicines no longer work. By the year 2050, annual deaths from AMR are predicted to increase to ten million. By their nature, epidemics come and go, but climate change and AMR have long represented the twin terrors of contemporary global population health. For this, we have nobody to blame but ourselves.

Human beings have been burning dead dinosaurs and prehistoric forests and pumping their fumes up into the atmosphere in increasingly frenzied fashion in the two hundred and fifty years or so since the Industrial Revolution. Then, after we were clever enough to 'invent' (or at least identify, by accident) the first antibiotic, in the form of penicillin, in the early twentieth century, reducing deaths from infectious diseases to a fraction of what they had been, the spectre of AMR has been creeping up on us ever since. The bugs have been developing resistance to the drugs not only through appropriate use of antibiotics to treat pneumonia and meningitis and the like, but through inappropriate (also referred to as 'irrational') prescribing of antibiotics for viral infections. Drugs that kill bacteria generally don't kill viruses. When you have a sore throat and your doctor gives you a script for antibiotics, a lot of the time that's irrational prescribing, as it's making the problem worse. You've most likely got a virus, meaning the antibiotics won't do anything for your throat, but the trillions of bacteria around your body will be exposed to that antibiotic and have the opportunity to evolve to become resistant to it. Then, of course, there's the mind-boggling amount of antibiotics that are used – often in the absence of any proper regulation – in the agriculture and livestock industries. The drugs get pumped into chickens and cows and pigs and sprayed across plants and then leach into rivers and we eat and drink the stuff so it gets back into our bodies and thus the deadly cycle continues.

AMR and the health impacts of climate change have quite a lot of things in common. For one, they're both known as 'wicked' problems – those that are considered difficult or impossible to solve – and will require an unprecedented level of cooperation between countries and industries.

'I guess I get a kick out of wicked problems,' I said to Mike.

'You're either a sucker or a masochist, that means,' he replied with a little chuckle as he drained his pint.

As we slapped some cash down on the bar table and gathered up our coats and bags, I had to ask the obvious question.

'So, listen, Mike, it's been great to meet you, thanks for the chat. But I have to know: are you inviting all the shortlisted candidates for this position out for beers?'

He paused for a moment, then broke into a cheeky smile.

'Nah, mate, just needed to check you out. Welcome to the cult. You sucker.'

*

I felt more at home in my first week with MSF then I ever did in years with WHO. After becoming so accustomed to WHO's formality, hierarchy, bureaucracy and chronic funding crises, the dressed-down, get-it-done, iconoclastic approach of MSF was a breath of fresh air. So was the fact that the organisation was, particularly following the 2013–16 West African Ebola outbreak, unexpectedly flush with funds.

MSF had been formed back in the late 1960s from a splinter group of French doctors who'd been working for the International Committee of the Red Cross (ICRC) but had become disillusioned with the ICRC's principles of neutrality and impartiality. Initially they viewed themselves – as did the public – as commando doctors doing emergency work in areas no one, including the Red Cross, was willing to go. Along the way, in their earliest forays in Nigeria, Nicaragua and Cambodia, these rogue medicos disavowed the ICRC philosophy of avoiding politics and instead took an aggressively outspoken approach, speaking out against injustice wherever they found it. That rebellious, argumentative, fuck-the-system spirit is still very visible in the way that MSF works today.

Despite the fact that the last fifty years have seen it become a slick, professional organisation, with its own inevitable forms of hierarchy,

MSF retains a relatively flat, open structure, where anyone from the international president to the volunteer in the comms office is encouraged and expected to share their views and contribute to the debate. Even at headquarters level, there was a strong sense of socialism. Salaries were kept notoriously low, no one had fancy offices, everyone wore jeans and flip-flops, you ate and travelled and got pissed together and time spent 'in the field' was the ultimate badge of honour. The longer you'd been out there and the sketchier the locations, the more kudos you accrued.

I was delighted but surprised to have been offered the job, given I was coming in from outside the cult and hadn't earned my stripes through years in MSF missions. When I mentioned it to Mike, he smiled mischievously and patted me on the shoulder.

'Yeah, we decided you'd done enough time in the field with WHO and all that other stuff in the Pacific to get the gig, but we'll probably need to give you a test run somewhere, just to be sure you've got the goods. I'm working on it,' he said with a wink.

That sounded promising. In the meantime, I had my hands and brain full. AMR was a relatively new area of work for MSF and my position had been created to raise the profile and level of understanding of the topic for the Access Campaign. The greatest challenge we had before us was figuring out what the key strategies should be to tackle drug-resistant infections in the seventy or so countries – most of them poor and many of them at war – where MSF worked.

One of the most fundamental problems with AMR is that clinicians frequently have to diagnose infectious diseases without the aid of confirmatory tests. Even in wealthy, developed countries, doctors often diagnose conditions like skin and respiratory infections and prescribe antibiotics without doing swabs, blood tests or x-rays. There is a fine line between using clinical judgement, thus avoiding wasting time and money doing unnecessary tests (and exposing patients to harm, such as the radiation used in x-rays), and using a blunderbuss approach, blindly giving antibiotics to patients and assuming they will work. In the settings where MSF operated, this problem was magnified to an extreme degree. Given the absence of suitable diagnostic tests, with only a few antibiotics available anyway, even the most well-trained, well-meaning clinicians frequently find themselves treating serious infectious diseases by what amounts to shooting in the dark.

The work I found myself doing as I led the Access Campaign's AMR team into battle – an intimidatingly bright bunch of pharmacists, diagnostics gurus and health policy hotshots – took place at a number of levels. We were lobbying WHO and its member countries to adopt policies to 'protect and preserve' antibiotics as a critically important resource and clamp down on indiscriminate and inappropriate use. We were pushing pharmaceutical and biotech companies to invest in research and development for new drugs and diagnostic tools that were 'field-friendly' (ideally cheap, portable and able to be stored on a shelf in a tent in forty-degree heat for a couple of years). At the same time, we were trying to educate the public and our peers in the field about 'rational use'. It was interesting, demanding, intellectually stimulating work. I felt like I'd reached the peak of my profession. I was finally able to combine my clinical training with my public health knowledge in applying myself to one of the most important problems in medicine in my lifetime, working at the headquarters of an organisation that I deeply admired.

But I had a problem. A number of problems, in fact.

My move over to MSF had come with the holy grail of a permanent contract and, with that, a residency permit to live legally in Switzerland. However, the full-time nature of the MSF job meant I was very limited in opportunities for clinical work. I could squeeze in a few weeks of rural hospital locums back in Australia, mostly during my annual leave from MSF, but I fretted that I risked having my medical registration lapse for lack of clinical practice.

I also struggled to find time to devote to Rocketship. I'd taken over from Graham as Chair of the Board of Directors, which meant I'd have to get up early in the morning to run Rocketship videoconferences before my official workday began at MSF, then work late into the evening, once I got home again, writing reports for Rocketship donors.

My financial problems were dragging me ever deeper into debt. I was now months behind on my mortgage payments and no longer had enough money to keep paying the school fees for the children back in Bene. The fact that I'd cut off their opportunities to get an education was a very heavy burden for me to carry. I felt terribly guilty for letting my family down. I made the difficult decision to liquidate all my remaining assets, but that was easier said than done. Vanuatu's already weak economy was in a downturn and the house I'd bought in Port Vila proved impossible to sell. I was haemorrhaging money just trying to maintain it from the other side of the world. I was genuinely worried I was going bankrupt.

For the first time in my life, I experienced insomnia. I'd wake up in the middle of the night and my brain would immediately flick into stress mode. I'd spend hours staring at the ceiling or tossing uncomfortably around on the couch, my mind churning endlessly over money and work. The frustration would build such that I couldn't sleep and I'd eventually resign myself to being completely knackered throughout the next day. I spent weeks at a time in a dull, headache-filled haze. I felt a long way from home. Inevitably, this intruded into my relationship with Viri. She, to her immense credit, put up with my moods and suffered through the long periods of me being distracted and distant. But we fought.

I was chronically tired and emotionally empty. It took all my energy just to get up and go to work every day. I didn't have the bandwidth to be a good partner. A fog filled my brain and I began to question my own judgement. Over an ugly period of three or four months, the ominous rumbling in the distance became a thunderous galloping of hooves as the four horses of my mental health apocalypse descended: work stresses, money problems, relationship issues and social isolation.

I broke down.

'Anhedonia' is one of those obscure, dry words we use in medicine. They frequently have interesting origins, usually Latin or Greek, sometimes with a French twist. This one literally means the absence (*an-*) of pleasure (*hēdonē*) and it refers to the inability to enjoy things. It's one of the principal symptoms of depression. I'd never thought about it very much, only in passing when I dealt with depressed patients, until it literally stopped me in my tracks. I've always been a keen and moderately capable runner. When I started high school, I was pleasantly surprised to discover that jogging through the bush – a routine part of life on the farm – was a competitive sport known as cross-country running. Back then, I'd get up at 4:30am, run down our dirt road with a torch, typically in the drizzle, run back, have a shower, practise piano for an hour or so and then have breakfast and leave for school. I was clearly way more hardcore at the age of 13 than I am now, but running has remained part of my life. I knew something had to be very wrong with me then when, on a gentle jog around the lake with Viri one spring afternoon, I just stopped. I wasn't physically tired; I just couldn't be bothered. As my grandmother would have said, my 'get up and go had got up and gone'.

Things just got worse from there. Within a few days, I could no longer function. I was hardly sleeping, barely eating, just existing in a cloud of worry, anxiety and foul moods. I could barely string a sentence together. Viri was beside herself with concern. We'd now been together for almost a year and the previous winter we'd got engaged. I'd moved into her little apartment and things had been great at the beginning, but by this point I was just an irritable, mopey shadow. I didn't know what to do. I didn't even know if I wanted to keep on living. Ending it all seemed increasingly appealing.

I reflected back on the exit strategy I'd had in mind after Dad died, which involved driving off the side of a rainforest-covered canyon. That still seemed like a scenic and briefly exciting way to go out. *There were plenty of cliffs near Geneva that would do the job*, I mused. I tried to buck the fuck up. I tried to convince myself that I was overthinking things and that I was fine, really. I wanted to believe that. But I wasn't fine. I was suicidal.

In the end, in desperation, I phoned home. My sister happened to be at Ma's house when I rang, so they both listened to me sobbing incoherently down the line from where I sat, hunched over and trembling, in a dark corner of a bedroom on the other side of the world.

'Use my credit card and book the next flight home,' Ma ordered.

I did as I was told.

I sent Mike a brief email to say I was flying home for a family emergency – which was true, as my grandfather had just had a heart attack, piling further pain onto the plate – and departed that evening. I left Viri, the love of my life, disconsolate, confused and worried beyond belief. Neither of us knew if I would ever come back.

Australia

I hunkered down at Ma's place. The day after I arrived, I went to see my GP. She arranged an urgent series of sessions with a top psychologist – a sharp-eyed, foul-mouthed fellow called Lou, with whom I instantly clicked. The three of us discussed the option of me taking antidepressants and decided together that a trial of non-pharmacological strategies was the best way to begin. I exercised every day, avoided alcohol and slept as much as my body would let me. After a few weeks of this, I felt strong enough to contemplate my next move. An email from Mike made the decision for me. If the 'family emergency' situation was sufficiently resolved, he asked, would I be up for a field mission? He'd heard some colleagues in South Sudan urgently needed medical support and, having spent several years there himself, he was keen to help. He'd pulled some strings and arranged for me to spend a month as the paediatric doctor in a project he charmingly described as 'the arse-end of MSF'.

I was tempted, but wary. Was I fit enough for a mission in South Sudan? Could I safely and competently care for patients in my current state of mind? Would subjecting myself to such an extreme environment make things worse? I talked through all these and many other concerns with Lou, as well as my GP, my sister and Ma. We weighed up the risks, both to myself and those around me, and agreed it seemed there was no air-tight reason to prevent me going ahead. I was markedly better than I was when I'd arrived back in Australia in full-blown crisis mode. I was healthy enough and confident enough now that I felt I could push on with the plan. Even though I'd missed (or, perhaps more accurately, ignored) the symptoms of depression over the preceding months, I knew that this was my calling. I'd spent almost twenty years dreaming of working in the field with MSF. All the studying I'd done and the experiences I'd gained through working in so many wild and crazy places had led me to this point in my career. I still had major money problems, but I was on the mend. This depression thing could go fuck itself.

I was fit. I was safe. I was ready.

I called Viri to tell her not to worry. I was feeling better, heading to a war zone and would be back in a month.

South Sudan

As we thumped upwards in our Ukrainian military charter helicopter, through the heavy clouds densely packed over the swollen, dense vegetation receding beneath us, I felt the familiar frisson of nervous excitement that typically accompanies the start of a new adventure. The remote village we were flying into, Old Fangak, was not only in the middle of a rebel-controlled area near the northern border with Sudan, resulting in a total absence of government services; it was also in the heart of the Sudd. By some measures the world's largest swamp, this sprawling wetland proved enough to prevent the Romans from pushing any further south in their expeditions into equatorial Africa in the early years AD. Even now, its impenetrability is impressive. No electricity, no running water and no roads – hence our helicopter – but plenty of dysentery, malaria and mud.

The dullish thundering through my sweat-filled ear protectors provided a painful reminder that I'd brought a respiratory virus with me, as the icing on my depression cake. I'd spent the previous couple of days in Juba – South Sudan's high-decibel, decrepit capital – having the briefest of pre-departure briefings and trying to remember how to smell, swallow and sleep. Fortunately, I'd managed to shake off most of that mess in time for my mission and was left with just a sniffle, a startling old-man-in-the-early-morning cough and a pair of blocked ears (which is to say, I was even more deaf than usual – damn those childhood days on tractors and adolescent evenings in garage band jams!).

We landed in a hectic swirl of grass and dirt on an airstrip flanked by a low building of timber and tarpaulin that reminded me what a terrific word we have in *ramshackle*. The airstrip, which was typically too wet for six months of the year to permit fixed-wing aircraft to land, was the subject of an ongoing diplomatic battle between the village elders and the main

NGOs active in the area – MSF, ICRC and the World Food Programme – regarding who was responsible for its maintenance. The result was that most of the time the landing area was left unattended, at the mercy of the swamp. The 'airport' itself was overseen by a pair of tall, skinny gentlemen in dark glasses. Their slightly sinister appearance and serious demeanour lent the timber and corrugated iron immigration-cum-customs hut quite an imposing vibe, offset somewhat by the semi-naked children running around outside making zooming noises with tiny toy aeroplanes made of mud.

There we – me and Marie, the French nurse returning from a brief period of home leave in Paris, which, having come from Old Fangak, must have felt like a six-day mini-break on Mars – handed over our official paperwork. This was duly perused, through the dim light and the sunglasses, and we were checked for cameras and cash, neither of which were permitted for foreigners in Old Fangak. By the time we'd been cleared for duty by the two stooges, boated our way up-river to the hospital compound and dumped our gear in our little mud-hut homes, my white MSF T-shirt was covered in dirt and my adrenaline levels were through the thatch roof.

I felt immediately at home in Old Fangak. It wasn't just the heat, mud and mosquitoes – I was accustomed to all that from my years in the tropics – but the living and work environments also felt familiar. This was helped enormously by the fact that I was made to feel instantly welcome by the array of characters that made up the little MSF team. I was one of three doctors, alongside Sabine, an exuberant Tunisian who was the medical team leader, and Albert, a laid-back Burundian, with whom I shared the clinical and on-call responsibilities. Albert and I became firm friends, as we quickly learned to trust each other's judgement and abilities – something, he confided, he hadn't experienced with the colleague I was replacing, a hard-working idealist whose frustrations had been evident from arrival and who ultimately quit his mission several months early due to burnout. I noted that silently and rehearsed a few of the deep-breathing exercises Lou had taught me to do whenever I needed to lower my own stress tempo.

On my first night, as I sat outside in the warm, still night air, passing around a bottle of rum with Tina, the Kiwi environmental engineer and Ahmed, the Pakistani logistics coordinator, taking in the brilliance of the stars in a sky free of interference from electric light, I felt truly happy for the first time in months.

*

I spent my days in Old Fangak treating the children that kept turning up in our Emergency Room, which, like most of the rest of the hospital, was nothing more than a muddy, mouldy, intensely humid tent. Many of these kiddies arrived comatose with severe malaria, having seizures and showing signs I'd only ever previously seen in medical textbooks. And I spent my nights sweating, swatting at the mosquitoes that bored their way like noisy, vampiric little ninjas through the multiple barriers of insecticide-treated net, then weapons-grade repellent, then my skin, and listening for (that is, hoping not to hear) the radio crackling into life with 'Dr Lachie, Dr Lachie for ER' – the summons to strap on my headtorch and stomp back through the mud in my gumboots to see what new sickness the swamp had brought forth.

By this point in my career, I figured I'd been around, seen some stuff, done some things. But I was still pretty shocked to encounter, on my first morning ward round in Old Fangak, a gorgeous little three-year-old girl called Akong, who'd been carried into the hospital in the arms of a stranger a month earlier, after her alcoholic mother had dumped her and left her to die in an open pit latrine. She was unconscious and severely malnourished, with both TB and kala-azar, otherwise known as visceral leishmaniasis – a parasitic infection spread by sandflies that is usually fatal if untreated. I'd never seen this before in my life but had to learn about it rapidly, as I was now in one of the world's hotspots for the disease. Outbreaks commonly occurred in settings of poverty, conflict, forced displacement, malnutrition and changing climatic conditions: Old Fangak had the royal flush.

Akong slowly recovered and her smile and outstretched, cuddle-seeking arms were the bittersweet highlight of every morning ward round. It was sweet to see her improve, but bitter was the knowledge that she still had no one to care for her.

It wasn't just the rare diseases that served as a reminder of where we were. Every day, young men would hobble in on makeshift crutches, clutching at dirty, bloody, pus-soaked cloths covering gunshot wounds. These were typically from days earlier and thus often infected, given the time it took to trek through the swamp to our hospital. The fighting between the loosely aligned rebel groups and the government forces rarely came close enough to make us feel in real danger, but there was a strict evening curfew and forays beyond the gates of our compound were few. That meant that I was particularly happy (albeit in a slightly guilty way) to be sent out on the motorboat for the occasional outreach clinic or emergency medical retrieval. The experience of skimming up and down the reed-choked river, grinning at the naked children cavorting in the shallows, watching the birds wheel lazily overhead and waving at the wiry men paddling along gamely in their handmade canoes – hollowed-out logs with the ends plugged with mud – was a rare, visceral, privileged pleasure.

*

One particularly sticky midday, as I finished my ward round and was squelching over to the communal dining tent to forage for some lunch, the voice of Jacob, the Nigerian Project Coordinator, came blaring over the radio.

'SOS call, Lachie. Young boy's been bitten by a snake in a village somewhere up the river. Need you to grab the retrieval kit, go with Marie in the boat with Wotjak, find the kid and bring him back if he needs treatment. You cool with that, over?'

'Copy that. On my way. Over and out.'

I swung by the dining tent, kicked off my boots at the door, shuffled through the mosquito net in my filthy socks, stuffed some stale bread and cheese in my satchel, then slipped my boots back on and stomped over to the pharmacy. I rummaged around in the drug fridge trying to find the snakebite antivenom. Eriko, the ever-cheery Japanese pharmacist, heard the ruckus and appeared smiling at my side.

'Do you need some help, Lachie?'

'Hey, Eriko, yes, thanks. Where do we keep the antivenom?'

'It's in the box behind the measles vaccines. Who do you need it for?'

'There's a kid in a village up-river somewhere who's been bitten. We're heading off in the boat to get him now.'

'Ah, I see. Okay. So, ah, are you sure?'

I yanked a couple of vials from the box and pulled my head out of the fridge. Eriko was still smiling politely, but she seemed a bit flustered. I tried to reassure her.

'Don't worry, I've treated plenty of snakebites in Australia. Thanks for this, see you when we get back.'

I stashed the vials of antivenom in the bag of emergency retrieval gear, hoisted the heavy backpack over my shoulders and staggered down to the muddy dock where Marie was waiting. A storm front was closing in as we set off up the river and, as we entered the mouth of a weed-filled lake, the rain came. We found ourselves chugging, achingly slowly, through the thick vegetation that covered the entire surface of the lake, as tropical raindrops the size (and density, it seemed) of sultanas pelted us from every direction. I peered through a hole in my anorak at Wotjak, the captain of our little vessel, as he stopped every few minutes to reach down behind the boat and unclog the outboard motor. Like many men from his Lou Nuer ethnic group, Wotjak had ritualistic horizontal scars on his forehead, but I thought he looked rather worried as well.

Eventually we arrived at the lakeside village that had sent the SOS. We sloshed through the knee-high water to one of the half-dozen little round mud huts and poked our heads inside. Packed into the tiny dark space were a man, two women and four small children, one of whom was wearing a calico cloth and a spooked expression. Fair enough, I supposed, from the little fellow's perspective, given he'd already had to deal with some nasty snake-related business and now a white man had just appeared in his doorway with a bright light beaming out of his head.

With the help of my trusty headtorch I gently lifted back the cloth and found one of his legs was blistered and swollen to twice the size of the other. I removed the makeshift tourniquet that had been applied around his thigh, as the risk of gangrene was already high. We carried our little patient back to the boat, where at least I had decent light and a flat, if wet, surface on which to work. The rain had stopped and the sun was out. I could see the steam rising off my T-shirt as I wiped the sweat from my eyes. Under the curious gaze of the patient's mother, father and about fifteen other folks from the village who'd gathered around the boat by now, I carefully inserted a cannula into a vein in the boy's arm, gave him some pain relief and fluid and drew up one of our precious vials of snake antivenom. These medicines were expensive, scarce, sometimes dangerous and – in this part of the world – occasionally ineffective due to dodgy manufacturing practices, but this was a 'life or limb' situation.

As I knelt down to give the injection, I felt a hand on my shoulder. It was Marie.

'Hey, Lachie, are you sure?' she asked, nodding in the direction of my syringe.

I felt mildly offended. Didn't my colleagues realise snakebites were common in Australia? We are perversely proud of our reputation as a country supposedly teeming with deadly creatures. Dealing with the consequences of their fangs and stings is the bread and butter of an Aussie rural generalist's job.

'Yeah, it's fine, I'm sure,' I replied, and very slowly injected the antivenom into the IV line, watching the boy's face intently as I did so. The immune response to this type of medication can occasionally be severe, in the form of an allergic reaction, which may, in the most extreme cases, manifest as anaphylaxis: a life-threatening emergency. The wee lad blinked back at me nonchalantly, then looked away and squinted into the sun. So far, so good. I gave a thumbs-up to Wotjak and he fired up the outboard.

The journey home was faster, as we were going down-river and could follow our earlier trail through the weeds in the lake. Our snakebite patient was joined the following day on the paediatric ward by another little girl who'd been bitten on the arm, but not so badly as to need antivenom. That was fortunate, as I had received a sharp slap over the wrist via email from the Medical Coordinator (MedCo) in Juba when she heard I'd given some to the little boy. The snakebite antivenom supply crisis was so severe in South Sudan, there had been a decision made by the MSF project managers to reserve the small number of vials of antivenom we had available in case one of our staff members was bitten and needed treatment. While I understood the reasoning behind this – namely that we had a duty of care to our own employees, and we couldn't expect them to work in a place slithering with venomous snakes and not ensure an antidote was available – this directive still made me deeply uncomfortable. How could we deny life-saving medication to the patient in front of us, knowing it was available but only for those with the right paperwork? I humbly accepted the reprimand from the MedCo, who assured me they were trying their best to rectify the supply crisis as soon as possible. But I wrestled with the knowledge, as I tossed and turned in my creaky cot, that – if faced with a similar situation – I'd probably do the same again. This dilemma represented so much of what I often struggle with as a doctor: the difficulties balancing the needs of the individual against those of a population; inequities in access to healthcare and medicines; and the impossible question of what value to place on a human life, particularly when it appears to be a zero-sum game.

*

The days in Old Fangak melted into each other like a muddy, sweaty, malaria-filled fondue. Every now and then something strange or interesting would happen, which helped break the routine, like the plague of locusts that, well, plagued us for several days, and the food shortage that saw Ahmed slaughtering a newly bought goat or two (with, it must be said, more than just a little gusto) for the grill. We had plenty of wins, like the kiddies who would wake up after days of lying unconscious with high fevers in our emergency tent and be able to shake my hand and ask for a biscuit. And we had a few losses, like the poor little boy I found dead on the morning ward round, suggesting he'd had a respiratory arrest while the nurses had slept through the night shift; the epileptic girl who convulsed to death, despite our best attempts at resuscitation; and the diabetic boy whom we'd managed to save after several days of the most intensive care we could provide, but for whom the MedCo refused to allow the outpatient clinic to provide the daily insulin injections he'd need to survive in the world outside our compound, on the basis that we were an 'emergency project'.

When my month was up, I left Old Fangak with mixed feelings. The field mission had helped me heal. The change of scenery and the clear sense of purpose had done wonders for my mental health. I'd taken to scribbling poetry at night by the light of my headtorch, sitting on the floor of my little mud hut, with the emotional outlet proving powerfully cathartic.

I'd miss the remote setting and the whacky medicine. Even more, I'd miss the camaraderie and the cold cans of beer at sunset, with Bevan, the Alaskan logistics assistant, serenading us on his guitar, tapping his filthy feet. I'd even miss the extra bucket of water over my head to which I'd treat myself in the shower tent from time to time. But my replacement had arrived and the helicopter awaited. Viri and I had managed to exchange a few WhatsApp messages while I was away, enough to reassure each other of our mutual love and commitment to getting things back on track.

It was time to go home.

CHAPTER TWELVE

2018
Switzerland

I opened the door to find Viri looking up at me with a shy smile. I wiped my sweaty hands on my jeans and invited her in. We opened a bottle of wine and took our glasses to the couch, sitting a couple of feet apart and chatting, haltingly at first, then with a little more warmth and rhythm. It was a surreal feeling – we loved each other, but a lot had happened in the previous few months and we'd drifted apart as a result. We hadn't seen each other since my breakdown, when I'd become a shadow of the man she knew, then I vanished altogether, and the next thing she'd heard was that I was heading to a war zone in a swamp. She'd spent a desperate summer, confused and abandoned, worrying about me and feeling pitifully sorry for herself. Her friends had offered her the full spectrum of advice, from 'Wait for him, he's worth it', to 'He's an arsehole, forget about him.' She'd lost weight.

When I got back from South Sudan, I'd rented another one-bedroom Airbnb for a few months to give us some extra breathing space, so Viri coming over this evening was at least accompanied by the incomparable thrill of a date, despite the slightly awkward vibe. We were still engaged, we agreed, but we needed to give ourselves time to regain the closeness and intimacy we'd enjoyed before depression dropped its filthy shroud of darkness over me. It was very strange not to know much detail about what the other one was doing in their daily life.

She asked how Rocketship was doing and I told her it was really taking off. The model we'd pioneered in Timor-Leste, flying experienced rural generalist medical educators over to support the local doctors training towards their Diploma in Family Medicine, had proved so successful that other countries in the region had taken note. We'd received a request from the Kingdom of Tonga to help them set up their own programme and we had a team currently on the ground there, doing a reconnaissance of the various options for donors, partners, trainees and facilities.

Viri's work was going well too, she told me, and her family were all fine.

Trying to sound casual, but yearning to reconnect, we found ourselves talking about our weekend plans.

'I'm going to see Archie next weekend,' she said, sipping on her wine. 'He's going to do a mushroom ceremony for me. I'm sure it will help with the healing process.'

Archie was a Mexican friend who was going through a slow and impressive transition from being a successful business manager to a full-time shaman. A party animal earlier in life, he'd forsaken drugs, then alcohol and eventually meat over the past year or two as his inward journey deepened and his awareness expanded.

I stared at her for a few seconds in silence.

'That,' I said slowly, 'is a pretty remarkable coincidence. I'm going on a healing retreat myself next weekend.'

'Wow, yes, what a coincidence,' she said, with a nod and a knowing smile. 'Mushrooms?'

'Ayahuasca.'

*

I'd been hearing whispers about ayahuasca for a while. It had come up in conversation at one of my best friends' wedding – which was chock-full of doctors – a couple of years earlier. What started out for me as mild inquisitiveness had gradually evolved into outright incredulity, as I read more and more of the scientific papers that were being published in what was evidently an explosion of recent medical research on the topic.

Ayahuasca, known by a long list of other names, including *Madre* – Spanish for Mother – has been used as a traditional medicine by Indigenous peoples of the Amazon for over a thousand years. It's a witches' brew that includes a specific type of liana, or woody vine, containing monoamine oxidase inhibitors (also used in modern pharmaceuticals to treat depression), boiled down with another plant to release dimethyltryptamine (DMT).

DMT is a naturally occurring molecule that has potent psychedelic properties. Psychedelics such as psilocybin (the neuroactive molecule in 'magic mushrooms'), mescaline (found in cactuses such as peyote and San Pedro) and lysergic acid diethylamide (LSD*), were the subject of a multitude of serious studies in the 1950s and 1960s, particularly in the US. Over that period, the scientific evidence steadily strengthened regarding their potential benefit in people with various psychological disorders, including addiction, post-traumatic stress disorder (PTSD), end-of-life anxiety, severe depression and suicidality. The initial clinical trials suggested that the therapeutic potential of psychedelics may be little short of revolutionary. One prominent psychiatrist, Dr Stanislav Grof, characterised psychedelics as having the same power for psychiatry – specifically their ability to peer deep inside the mind to enable glimpses of its workings – as the microscope did for biology and the telescope for astronomy.

---

* If you're wondering why the compound is abbreviated 'LSD', rather than 'LAD', this is because it's based on the original German Lysergsäurediethylamid.

Sadly, the dogma of the cynical conservatives who dominated American politics in the 1960s and 1970s, grossly and disingenuously oversimplifying the links between all types of 'drugs' and crime, led to psychedelics being categorised as 'Schedule 1' controlled substances. The vital research work was thus suspended until more rational thinking began to prevail once again from the late 1990s. What started as a slow renaissance, with neuroscientists, psychiatrists, clinical psychologists and other researchers scrambling for funding and advocating for the necessary regulatory changes to try and make up for the lost decades, has gradually gained momentum and we are now witnessing an exponential increase in our knowledge of how these medicines work and what beneficial effects they can have.

The Indigenous custodians of traditional medicines such as ayahuasca and peyote of course possess, from experience gained through the centuries, a vastly greater understanding and respect for the substances they consider to be direct links between the natural world and the divine. Ayahuasca, in particular, is regarded as the most powerful entheogen – a substance that induces visions, enables profound personal insights and inspires spiritual development – on the planet.

I read through the latest findings from some of the world's most eminent medical research institutions, such as Johns Hopkins University in the US and Imperial College in the UK, along with summaries of the latest evidence in books such as Michael Pollan's excellent *How to Change Your Mind: The New Science of Psychedelics*, and marvelled at how relevant and timely this research appeared to be, both for society in general and for me personally. Although I was miles better mentally than I had been months before, I still felt the cold, bony hands of depression encircling my neck every now and then, and I knew there was a lot of healing work ahead.

Perhaps psychedelics could provide the kind of reset that I felt my battered brain might require.

I set up a Skype call with Lou, my psychologist back in Australia, to see what he thought of it all. I wasn't sure he would approve of the idea of me experimenting on myself with psychedelics in what was a fast-changing but still unregulated environment, but he was frank and fearless and I trusted his judgement.

'What do you have in mind, exactly?' he asked, leaning closer to the screen and adjusting his glasses, his curiosity clearly piqued.

'Well, I guess I could probably get my hands on some mushrooms or LSD, but that seems pretty risky. So I've been looking into other options and it seems there are ayahuasca retreats held regularly over here.'

'Really? Ayahuasca, hey? You're a long way from the Amazon, mate. Is it legal there? Who runs the retreats?'

'I think it's more a matter of being tolerated, rather than regulated, at least at this stage,' I replied. 'There are several groups who do it, and it's mostly out in the open. They have websites where you sign up, fill out a medical questionnaire, have a pre-departure counselling session and if they think you're fit for it then off you go.'

'Hmm, okay. Pretty different situation here in Australia, as I'm sure you're aware. In the sessions you're looking at over there, is there psychological support provided?'

'More or less. Depends on the group. Some have counsellors doing what they call "psychotherapeutic integration", but I'm not sure how much formal training they have.'

'Steer clear of those,' Lou said firmly. 'If you're going to do this, and you want my blessing, there has to be a mental health professional present.'

'Fair enough,' I nodded. 'There's one group someone told me about that is run by a clinical psychologist. Did her master's degree working with traditional medicine practitioners in Brazil, where a lot of the most original research is being generated. From what I've heard, she's superb.'

'Okay, send me her bio and some info on the retreat. I want to do a bit more of a background check. I'll email you later in the week. Don't do anything stupid before then.'

'Copy that. Thanks Lou. Appreciate you being so open-minded about it.'

'Don't thank me yet,' he growled, and hung up.

The email I received a couple of days later from Lou was reassuring, but clear where the responsibilities for the decision lay.

> *I looked her up. Seems legit.*
>
> *Obviously I can't give you my professional approval, as it's outside my experience and jurisdiction, but I respect the fact that you've done your homework and discussed it with me.*
>
> *Let me know if you go ahead, and if you do, I expect you to check in with me within 48 hours afterwards.*
>
> *Got that?*

I shared my plans with a couple of health professional friends I trusted in Geneva and it turned out they'd both been looking into it too. Stuart, a psychologist, had recently returned from a two-week ayahuasca retreat in Peru, and told us how it had been one of the most intense experiences of his life. He'd come back a man changed distinctly for the better. Karel, a medical doctor like me and similarly uninitiated, decided to join me and we booked ourselves on the next retreat. We went through the recommended preparation phase, including avoiding alcohol and meat for a week, and reflecting on a specific 'intention' to bring to *Madre*. My intention was simple, although I wasn't sure it was achievable: I wanted to try and identify my true purpose in life.

When the day came, I squeezed into the passenger seat of Karel's coupé to wind our way up into the mountains in search of enlightenment. It was a low-key beginning. We arrived after dusk at an intersection with three large barns and a small cluster of chalets that together barely deserved to be called a village. Still, as that's where our patchy sat-nav was insisting we stop, we pulled up alongside a few other vehicles and wandered nervously up to the old stone buildings to peer at the numbers above the battered timber doors. One swung open with a gentle push, so we edged up the stairs, preparing to either enter the warm embrace of shamanic medicine or apologise for interrupting someone's dinner. The acoustic guitar sounds, smell of herbal tea, and smiles and hugs that greeted us suggested we'd found the former.

Our retreat was to be co-facilitated by Francesca, the clinical psychologist about whom I'd heard such good reports, who radiated positive energy, and Nico, the shaman, who was to be our spiritual guide for the weekend. Nico did, to be fair, show an unusually high level of self-awareness from the outset.

'I might not look like it,' he acknowledged, after the dozen of us had stashed our bags and settled down on thin foam mattresses circled around the floor, 'but I trained with some of the best *curanderos* (healers) in Peru and I've been doing this for many years.'

The lights were dimmed, candles were lit and to kick things off we lined up to have Nico blow wild tobacco up our nostrils through a carved, wooden, well-worn pipe. It stung like blazes from the back of the nose, through the eyeballs and up into the brain.

'Use the tissues, if you need to,' Nico said gently, pointing to the small pile of supplies beside our mattresses as we all gagged and sneezed for the following few minutes. The pile also included a plastic bucket and several garbage bags.

'For the purging,' Francesca had explained as she distributed them. 'But for vomit only,' she warned. 'If you need to shit, we recommend you use the bathroom.'

Good to know.

'Purging' on ayahuasca, I'd read beforehand, was almost guaranteed and was welcomed by many of its practitioners as a necessary part of the purification process. Once we'd recovered from the tobacco snorting and each silently plotted out our purging strategies, Nico talked us through the journey ahead.

'You will see things and experience things you've never seen or experienced before,' he said. 'Some of it will be incredibly beautiful, some of it may be extremely painful. You might laugh; many of you will cry. Some of you,' he paused thoughtfully, looking around, 'may even die.' He let that hang in the air for a moment before carrying on calmly, 'Not literally, of course, but it may feel very real. And if that happens, don't try to resist. It must be important, as it will mean *Madre* is trying to teach you something. So, if that happens, you should just let yourself die.'

He stood up to rearrange some talismans on the low altar in front of him, jangled some wooden maracas and flapped a palm and feather fan vigorously for a few seconds. Satisfied, he settled back in an old leather chair, draped a quilt over his shoulders and offered some final advice.

'Whatever happens, I will be there to guide you. Whatever you experience, it is likely I have been there before. You will be safe, and you will survive.' Then, as he picked up the glass jug and stirred the thick brown brew briskly with a long wooden spoon, he added, not entirely reassuringly, 'Just don't leave the room.'

Pre-departure briefing completed, we all sat, obediently cross-legged, most with their eyes closed and hands resting lightly on their knees, waiting for our signal to approach the altar.

'Bon voyage, buddy,' Karel said softly from the mattress next to mine.

'You too, mate,' I whispered back. 'See you on the other side.'

When my turn came, I got up, walked over and knelt down respectfully in front of Nico. He muttered an incantation, raised his eyes skywards and offered me the little cup. Not knowing what else to do, I also glanced upwards and mumbled a few words of gratitude, then lifted the glass to my lips. The stuff had the taste and consistency of fresh mud, with a hint of vinegar. I retched slightly but got it down in one go, as seemed to be the expected method. Back on my foam mat, I sat upright for a while, observing the rest of the ceremony while swallowing hard and often to try and clear my suffering oesophagus. Once all had partaken, we sat in silence. After half an hour or so, with less of a taste of rainforest in my mouth, I wriggled down into a semi-recumbent position and closed my eyes.

I fell asleep. It was, after all, midnight on a Friday, and I'd had a typically jam-packed working week. My body clock didn't care that my mind was about to become one with infinity. It was past my bedtime.

I woke up about half an hour later to a nudge from my subconscious. With my eyes still closed, images appeared: rabbits bounding across my vision like a carnival duck shoot.

I fell asleep again.

When my subconscious woke me a second time, it wasn't so subtle. With a wham and a roar I was catapulted out into space. I saw the universe as a moving, pulsing energy. An alive, interconnected entity – not an organism, nor a machine. Just an *it* that *is*. An ageless, self-consuming and ever-regenerating being that incorporated everything. It had a reptilian quality in the way it seemed to twist on itself and it completely filled me with awe. And yet, despite my lifelong phobia of snakes, I wasn't afraid. It had no emotion, it didn't care, it simply existed – always had and always would – and we were all part of it.

And that was just the beginning.

I spent the next four or five hours on a voyage through my life and place in the cosmos. The latter, of course, was shown to be entirely insignificant, but in a way that was oddly comforting as I now understood it. Viri appeared early on in my journey. She wore a long white dress, embroidered with brightly coloured flowers, and had hair braided with ribbons like her Indigenous Purépecha ancestors. She had a crown of feathers and bracelets of silver. She smiled at me lovingly and had never looked more beautiful. The joy I felt was so intense that I burst into tears.

When she'd finished kicking my consciousness around the solar system like a football, *Madre* plugged my mind into the network of life on Earth. I didn't just *see*, I *felt* the humming, throbbing, moving density of creation. The strongest impulse came from the plant kingdom – the noblest, strongest and longest-living of the lot. I understood why ayahuasca was treated with such profound reverence and how it was considered to have such potent, feminine energy. My mind then turned to the creatures scuttling all over the surface of the Earth on their short-lived little missions. I saw humans clearly as animals, but with undeniably unique characteristics. For all our infinite follies and unparalleled arrogance, we have come to be distinct from our animal kingdom cousins and now find ourselves – far more by accident than design – with the capacity to inflict unprecedented damage on the very planet we inhabit. Individually, humans are truly remarkable biological machines. Collectively, our abilities are miraculous. As a species, however, we're diabolical. Inside of me dawned an insight that helped me comprehend my intermittent existential crises. I need not feel so torn between my responsibilities as a clinician (providing individual care to patients) and those of a public health professional (trying to protect the human race from itself). Rather, these could be invaluable, complementary perspectives.

I felt the tremendous privilege of being a doctor, to be armed with a little extra knowledge of how humans worked and be charged with using that to do what could be done when things went awry. The revelation was in equal parts humbling and affirming.

Nico's chanting brought me softly back to earth. The candles flickered low and many figures around the circle were curled up in sleep. A faint smell of vomit wafted across the room, but Nico, Francesca and their assistants had been very attentive in emptying the buckets and blowing wild tobacco smoke over us periodically as a part-ritual, part-deodorising technique. I had mercifully avoided puking and my purging – in the physical sense – had been limited to a couple of brief scurries to the loo.

With the first slivers of daylight peeking through the curtains, I bunched up my sleeping bag and dragged myself wearily upstairs to find my bunk. I felt physically spent, but more aware and alive than I'd ever been in my life. My mind and spirit had been jolted awake with a biochemical cattle prod. Right now, though, my body reminded me, it was time to get some shut-eye – we were doing it all again the next night.

Viri and I shared our stories over dinner one evening later that week, both of us profoundly re-energised by our respective psychedelic encounters. The coincidences of us having independently planned healing retreats on the same weekend, and the similarities in what we experienced, were starting to feel less and less like coincidences. We were regaining most of the closeness we'd lost in the lead-up to and fall-out from my depression and were ready to merge our lives together again after the months we'd spent officially together but physically apart.

Over the following weeks, we moved into a lovely old crumbling villa with a large garden backing onto a river that we could afford because it was destined for demolition. I felt intellectually and psycho-emotionally super-charged. That was fortunate, because things were heating up with my role at MSF. I had been appointed to represent the Access Campaign on MSF's newly established Antibiotic Resistance Taskforce and we had identified a hotspot for our antibiotic resistance problems. Together with Maarten, the Taskforce Leader, I was despatched to the Middle East.

Lebanon

When I was a kid, the name 'Beirut' conjured images of car bombs and bullet-riddled buildings and the word 'Lebanon' was synonymous with civil war. Leap forward a few decades and the downtown area of the capital city bristles with glitzy shopping malls, with well-heeled Lebanese in designer sunglasses and fake tans blaring the horns of expensive cars jostled together in the narrow streets. However, juxtaposed against that are the pock-marked apartment blocks and ambiguously vacant lots that could be sites of destruction, construction or both. The country has experienced spasms of violence, political and economic shocks and social upheaval between periods of relative stability, as it sits uneasily alongside its neighbours in that ancient, proud, densely populated, volatile pocket of the world. The tension between the country's Christian and Muslim populations and their respective sub-groups still simmers, and the cross-border links between organisations such as Hezbollah and the chemical-weapon-loving government of Syria are a festering sore. Fair to say it's not the easiest place to be posted.

'Ah yes, MSF,' huffed Dr Laila, the Lebanese infectious diseases physician appointed as WHO's national AMR tsar, as she strode past, waving us into her office and collapsing into her chair. 'I should mention, before we begin, WHO is against field hospitals.'

Maarten and I glanced at each other, wondering if we should take the bait, given how she was referring so blatantly to one of MSF's main ways of working. That seemed an inauspicious way to kick things off.

'Okay, well, thank you for agreeing to meet us anyway,' Maarten replied politely. 'Perhaps we could start with some introductions?'

As she eyed us with suspicion, Maarten explained that we had been sent on behalf of MSF headquarters to improve our understanding of the main drivers of drug-resistant infections in the region. Our colleagues in the MSF country office in Lebanon had taken up the cause and were enthusiastically preparing to host a multi-country meeting on antimicrobial resistance (AMR), in which Maarten and I would participate before we departed. As Lebanon was one of the wealthier and more stable countries in the region, occasional mortar attack or presidential assassination notwithstanding, it was viewed by many, including MSF, as having a significant responsibility in attempting to tackle the problem of bacterial infections that were proving increasingly difficult to treat. Some had even reached bacterial nirvana: total antibiotic resistance.

'Yes, these are deeply rooted problems that are difficult to undo,' Laila said wearily. 'We have set up a national infectious diseases committee that restricts antibiotic use in all public hospitals, but these only represent a fifth of the health sector. The other 80 per cent is private and completely unregulated. There are many pharmaceutical companies in Lebanon and they have a lot of influence. They encourage pharmacists to dispense antibiotics without prescriptions. Anyone off the street can buy any antibiotic they want in a private pharmacy. The pharmaceutical representatives also give rewards to the doctors who prescribe their products in the largest quantities in the private hospitals.'

Maarten looked up from his notebook. 'Rewards?'

'Yes, you know, like expensive dinners and sending the doctors and their families on holidays to the Seychelles.'

'Doesn't the government try to clamp down on those practices?' Maarten asked.

'There is no real leadership in the government to tackle these complex issues,' she sighed. 'Their capacity to impose limitations on the private sector is, let us say, negligible. They tried some time ago to regulate the pricing to restrict the inappropriate sale and use of broad-spectrum antibiotics. But rather than increase the prices of those last-line drugs, which would have angered the private sector, they decided to reduce the costs of first-line drugs instead. So, what happened? Sales of those common antibiotics skyrocketed!'*

Maarten raised his eyebrows and went back to scribbling notes.

'What about microbiology lab services in Lebanon?' I asked. 'Are they producing reliable data on antibiotic sensitivity and resistance patterns?'

'Ha!' she snorted. 'We did our first round of laboratory accreditations for the national AMR programme this year. We assessed thirty-five labs. None of them passed. It was, to be honest with you, a complete catastrophe.'

She went on to confirm what we'd heard from other sources. Many

---

* 'First-line' antibiotics, as the name suggests, are those intended to be used as the first-choice option for doctors prescribing antibiotics for bacterial infections, particularly in settings where diagnostic capacities are limited (i.e. where the specific bacteria causing the infection, and its respective resistance patterns, cannot be identified). These tend to be the cheapest and most common antibiotics. 'Second-line' and 'third-line' antibiotics are the next levels of defence, which typically come with higher prices and/or riskier side-effect profiles. 'Fourth-line' and 'last-line' drugs are those that should be kept in reserve for only the most resistant and difficult-to-treat infections. They tend to be more expensive and some have potentially very serious side effects.

laboratories in Lebanon were quite well resourced, with the ability to receive bacterial specimens (such as blood, sputum or wound swabs), grow the organisms and test them against different antibiotics to see which ones worked (that is, killed or limited the growth of the bug) and which ones didn't. One of the problems was that high rates of bacterial resistance do not reflect well on the control measures that are supposed to be in place, so publishing that kind of information can be politically risky. Lebanon, it seemed, like many other countries, was not keen to accept, much less advertise, the fact that the levels of antibiotic resistance in the community and its hospitals were so high.

'What about other countries in the region?' Maarten asked.

Laila leaned back in her chair. 'Before the war, Syria was very good. Many things worked well there. You couldn't get any antibiotics without a prescription. Now, anything goes. Jordan has sensible regulations, but they are always breached. And Egypt looks solid on paper, but who knows?'

We wandered out of the WHO office in a daze.

Maarten looked at me with a wry smile. 'I think you have a term in English for this: "cluster-fuck". Is that correct?'

I nodded. 'It is indeed.'

Jordan

A few days later, we arrived in Jordan. The MSF-run Reconstructive Surgical Project (RSP) in the outskirts of the capital, Amman, is one of the busiest and most sophisticated facilities across all of MSF's operations. The initiative was set up in 2006, converting Al-Mowasah Hospital into a dedicated war trauma centre, with specialist orthopaedic, maxillo-facial and plastic surgeons collaborating with physiotherapists and prosthetists to manage patients with horrendous injuries from bullets, blasts and burns. Many were civilians, including children; others were combatants, either from government armed forces or militia.

The hospital squatted on a hillside, coated with the residue of the frequent sandstorms, surrounded by a sprawl of adobe-like buildings as Amman's outer suburbs disappeared into the haze. The entrance was guarded by soldiers with machine guns, but they were the only weapons allowed on the premises. MSF does not politicise the medical care it provides nor discriminate between patients. Military uniforms and weapons are banned inside MSF facilities. This is not as much of a no-brainer as you might imagine; kidnapping of hospital patients for torture and/or assassination is a tragically common problem in other MSF projects. Inside the hospital, much care was taken to try and separate individuals known to belong to warring factions onto different wards.

Jordan is a mostly stable, peaceful country – an oasis in the region – and Amman was a relatively long way from the active fighting in neighbouring Syria and Iraq, and even further from the civil war in Yemen. Patients in this hospital, therefore, had experienced long and difficult journeys, in more ways than one. Whether they'd been shot, blown up or injured by falling rubble or flying debris, they'd all had to survive not just the initial impact, but the first, second and subsequent attempts at surgical repair of their injuries before eventually being referred to the RSP. In the process, they all inevitably received multiple rounds of antibiotics, meaning the generations of bacteria contaminating their wounds, burrowing into their muscles and embedding in their bones had gone on resistance-gene-producing rampages. By the time they turned up in Amman, these patients had some of the toughest and most drug-resistant bacterial infections known to humankind.

There was mounting evidence that the bacteria circulating freely in the environment had sky-high levels of resistance. That meant any projectile – bullet, metal fragment, chunk of concrete – that pierced a human body could be coated in antibiotic-resistant bugs. Some of the academics and advocacy groups with whom we met were beginning to bang the drum about conflict being a driver of antibiotic resistance and therefore a violation of human rights. I must admit I never quite got my head around that part of their argument. Wasn't getting shot or blown up already a 'violation of human rights'? In any case, their idea appeared to be that armed groups could therefore be brought before the International Criminal Court (ICC) for contributing to the meteoric rise in drug-resistant infections. *Good luck with that*, I thought. The ICC didn't seem able to do much about the multiple war criminals already on its Most Wanted list, so I very much doubted they would wade into the mess of drug-resistant infections as weapons of war.

We spent several days pounding the well-worn concrete floors with Dr Fatimah, the warm and garrulous Iraqi physician appointed to be the hospital's Antibiotic Steward. Her job was complicated. Not only did she have to carefully monitor the results from the microbiology lab to see which bugs were growing from the pus retrieved from which patient's tissues or bones and which antibiotics might be effective to treat the infection. She also had to deal with the surgeons.

Now, I should mention here that some of my best friends are surgeons and I have nothing but the greatest respect for the vital, amazing work they do. There's no way I could do it – hours of painstaking labour, fiddling around inside a human body, fixing someone's broken bits with tiny, sharp tools while hunched awkwardly over an operating table. My bladder's too small, for one thing. Doing the odd cameo in the operating theatre as an anaesthetist at least means I can pop out for a tea and a wee once in a while. But for all their fine motor skills, surgeons are not known for their finesse when it comes to management of medical problems – that is, anything for which the solution doesn't involve bright lights and cold steel. Thus when it comes to issues beyond the operating table – heart attack, brain death or infection resistant to most antibiotics – the surgeons usually aren't the best ones to ask, as their approach, quite naturally, tends towards the mechanical.

Fatimah's role, therefore, involved as much diplomacy as clinical acumen. Every morning, as she did her ward round, she'd see the post-operative patients and would gently but firmly advise the nurses that she was changing the medication chart to remove the expensive, broad-spectrum, scattergun-style antibiotics her surgical colleagues had prescribed and replace them with a drug specifically tailored to the patient's laboratory-proven antibiotic sensitivity pattern. It drove the surgeons potty, of course, but that was her job and she had ultimate authority within the hospital for all antibiotic prescriptions.

The results showed. After her role was created, some seven years earlier, the use of broad-spectrum antibiotics decreased dramatically, with the corresponding savings making the project coordinator and finance team in Paris very pleased. A single course of third- or fourth-line antibiotics could cost north of four thousand US dollars and the supply of these precious drugs was precarious at best. The worry now, however, was that usage of those heavy-duty drugs was on the rise again, not from inappropriate prescribing but because, year by year, the rates of resistance were creeping up.

Fatimah was very generous with her time, slowing down her seemingly endless ward rounds to make sure we had the chance to chat briefly with each patient. Around half were Iraqi, with the remainder a fifty-fifty split between Syrian and Yemeni. All were very polite, greeting us softly with tobacco-stained smiles before we peeled off their bandages and dressings to inspect their wounds. Many patients had amputations and many more were clearly heading that way. The foul odour of pus warned of rotting muscle beneath and the gnarled twists of sinew clinging to discoloured bones suggested our battle with the bacteria was all but over, and those little fuckers had won. From time to time, I would see Fatimah cross something out on a patient's medication chart and mutter a few words to herself. Assuming she was correcting yet another surgeon's antibiotic order, which must wear thin, day after day, I guessed she was quietly swearing to herself. That was certainly what I would be doing in her position.

'Maybe one day they'll learn, hey?' I joked.

She looked at me, puzzled.

'Who will learn what, excuse me?'

'The surgeons and their antibiotic orders. I saw you cross out the order and I thought you must have been cursing them.'

She was shocked.

'Of course not, Muslims don't use profanity!'

I felt my face turn red. 'I'm really sorry, Fatimah, I didn't mean to offend you. I just thought, when I saw you crossing out the orders . . . '

Her eyes widened briefly and she bowed her head. 'Ah yes, I understand. You see, for those patients, I'm not changing the prescriptions from the surgeons. I am cancelling the antibiotic orders completely.'

'Why would you do that?' I asked, feeling like more of an idiot with every second.

'Because their lab results show that they have total antibiotic resistance. I am cancelling the colistin order. It is a difficult decision, because that's our last-line antibiotic.'

'What do you do then?'

She looked out the window and repeated the same phrase she'd been saying when I thought she was abusing her colleagues under her breath. Then she looked back at me.

'We pray.'

*

Before leaving Amman, Maarten and I met with Dr Hakeem, the Iraqi lead surgeon and project director. He'd been there from the very beginning, when MSF opened the Reconstructive Surgical Project 12 years earlier. His handshake was warm and he spoke with energy but his clothes were rumpled and his eyes were tired. He was desperate for MSF to speak out and flex its muscles on the issue. His message echoed that of Dr Laila, the WHO doctor we'd met back in Beirut.

'The problem is overuse,' he explained. 'Access to antibiotics is too easy here. There is very little rational prescribing and almost no restriction. Our patients have been exposed to these drugs again and again and again, before they even make it to our hospital. Even with the best surgery, we can't fight bacteria that are resistant to all of our drugs. What can we do? What can you do to help us?'

Maarten and I looked at each other and down at our notes.

I cleared my throat. 'Well, I work for the Access Campaign, which has always been about trying to improve access to essential medicines for patients who really need them. Maybe there's a way to use the Access Campaign's expertise to tackle this problem from the other way around. We could develop a campaign to try to improve the way we use the drugs we already have and protect them as a resource, rather than to increase supply and drive down cost, which is what we're usually trying to do. It's still ultimately about access, right?'

Maarten nodded thoughtfully.

Hakeem's weary eyes flickered into life. 'Yes, we harness the power of the Access Campaign! I like that idea,' he said. 'How do we do that?'

'I'd suggest we start by telling your stories,' I replied. 'You and your team are among the best examples MSF has of how to identify and manage the problem. You have the most experience and you know what works, so you represent the tip of the spear. What's happening with your patients and their totally drug-resistant infections is the worst-case scenario for the rest of MSF, and the rest of the world, if you think about it. Know what I mean?'

'I know exactly what you mean,' Hakeem said proudly. 'We have been doing this a long time now. We are, as you say, the "tip of the spear". After 12 years of fighting this fight, we should surely have the grounds to speak out.'

We shook hands. I told him I'd take the message back to Geneva and be in touch.

The following morning, Maarten flew out and Viri joined me in Jordan for a few days of R&R. We survived a flash flood on camel-back in the 'lost city' of Petra – an architectural treasure carved some two thousand years ago out of an orange- and rose-coloured canyon – and bobbed around for a few days in the super-dense Dead Sea. As we baked on the mountainside after one such surreal swim, I shared with Viri some stories of the patients we'd seen and the problems our colleagues were trying to deal with in this most complex of regions. I told her about our final conversation with Dr Hakeem and the idea we'd hatched about the Access Campaign becoming a voice for better use of antibiotics within MSF and beyond.

'You're a communications guru, what do you think?' I asked her. 'Does that even make sense?'

She thought about it for a few moments. 'It makes sense, but it sounds ambitious,' she said at last. 'Do you think your bosses will go for it?'

'I don't know,' I replied. 'I made a promise, though, so I'll have to try.'

Viri looked out across the sea with an enigmatic little smile and then lay back on the warm rocks. 'I'm sure you will.'

CHAPTER THIRTEEN

2019
Democratic Republic of the Congo

Three months later, I found myself heading deep into the beating heart of MSF: the 'Democratic' Republic of the Congo (DRC). The report that Maarten and I presented to the Antibiotic Resistance Taskforce about our findings in Jordan and Lebanon had been well received and it was agreed that these stories from the Middle East represented the unwanted endgame in the fight against drug-resistant infections. I'd also delivered Dr Hakeem's message and the proposal to use the Access Campaign to advocate for better use of antibiotics in MSF projects.

The idea was taken up enthusiastically by the Taskforce, but had been met with a rather more lukewarm reception by the Executive Director of my department. It was proving more difficult than I'd imagined to aim the Access Campaign's firepower in the direction of the critically important problem of how to use antibiotics more responsibly. The key obstacle I was encountering was the deeply entrenched belief that new antibiotics would be the miracle that would save us all from death by drug-resistant infections.

Now, new antibiotics are urgently needed, certainly, but there's one fat, filthy dead fly in the ointment of that idea: the pharmaceutical companies can't be arsed. From a commercial perspective, why would they bother? Developing a new antibiotic typically takes over a decade and upwards of a billion bucks, or so goes the claim. Then, even if it makes it to market, the whole point of an antibiotic is for it to be low-cost and taken for as short a period as possible. When the alternative is to invest in research and development of new drugs for cancer (that is, short-term but expensive therapies) or chronic conditions such as high blood pressure and cholesterol (that is, tablets that are cheaper but typically taken for many years), there's no doubt what appeals more to the shareholders of these insanely profitable companies. As a result, no new classes of antibiotics have been developed since the 1980s – not because it's necessarily *that* difficult, but because there are minimal financial incentives to do so. This was a long-term battle, into which the Access Campaign had already sent a small army of pharmacists, lawyers and regulatory experts, so I left them to it. I'd been directed by the Taskforce to identify other examples of problematic antibiotic use in MSF's projects, along with any potential solutions. A large, long-term, relatively stable project in north-east DRC had been selected as the next one to investigate, so with Mike's support, a fast-tracked humanitarian visa and a few weeks of intensive French tutoring behind me, I boarded a flight to Kinshasa, the notoriously chaotic capital of the country otherwise known as Congo-Kinshasa.*

After a few hours spent gazing out of the window as the snow-covered Alps flattened into the subtle colours of the vast Sahara, then slowly morphed into strikingly dense jungle, we bumped down onto the tarmac. I glanced around at my fellow passengers jostling against each other impatiently as we waited to disembark. Overweight women in brightly

---

* This is to distinguish the Democratic Republic of the Congo from its tiny neighbour across the Congo river – a country called Congo, whose capital is Brazzaville, and is hence known as Congo-Brazzaville. All the more confusingly, DRC is also commonly referred to simply as 'the Congo'. One can't help but think that those colonial administrators and early independence leaders could have had a little more imagination when it came to naming and saved us all a lot of bother.

patterned dresses, tottering unsteadily on their cheap heels in the narrow aisles; buttoned-up businessmen with glinting watches; flashy young fellows bedecked in designer jackets and redundant sunglasses; a middle-aged pair of missionaries clutching religious pamphlets and sporting leather bum-bags that anywhere in the world scream 'Rob me!'; and a handful of grungy development-worker types with dusty boots and over-stimulated livers (the latter not visible but safe to assume).

I got as far as the compulsory health check, between the immigration desk and baggage carousel, before I got shaken down. I proudly whipped out my vaccination record – the dog-eared yellow card that was as essential for me to travel as my passport – and was told my temperature was normal by the lady who zapped my forehead with an infrared thermometer. This was in the pre-Covid era, but the spectre of Ebola was everywhere. The same lady then stuck her hand out.

'Where's my money?'

I didn't know if it was a joke, a half-hearted but hopeful scam, or a legitimate demand for a real fee. I decided to call her bluff. I brazened it out, tried to turn on some scruffy charm, gave her a broad smile and strolled on through. I wasn't arrested, but I sensed this place would test the limits of my comfort zone.

DRC, like countless other countries in the world, isn't really a country at all. Lines on a map, hastily and mostly arbitrarily drawn by a bunch of rich white guys in the stampede that took place towards post-colonial independence, attempt to fence in hundreds of different cultural, ethnic and linguistic groups in one of the most diverse and combustible regions on Earth. The Algerian writer and philosopher Frantz Fanon described it neatly: 'Africa is shaped like a gun, and Congo is its trigger.'

The history of DRC is absurdly complicated. It stretches back some one hundred thousand years, with the first known kingdoms present from at least the fourteenth century. Its modern history features the infamously rapacious Belgian King Leopold II, who treated the region as his personal fiefdom throughout the nineteenth century. He employed the Welsh explorer Henry Morton Stanley (he of 'Dr Livingstone, I presume?' fame) to navigate the Congo river and locate potential hubs for transport and commerce. Leopold II then proceeded to extract maximum possible profit by enslaving the local population, ordering the killing of those whose daily rubber harvests were considered insufficient (and their hands to be hacked off as proof of their punishments), and exploiting the remainder of the region's natural resources as quickly as he could before anyone else noticed.

In a little over twenty years of remote rule – he never set a dainty royal foot in the Congo – Leopold II oversaw the massacre of some ten million Congolese. Among those who eventually paid attention were the authors Mark Twain and Joseph Conrad, the diplomat Roger Casement and a range of missionaries, whose collective writings condemned the bloodthirsty Belgian king and caused a moderate level of outrage among the Western gentry. The Belgian parliament, finally spurred into action, voted to take over control of the Congo Free State, generously compensating King Leopold II for his loss in the process. The Belgians then went on a half-century-long colonial development and construction spree before the first few Congolese educated within the Belgian system were able to organise and lead the country towards independence. Unfortunately, like many recent efforts in that direction, this did not go particularly well.

After observing the initial couple of feeble presidencies in the first five years of independence, a journalist and soldier by the name of Joseph-Désiré Mobutu seized power. Mobutu, who modestly awarded himself the title of 'The All-Powerful Warrior Who, Because Of His Endurance

And Inflexible Will To Win, Goes From Conquest To Conquest, Leaving Fire In His Wake', took up where Leopold II had left off. For the next 30 years, he siphoned the country's revenue directly into his own private palaces, planes, French chefs, top-shelf champagne, a fleet of Mercedes-Benzes and at least one leopard-skin hat. He stole a fortune estimated at five billion US dollars while the population of the country he was supposed to be leading fought, suffered and starved. The product of these decades of pillaging is a country of around one hundred million Congolese who have somehow learned to survive despite their governments. They are hard workers, hustlers and entrepreneurs. Their music is famous throughout the French-speaking world.

What the country is probably best known for in this century, though, sadly, is war. And Ebola. These double-barrelled humanitarian crises make DRC the most poker-hot of MSF's projects. All five of the organisation's European headquarters have projects there and it remains by far the most expensive country in terms of MSF's operational investments. Knowing all that, I was pretty bloody nervous. But I couldn't deny being a bit excited at the same time. This promised to be one of the most radical experiences of my career.

Up to my eyeballs in antimalarials and covered in a half-inch-thick layer of insect repellent, I spent the first few days in Kinshasa balancing my laptop on my knees and slapping mosquitoes on a wooden bench in a corner of the MSF country office. The Belgians, with history weighing rather heavily on their conscience, one might suspect, were MSF's lead operational centre in DRC. I strained through my initial briefings to understand the mix of French spoken by my Belgian, Congolese and Canadian colleagues, while poring laboriously over the internal reports on infectious disease burdens and antibiotic use. It seemed that, from the few samples MSF had managed to test in this deeply impoverished country, with its armed conflict, kleptocratic government and scarce laboratories, bacteria here were evidently developing resistance to antibiotics. Even in the most remote communities, there were increasing reports of antibiotic treatments failing and patients were losing faith in the medical system as a result. This meant that the traditional healers and ubiquitous roadside pharmacists were doing a roaring trade. Unfortunately, such improper use of antibiotics and widespread sale of fake medicines were only making the problem worse.

Jérôme, a friendly, hyperactive French logistician, turned up at the office, cracking jokes with the cleaning staff and giving high-fives to the drivers. As we slurped lukewarm instant coffee together on a crumbling stairway, seeking the welcome relief of the breeze, we realised we were staying in the same share-house that evening and heading to the same project the next day: Masisi. After a fitful, mosquito-bitten sleep, at 5am I woke to the sound of the MSF Land Cruiser beeping its horn from outside. On the road to the domestic airport, we peered through the smoke, the early morning mist and the *No Machine Guns* stickers on our windows at the tumbledown buildings and turgid river in the distance. We pulled up on the tarmac, fanned ourselves with our permission paperwork and sweated into our MSF vests while the no-frills Red Cross charter plane was fuelled for boarding.

Several hours, some soggy home-made sandwiches and three hops east across the country later, we bumped down in Goma. Even by the standards of a border town, Goma is extremely edgy. It sits between an active volcano – whose eruptions in recent decades have killed hundreds of people, displaced hundreds of thousands more and left black lava congealed around the city's streets – and a parasite-filled lake that is prone to exploding.* The surrounding mountains are home to a hundred different militia groups and a dwindling population of gorillas. It's the transit point for the Congolese and Rwandan armies as they periodically invade each other, and it was our final stopover en route to our destination.

After a night in the MSF safe house on the shores of Lake Kivu, Jérôme and I were joined by Ricardo, a genial Italian surgeon on the verge of retirement, as we piled into the Land Cruisers the next morning. We travelled in convoy, stopping off at a couple of local hospitals to pick up patients MSF had referred to Goma who had survived the experience and were ready to go home. Five ladies clutching tiny babies wrapped in colourful blankets shuffled up the bench seats in the back of the Land Cruiser next to me. They smilingly accepted my offer of torn bread smeared with ripe avocado. We munched on our breakfast as we sped along the dirt road, past boys pushing large, clunky wooden bicycles piled high with heavy loads, my travel companions nodding politely at my garbled attempts at conversation. It took almost eight hours for our convoy to haul itself the eighty kilometres up into the mountains, over the roughest roads I've ever seen. Our four-wheel drives were swallowed up to the windows in potholes, and river crossings were only possible because of the snorkel exhausts that popped up like periscopes at the front of the vehicles. The landscape changed as we ascended and I was startled to see black-and-white dairy cows grazing peacefully on green slopes at the cooler altitudes. It looked a lot like the hills around my hometown of Millaa

---

* The parasite is schistosomiasis – a flatworm whose larvae are released by freshwater snails and which can penetrate the skin and cause inflammation, bleeding, organ damage and infertility. The lake explosions – technically known as limnic eruptions, which are thankfully very rare but potentially exacerbated by the release of volcanic gas – are due to accumulation of carbon dioxide and methane in the water.

Millaa, although admittedly with more kids toting Kalashnikovs. With our tailbones aflame, we finally rolled in to Masisi.

Considered 'the jewel in the crown of MSF Belgium', as it was described to me in my briefings, *l'Hôpital général de référence* (HGR, or General Referral Hospital) in Masisi is one of the organisation's longest-term projects. MSF has supported the hospital and several smaller facilities in the area since 2007, during which period it has witnessed numerous attacks against the local populations, as the violence that erupted during the First and Second Congo Wars has blazed on. The surrounding area is now home to around a million 'internally displaced persons', or IDPs – one of those bland terms used in political and humanitarian discourse that completely fails to capture the tragedy of the people in question's plight.

With the physical peril and displacement come malnutrition, infectious diseases and sexual violence, much of which was being treated in the MSF-supported hospitals and clinics and much more of which rumbled on outside, unseen. The violence had occasionally crossed the threshold of the health facilities themselves, with militia storming in to haul patients out of their beds and off to meet extremely unpleasant fates, despite the agreements earnestly negotiated between MSF's project coordinators and the representatives of the various armed groups. I'd chosen to omit those details from my farewell phone call with Viri. I also thought it best not to mention the more alarming aspects of our orientation to the project in my WhatsApp message to her after we arrived.

We were given a short welcome briefing by Bart, the burly Belgian project coordinator, and were then handed over to Piotr, the lanky Polish logistics coordinator. Piotr handed out our radios and then led us through the compound, pointing out the dormitories, flimsy timber shower cubicles and communal kitchen–dining area.

'Now, the most important thing I need to show you,' he said, speaking over his shoulder as he descended a concrete staircase, 'is the bunker.'

That turned out to be the basement of the main building, protected by a single, stout, double-locked door. Inside were a pile of mattresses, a small toilet, a satellite telephone and several crates of water and tinned food.

'If you hear gunshots, you are to stop what you're doing immediately, come directly to the bunker and stay here until I tell you it's safe to leave. No exceptions, no excuses.' Piotr looked around with a frown that would make a grizzly bear mind its own business. 'Any questions?'

I had one and was willing to brave the scowl to find out.

'When was the last time you had to use the bunker?'

He squinted up at the concrete ceiling and scratched his stubble.

'Tuesday.'

*

We had a few lukewarm beers on the terrace by way of welcome on our first evening and I woke under the mosquito net in my small, thin-walled room the next morning fresh and ready for action. First item on the agenda was a meet-and-greet with the hospital's Medical Director, a jolly Congolese surgeon, following which Ricardo and I joined the rest of the hospital medical staff for their morning meeting. This consisted of a monotonous reporting by the head nurse of the previous night's action on the wards, then a rather more enthusiastic communal prayer. Ricardo then pottered off to the operating theatre and I finally found the person I'd been searching for: Dr Clémence, the hospital's Antibiotic Steward. She was short and smartly dressed, with a plaited weave and more make-up than I'd seen since boarding my flight back in Brussels. She was also, I quickly realised, a very sharp doctor indeed.

Since taking on the responsibility of being the hospital's antibiotic watchdog, Clémence had, mostly of her own initiative, developed a system for evaluating the appropriateness of antibiotic use. She would take a random sample of patient files from each of the hospital wards every month and compare those prescriptions to the official MSF guidelines. She had thus collected almost two years of data, including not only the proportion of antibiotic prescriptions that followed the guidelines, but categories of prescribing errors and patterns of inappropriate antibiotic use. She'd then gone even further, not only by presenting that information back to the hospital's medical staff and running tutorials on antibiotic stewardship using examples from their own cases, but by implementing the same system in a second, smaller hospital another 30 kilometres distant up in the mist.

I was seriously impressed. 'This is excellent work, Clémence,' I said, scrolling through her meticulously prepared spreadsheets in awe as we huddled in an unlit corner of the grotty medical ward. 'How did you come up with this system?'

'It just seemed like the right thing to do,' she replied with a bashful smile.

'It's brilliant. This is one of the main jobs I thought we would have to do together while I'm here, and it would have taken us weeks. You've saved us so much work! We need to use your system across all of MSF's projects. But I don't understand: why is this information not in any of the reports sent to headquarters?'

'No one has ever asked for it,' she shrugged.

What a champion, I thought, as I followed her off to do the ward round.

We went from bed to bed, reviewing each patient, their diagnosis and the medication chart. Most had antibiotics prescribed for something – if you didn't have an infection when you arrived, you'd almost certainly get one while you were there. I'm not one to cringe, but the place was a germophobe's nightmare. For all their great work on the antibiotic stewardship side of things, Masisi HGR had a long way to go with infection prevention and control (IPC). IPC, which ranges from basics such as hand hygiene and cleaning through to more complex processes such as sterilisation of instruments, is one of the three main strategies to attack drug-resistant infections, along with stewardship and improved diagnostic capacity, and this hospital looked like a bacteria breeding factory.

Skinny lads with amputated limbs lolled in filthy beds, their wounds soaking up bugs like sponges. Tiny babies with meningitis were developing pneumonia by the minute. It was a wonder the staff survived each day at work with their immune systems intact. These folks were about as robust as you can get, but I could see the difference that even some small improvements in hygiene practices would make, along with some judicious use of bleach. *That would give me something useful to do while I'm here*, I pondered, now that Clémence had radically rejigged my agenda thanks to her wonderful stewardship work.

We finished our antibiotic ward round and I headed back up to the common room to find some lunch. As I sauntered up the stairs, I heard someone urgently calling my name. Piotr was beckoning me to follow him as he jogged over to the main office. I hustled over behind him to find a large group of people gathered around the Land Cruisers. There was a loud screech and I turned to see Bart striding into the middle of the crowd with a megaphone.

'Friends, colleagues, I have some very difficult news. This morning, on their way to deliver supplies to the maternal and child health clinic, two of our drivers were ambushed and kidnapped. One of them was able to make a quick radio call before they were taken. At this stage we do not know where they are, how they are or whether they are still alive.'

What the fuck? Had I understood Bart's French correctly? Ambushed? Kidnapped?

Alarm swelled through the crowd, with questions shouted out in multiple languages.

Bart raised his hand in a plea for calm. 'Of course, we are doing everything we can to get them back. Piotr and I will be in non-stop contact with Kinshasa, Brussels and the armed party or parties until this is resolved. Until then, our beloved Masisi project goes into emergency mode. That means all non-essential activities are suspended and all non-essential staff will be evacuated. You must go to your rooms and pack your bags immediately. The convoy leaves for Goma in an hour.'

My heart rate doubled. This was serious shit.

I knew my role was distinctly non-essential, so I hurried to my quarters and repacked what I'd just unpacked the night before. I rushed back to the hospital to find Clémence. I apologised for having to leave so suddenly, begged her to keep up the terrific stewardship work and promised I'd be in touch again when I could. Then I made one of the strangest and scariest phone calls of my life.

'Baby, it's me. Can you hear me?' I tried to sound relaxed.

Viri's digitally distorted voice came faintly through on WhatsApp. 'Yes, I can hear you, but you sound stressed. Are you okay?'

'Listen, please don't worry, but there's been a security incident and the project is being suspended. Most of us are being evacuated, including me.'

'You mean right now?' She sounded scared.

'Right now. We leave in less than an hour.'

'Where will you go? Will you be safe?'

'We're going to the safe house in Goma. We should be okay there.'

'And then what? Will you have to go back?'

'I don't know, sweetheart. I'll let you know. I have to go now. I love you.'

Poor Viri. The shit I put her through. *It can't be easy to be with me*, I reflected ruefully, as I scrambled back up the stairs, stuffed my backpack on the pile in one of the Land Cruisers and squeezed in behind it. Ricardo clambered up behind me looking terrified and Jérôme bounced in behind him, his eyes alight.

'Exciting, isn't it?' Jérôme said, jiggling his knees. 'Been a while since the last time I was evacuated.'

The journey back down to Goma was quicker, but no less bumpy. We fretted and speculated as we jolted and lurched. Anxiety was in the air. As the conversation spiralled and the temperature rose, Ricardo reached over and opened a window.

'Shall we sing a little together?' he suggested.

Ricardo, it turned out, was a classically trained opera singer, so he had us over a barrel, but his rich, deep voice calmed our collectively jangled nerves. Our spirits lifted as we caterwauled our way down the mountain. The lights of the MSF compound in Goma were a welcome sight as the security guards rolled open the spiked iron gates. Derek, the safe house manager, was well prepared.

'I know you've all had a rough day,' Derek said as he helped unload the trucks. 'We'll debrief tomorrow and I'll update you on what's happening back in Masisi. For now, just find a bed in the dorms, grab a drink and chill out.'

The communal fridge was packed with cold beers and a dozen large pizzas arrived minutes later. Within a couple of hours, we were all rugby-league drunk. Adrenaline definitely works up a thirst. Jérôme and I took our beers out to the balcony to admire the glow from the volcano across the lake. We sat perched precariously beyond the railing, our legs dangling in the breeze over the water.

'Cigarette?' he offered.

'Sure,' I said. 'Thanks.' I don't usually smoke. But again – adrenaline.

As he sucked with pleasure and I nearly coughed myself off the ledge, we spoke of home. Jérôme was from a small village in France on the opposite side of the lake from Geneva. We were basically neighbours.

'When do you think they'll send us home?' I asked.

Jérôme was several years younger than me but already a veteran of six MSF missions. He exhaled slowly.

'I don't want to go home, man,' he said. 'There's nothing for me there. I love my family, but I live for this shit. I was looking forward to this mission. I hope in a few days we can get back to Masisi.'

I grunted, took another quick pull of my cigarette, spluttered again and flicked it away with disgust into the darkness. 'Not me. I think this is a sign. I gotta get home. My fiancée will be worried out of her mind.'

'Fair enough,' he said. 'A toast, then: to getting where we need to go.'

We clinked our bottles, took a long swig and stumbled off to find our beds.

The next day, we gathered with our hangovers on wooden benches in the garden. As we smacked at the mosquitoes, Derek read out the situation report. Contact had been made with the kidnappers and the drivers were confirmed to be alive. Negotiations were underway for their release. In the meantime, the project would remain suspended.

The MSF head honchos in Kinshasa and Brussels were confident that the local population in Masisi was strongly supportive of MSF's presence there, so the word was being spread about what had happened. The reputation of the militia group who'd carried out the kidnapping would likely suffer as a result, the theory went. As these ragtag but still very dangerous groups depended on some level of local political support, this would be a small but significant outcome.

Derek then read out a list of names. 'Alice, Françoise, Guillaume, Khaled, Lachie, Paul and Thomas – we're booking a Red Cross charter flight back to Kinshasa for you on Monday. You'll have to wait here for a few days until then. The rest of you will stay until the Masisi project reopens. The Wi-Fi is shitty but we have books and beers and views of the lake. Relax, be patient, take care of each other and catch up on some sleep. Wherever you're going, you have long journeys ahead.'

I caught Jérôme's eye. He winked.

Switzerland

I made it back to Geneva several days later, presumably with one hand on the MSF trophy for Shortest Field Mission Ever. Nevertheless, despite the brevity of my visit, I felt I was returning with a valuable prize. Clémence's antibiotic evaluation system was so similar to the 'best practice' models used in developed countries, yet so simple in its effectiveness, I was sure it would be something we could adopt across MSF's projects. I'd also received word from the gang back in Goma that the two kidnapped drivers had been released. They were physically unharmed, but had been forced to walk from the militia's mountain redoubt through the bush for two days to safety. Under the circumstances, I should have been relieved to be home. And I was. But I also felt strange. Unsettled. Wary. Even a little hostile – not only towards myself but almost everyone around me.

I was reluctant to admit it, even to myself, but the DRC experience had me rattled. Kinshasa was a perilous abyss of a city that threatened to swallow you up the minute you let your guard down and Goma was a border town that made Tijuana look like Disneyland. The day before my Red Cross flight out, I'd been robbed, in broad daylight, just outside the gates of the safe house. I caught the teenage thief with his hand in my pocket and he glared back at me with a sullen confidence that said he held the aces. The onlookers in the street, I sensed, had his back. I shouted at him and scurried the few metres back inside the compound, shaken, to find my emergency wallet gone. The fact that our drivers had been ambushed just two kilometres from our hospital by thugs with AK-47s, then held captive for days while negotiations took place with MSF headquarters via radio, was a frightening one. Inevitable questions arose. What if I'd been in that vehicle? How would I react in that situation? What if the negotiations hadn't been concluded to the kidnappers' satisfaction?

Stuck in the safe house together for those few days, treading water nervously, our group had opened up and got to know each other. With little else to do and in need of distraction, we told each other stories. We spoke of our partners, families, dreams and fears. It was an intense, intimate environment. I shared things with my colleagues there that some of my best friends didn't know about me. In a bizarre way, it was hard to leave that safe house. I kept thinking about Jérôme, Ricardo, Piotr, Bart and the rest long after I departed. I missed them, somehow, and admired their apparent fearlessness in the face of such obvious danger. I had so much respect for that world and the people who worked in it that I felt guilty to have left, escaping back to the safe sterility of the Geneva bubble. As I took a long, hot shower and unpacked my bag, waiting for Viri to get home from work, I knew I'd have a hard time explaining to her what had happened.

It was weird. From the moment she walked in the door, it was weird.

Our much-anticipated reunion was cool and cautious, rather than warm and joyful. She was glad I was home and I was safe, but she knew immediately that there were things I wasn't telling her. I simply didn't know how. Partly to protect her from the trauma of my experience and partly to avoid having to relive it myself, I turned inwards instead. I was moody and irritable. I slept in the spare room for a few days, claiming jetlag. Viri raised an eyebrow – she knew exactly where DRC was on a map and the fact that there was a grand total of one hour's time difference – but she let me be. She worried, while I brooded. I'd felt symptoms of depression niggling at me again in the weeks leading up to my departure for DRC, but I hadn't mentioned it to Viri. I didn't want to make her anxious. It felt like we'd not long recovered from my last meltdown and I didn't want to believe it could happen again so soon, when the wounds were still so raw. But she could see what was happening to me now and it made her anxious anyway; probably more so than if I'd been able to explain.

I tried the usual things, including venturing out for a jog or two to get the mojo flowing, but it didn't work. I'd mangled the meniscus in my knee the previous year in a canyoning incident, followed by a botched repair by an over-confident Swiss surgeon, so I was physically broken as well as psychologically and emotionally. I was, to be frank, fucked.

As we sat glumly together at the kitchen table one morning, Viri reached across to take my hand.

'I don't know what's going on with you, but I will do whatever I can to help.'

'Thanks,' I said, not looking up.

She withdrew her hand. 'That's if you want me to. If you want . . . me.'

I nodded, staring down at my cold breakfast.

'Lachie, I need to know. Do you still want me? Do you still want this?'

'I don't know.'

One of the shittiest things about depression is how it clouds your thinking. Most of us rely on our brains to provide us with the essential combination of reason and instinct to make the decisions to get us through every day. When I found myself doubting my own decision-making ability and not trusting my own judgement, I felt cognitively adrift. I loved Viri, but did I want to be with her? Of course I did, she was my soul mate. Or was she? She wasn't the problem; I was the problem. Or was it her? I needed her. But maybe I'd feel better by myself. Maybe I'd feel better by not feeling anything at all.

I'd updated my 'suicidal ideation' (the banal medical term for it) from the brutality of a car crash to the tranquillity of a long, solo scuba dive. Nitrogen narcosis – the feeling of being drunk or high that you get when you spend long enough below – seemed like the way to go. Just suck in the bubbles and sink down into the deep. I had all the gear, and the lake was right there . . .

'Lachie!' Viri's heart-wrenching sob broke my dark reverie.

I looked up. She was desperate, defiant, holding back tears.

'You have to get your head together.'

*

I sent an SOS text to Lou, my psychologist back in Australia. He listened sympathetically as I poured out my story to him via Skype.

'Geez, mate, that's wild,' he said, shaking his head. 'No wonder you're feeling fucked. You've probably got more than a touch of PTSD, you poor bastard. Are you having any thoughts of self-harm or suicide?'

I silently bowed my head, unable to look him in the eye.

He sighed. 'You need to talk to me, Lachlan. I'm trying to do a risk assessment here. How can I be assured you're not going to run off and top yourself? It's a pretty long way from here to Switzerland, but if I think you need to be committed to hospital you know I'll find a way to fucking do it!'

I snorted a half-laugh. Lou was smart. He knew how he needed to speak to me.

'Do you have a GP or a psychologist there in Switzerland?' he asked.

'Nope,' I said. 'Can't afford it.'

'What about MSF? Shouldn't they be paying for you to see someone?'

'I haven't told them. Don't want anyone to know. Can't risk losing my job.'

He puffed out his cheeks and let out a slow breath. 'Well, if that's not a catch-22 then I don't know what is,' he said. 'You're a medical professional, working for a medical organisation, and you need medical assistance, but you say you can't afford it and don't want to ask for it anyway because you're worried that would mean you'd lose your job. That is some seriously back-to-front, through-the-looking-glass bullshit.'

I shrugged. 'I might be wrong about MSF. Maybe they'd be supportive. I just don't know. I know I'm definitely being paranoid – it's pretty much my default state these days – but I just want to keep this between you and me for now.'

'What about Viri?' he asked. 'Are you able to talk to her?'

'She wants me to, and I'm trying, but I just don't know what to say. I don't have words for how I'm feeling.' I felt the warm sting of tears.

'Hmm,' he said, and paused for a long moment. 'Look, I wouldn't normally be suggesting something like this, but I'm really wondering if you should reach out to Francesca again.'

It took a few seconds for that to make sense. 'You mean you think I should go on another ayahuasca retreat?'

He leaned forward. Through his glasses and our two screens, his grey eyes fixed me with their gaze. 'I want to be clear about the fact that this is not a formal recommendation. As you know, I am unable to do that, particularly under the circumstances,' he said, gesturing at his laptop. 'But I saw how that last ayahuasca experience got your engines fired up again. The evidence is pretty compelling regarding its short-term use for depression and PTSD. I think there's at least a fair chance that it might have a beneficial effect on you now. It's up to you. But you need to do something, and it seems like it's going to have to be that, antidepressants or hospitalisation.'

Shit. 'I'll think about it.'

'Okay, but I expect you to be in touch with an update in the next twenty-four hours. I'll give your GP here a call and I'm going to send an email to Francesca. That's her name, right? The clinical psychologist you mentioned led the sessions over there? She needs to have the heads-up about you. Consider it a referral.'

*

Francesca welcomed me back with a sisterly hug. It was a different shaman this time. Nico's weedy but powerful presence was replaced by Manuel, a gentle Spaniard who projected the same aura of quiet strength and other-worldly wisdom. I was better prepared, forsaking the pretentiousness of white linen for the warm comfort of an old hoodie and my Ugg boots. I supplemented the thin foam mat with my inflatable camp mattress and a second pillow and settled back to let my nostrils absorb the wild tobacco inhalation and my gut the bitter witches' brew. I understood by now why the optimal strategy was to bring an 'intention' to the journey. This allows the idea to simmer in the subconscious until it is flambéed by the Amazonian potion. This time I intended, then, to raise the stakes and present *Madre* with my existential dilemma: I would try to find both the will and the way to keep on living. It was a tall order, so I planned to ease into it gently, not expecting too much by way of answers up front.

Naïve of me.

When the shamanic magic kicked in and I was hurled into space, the first thing I was confronted with was a vivid scene of me standing on the front doorstep of our house. Viri was backing out of the driveway in her little white Fiat, her glasses and winter jacket on, looking desolate. She slowed, turned towards me and gave me a sad wave that I suddenly realised was a final goodbye. She was leaving. For ever. Then she drove away and was gone.

I knew I was witnessing our future. It was no future. We were to become nothing. I was crushed. The sadness that welled up inside me was overwhelming, catastrophic. I grabbed my bucket and vomited, violently and repeatedly. I don't know how long later – maybe five minutes, maybe an hour – I slumped back, wrung out and empty. I curled up, shuddering, in my sleeping bag, trying to process the pain that flooded my body from the loss.

I passed out.

When I regained consciousness, I was met with another revelation. Not a vision this time, but an insight. The cosmic kick in the balls that *Madre* had just given me was not to show me my future, but my alternative reality. The scene I'd witnessed of Viri leaving me wasn't inevitable; it was what awaited if I didn't get my shit together. I had a choice.

I chose love. I chose life.

Sabotaging the relationship with Viri would be idiocy and killing myself surely wouldn't be the wisest thing to do either. Once again, the biochemical cattle prod had come to the rescue, zapping me awake and saving me from myself.

I hobbled through a field in the mountain sun the next morning and phoned Viri to tell her I loved her, I was feeling better and I'd be home for dinner.

I had work to do.

*

My medicinal voyage had taught me that I needed to take control of the driving forces behind my depression. It wasn't just the trauma from the DRC experience that was messing with my head. That was just the top block in a game of Stress Jenga, the lower, rickety layers of which consisted of money problems, frustrations with the Access Campaign and a sense of lost opportunity with both my clinical role and Rocketship. The tension between Viri and me was a symptom, I realised, not a cause. My resolve to deal with these issues definitively led me to understand that they were impossible to disentangle. Each affected the other, so I had to address them all.

Number one on the list: I was bankrupt. My attempt to continue meeting all my financial commitments on my reduced income and with the increased cost of living in Switzerland had led, inexorably, to insolvency. I had banks in two countries threatening legal action over my unpaid mortgage in Vanuatu and I had received a 'Letter of Pursuit' from the Swiss police for failing to pay the obligatory health insurance premiums. My full-time MSF job meant I was having to use my vacation days or take leave without pay to do the occasional week or two of rural hospital work back in Australia. However, the extra money that brought in wasn't enough to cover my debts, nor would those short bursts of clinical work be sufficient over the long term to keep my clinical registration current and maintain my procedural skills at the necessary level. Two years had passed since I'd been able to send money to Nixon to pay for the Bene children's school fees, and even that I'd had to borrow. I was so strapped for cash I'd resorted to shoplifting at the supermarket to get groceries. Unpayable fines and/or prison beckoned.

I'd also hit a wall in my role at the Access Campaign. The messages I'd brought back from the Middle East and DRC about how to protect antibiotics and improve their use in MSF projects had still not gained any real traction. The ideas I was pitching for new projects and campaigns were getting rejected and I felt like I was wasting my time. The advocacy work in which the Access Campaign was engaged on antimicrobial resistance was at an ultra-high level. I'd attend meetings at WHO Headquarters that would drag on for days, as countries debated their respective rights and responsibilities when it came to preserving antibiotics for human use, as opposed to their widespread application in agriculture and livestock industries. The right to economic development was a difficult one to argue against, but at what price for human and environmental health? Technological solutions were possible, in theory, all agreed, but who should foot the bill? I felt the familiar, cynical echoes of the climate change debates.

Meanwhile, on the other side of the globe, despite my patchy leadership, Rocketship was going from strength to strength. We'd launched the new training programme in Tonga, with four doctors now on track to become the kingdom's first family medicine specialists, studying towards their diplomas while remaining living and working in their own country, supported by remote mentorship and regular clinical teaching visits by our Rocketship Trainer Team. The model was working well. The programme partners were happy, the donors were showing off the results and Rocketship was becoming the go-to organisation for primary healthcare systems support in the Pacific region. We'd been offered a new contract in Solomon Islands to help them set up a rural medical training programme and had even got back into bed with the ever-fickle Ministry of Health in Vanuatu, after they'd requested crisis support during a period of extreme medical workforce shortage. We had some modest funds thrown at us, sufficient to send a dozen rural generalists to work in Vila Central and Northern Provincial Hospitals over a period of six months. During that time, we extended the programme to include support for the Cuban-trained junior doctors who were finishing their internships and being despatched to the outer-island facilities, most of them alone, to sink or swim. Our volunteers, all experienced medical educators, were shunted around the islands on six-seater planes and aluminium dinghies to track down the junior docs, spend some time with them, evaluate their progress, do some on-site teaching and reassure them that someone senior actually gave a shit about them.

I felt sorry to be missing out on that action and regretted not being able to contribute more. The organisation that my buddies and I had dreamed up and sweated blood to build was finally taking off and I was a mere witness, waving impotently, from a distance.

I came to the long-overdue conclusion that, my deeply held generalist principles notwithstanding, I couldn't do it all, and certainly not all at once. I needed to prioritise. Prioritise my relationship, prioritise my mental health and prioritise how I spent my days.

EPILOGUE

Switzerland

I met with Mike and gave him my letter of resignation. He was sympathetic and discreet about my reasons. I regretted not being more open with him when I was deep in strife, as I realised he probably would have done whatever he could to support me. But it was too late now.

My first priority was to haul myself out of debt, once and for all. Having finally sold, at an eye-watering loss, the house back in Vanuatu, I had nothing left to sell but my time, energy and sweat. I cast myself out into the wilderness of the gig economy. I juggled multiple short-term contracts from Geneva, interviewing experts and writing reports on Ebola vaccine developments by day and chain-drinking coffees to get through videoconferences with the Australian government about Pacific health funding by night. I barely left the house. But that didn't mean I was really there. When I was in Geneva I was consumed by work and I would leave for long periods to do rural hospital locums back in Australia.

Viri had graciously accepted my decision to quit MSF, choosing not to poke holes in my flimsy plan and make a big deal out of small details, like the fact that I needed a Swiss work permit to stay in the country. She trusted my judgement and believed in my commitment to getting us out of the predicament I'd put us in. But as the months dragged by, and my promises of being away for 'just a couple of weeks this time' were broken again and again, her confidence in me started to slip.

Even worse, I could tell she wasn't happy. She was working her backside off as well, doing her best to contribute to righting our financial ship and keep up with the increasing demands of her global communications role. Once again, we found ourselves drifting apart. We were often in different time zones, not really aware of what the other one was doing and finding it increasingly difficult to pin each other down over the phone.

The difference now was that I felt psychologically strong. I wasn't depressed; I was determined. I could clearly see the goal and I was single-mindedly, teeth-grittedly churning through the days, nights and ED shifts to get there. I was sure this was a short-term situation and the time apart would be worth it in the end. To be free of debt and able to start building a real future with Viri was my sole objective.

In the process, though, I lost sight of the bigger picture.

Viri needed me. She needed me to be present. She saw the mission creep of the work-related travel and felt like our relationship was becoming a long-distance one. It didn't occur to me that she would have gladly lived on rice and pasta for months on end, just to have me home more. She knew the value of cuddling in bed, making each other breakfast and spending evenings and weekends together, whereas I'd become obsessed with using every opportunity to fill in the debt hole that I'd dug. The pressure was building up for her. She was anxious, stressed, not sleeping, suffering.

I should have seen it coming.

Australia

She called me from Morocco, where her company was holding its annual corporate bash. I was on the other side of the world, hammering out another month of non-stop shifts in a rural hospital back in Australia.

'How's the conference going?' I asked.

'It's fine,' she said. 'Busy.'

'You sound distracted.'

'I am. It's crazy here. I'm in charge of all the digital communications and no one here seems to know how to download an app onto their phone. I'm getting hassled non-stop.'

'I'm sorry.'

Silence.

Was she working while on the phone to me? Was she pissed off?

'I've been offered another short-term consultancy job,' I said.

'Where?'

'Somalia.'

'How long?'

'The job is for two weeks. But I have to go two weeks earlier for security training.'

Silence.

'Are you okay?' I asked, as gently as I could.

Fireworks.

'No, Lachie, I'm not fucking okay! I don't have time to eat, I don't have time to sleep, I can't do any exercise, I feel like shit and I haven't seen you in months. I'm not okay, okay?'

Silence.

'Well, it's really important that you eat, sleep and exercise,' I said at last, lamely.

'I know. I have to go. We can try and talk again tomorrow. Take care, Lachie.'

She hung up.

She never called me by my first name when things were fine. And 'Take care'? That wasn't good.

I felt sorry for her, but I was frustrated too. Could she not see that I was doing everything in my power to get us back on track? Couldn't she at least be a little grateful for the sacrifices I was making? Reflecting on that, as my bitterness subsided, I realised we simply didn't see our priorities in the same way. I'd assumed she shared my resolve to get our finances sorted as quickly as possible. Instead, she saw me turning into someone motivated only by money. It was getting ugly. There had to be some middle ground. I had to find a way to drag us out of debt, but at the same time be home more and able to contribute to the relationship in other ways, not just by paying the bills.

I found myself back in Innisfail, the tropical cane-farming town where my sister and I had attended high school and Dad had been the principal of the special school. I was rostered on for as many shifts as I could get, dividing my time between the ED, the general ward and the operating theatre. I was working hard but quite enjoying the occasional encounter with an old high-school buddy in the local coffee shop or supermarket. We chuckled about how we were all grown up now, with more weight around the middle and less hair on top, and they proudly showed me photos of their partners, kids and farms. I could see how easy it would be for me to slot into a rural hospital job and a relatively comfortable life back in Australia, where there are plenty of health needs and doctors are very well paid. But I doubted that would be enough for me. Australia has lots of problems, and people who are poor, Indigenous and live in rural areas across the country shoulder far more than their fair share of the burden of illness and injury. Yet, elsewhere in the world, there is even more suffering, even greater injustice and even less access to medical care. By now, I'd learned enough about myself to know that I needed to find a balance between clinical medicine and public health: interesting, stimulating work that kept me on my toes and pushed me to the limits of my skill and comfort zone. The heartburn-inducing dilemma I had was just how the hell I could possibly do all that together, while staying sane and building a life with Viri.

It was late at night.

My mind drifted, freed from the tension of Innisfail's ever-busy ED. The ceiling fan squeaked overhead as I sprawled shirtless, laptop open, on the stained couch in the rickety timber duplex by the river that was the locum doctor's accommodation. I wasn't searching for anything in particular. I aimlessly landed on the homepage of the Australian College of Rural and Remote Medicine, checked to see that my information was up to date and glanced at the 'Jobs Board' at the bottom.

Virtual Rural Generalist Service.

The four words burned into my retinas for a few seconds, my mind refusing to believe they could be real. Then I read the position description. A new system had been set up to provide round-the-clock medical care to the thirty-something health facilities in western New South Wales where there were too few doctors for the population of close to a quarter of a million, scattered around a frequently drought-stricken region the size of Germany. The work was to be conducted via videoconference, with a requirement that each team member also spend a quarter of their total shifts on the ground, in the rural hospitals across the district. A team of experienced rural generalists was being assembled to be the guinea pigs for the service, which would be the first of its kind in the country. It would be a revolution in medical care for rural communities.

I scanned the application information.

Enquiries to Dr Ryan Hamilton, Director of Rural Medical Services.

I knew that guy! Ryan was a young gun, already well known and widely respected within rural generalist circles in Australia. I'd noticed him coming up behind me while I was training. He'd made waves from an early stage, showing an unusual aptitude for networking and technology, involving himself in a variety of organisations and projects. I was also sure I remembered hearing over beers that the bloke was a professional athlete – an endurance horse-rider who'd narrowly missed out on winning a multi-day race across Mongolia because he'd suffered the inconvenience of falling off and breaking his neck.

I had his number.

'Ryan, it's Lachie. I'm calling about this new service you're setting up. Looks really impressive!'

'Thanks, mate, yeah, we're pretty excited about it. You interested?'

'Honestly, it looks perfect. I'm fucking desperate for some clinical work that would enable me to be home more. I just have one little problem.'

'Oh yeah? What's that?'

'I live in Switzerland.'

He laughed. My heart sank.

'Wouldn't work, hey? Ah well, thought I'd ask anyway.'

'No mate, sorry, bit of a misunderstanding there,' he said. 'I was having a laugh 'cos I was thinking it could actually work really well. Someone's gotta do the night shifts, right?'

The Virtual Rural Generalist Service saved my clinical career, and quite possibly my relationship. I was finally able to work as a rural generalist in Australia, from Switzerland, thanks to the miracle of digital technology. With two laptops set up on my desk, I would spend my shifts being beamed in via video camera to the Emergency Departments of dozens of little rural hospitals in the farming and mining towns scattered across the wide, brown lands on the other side of the world. Through the screen, talking to the patients, with the nurses at the other end acting as my hands, I would treat everything from coughs and migraines to trauma, strokes and cardiac arrests.

It was a bizarre, thrilling experience. Obviously a virtual doctor cannot replace one physically present, and it was frustrating not to be able to reach through the camera to peer into the ears, stitch up the wounds or insert the tubes that many patients needed, but a virtual doctor was certainly better than no doctor at all. I was still working 80-hour weeks, but at least I could be with Viri and didn't need to disappear for months at a time just to pay the rent. After a year of almost constant travel and work, I finally got my head above water and the banks off my back. I even managed to restart paying the Bene children's school fees and escaped from the shadowy threats of insolvency and incarceration.

Viri was delighted, and more than a little relieved.

It was just in the nick of time. The Virtual Rural Generalist Service had only recently been established when the Covid pandemic hit. Telemedicine went from being a useful but peripheral service to being central and essential to providing safe, sustainable care to patients when hospitals were overflowing, clinics were shut and frontline health workers were stretched beyond any conceivable limits. Our new service was suddenly in the spotlight as health facilities all around Australia scrambled to figure out how to keep their doors open.

I pushed grimly through my shifts, horrified at the sight of patients gasping for breath at the other end of my camera and humbled by the commitment and professionalism of the nurses at the bedside, doing their absolute best in these tiny outback hospitals where no doctors seemed willing to work for love nor money. More than ever, I felt profoundly guilty about not being on the ground, in the action, sweating into my personal protective equipment in the ED, or at least contributing to the public health response. I was torn. I'd been trained for this. The world was burning and I was skulking at home behind a computer screen. Part of my brain was screaming at me: *Get out there, you fucking coward!* Another part whispered seductively: *Stay right where you are, safely out of harm's way.*

Then I got a call from Martha, a colleague from the tropical medicine team at MSF's Operational Centre in Geneva.

'What are you up to these days?' she asked innocently.

I was cautious, but I couldn't deny I was curious too. We weren't close enough to warrant a purely social call. 'This and that. Why do you ask?'

She explained how, since the start of the pandemic, many of MSF's projects had been in states of suspended animation. With Covid spreading its invisible, deadly tentacles across the world, MSF staff couldn't travel, patients couldn't access healthcare and vaccines were barely available in many countries where the organisation worked. There were already signs of diseases like malaria surging due to the reallocation of scarce resources to try and stem the tide of coronavirus. The evidence pointed to this pandemic being caused by a virus spilling over from animals to humans, as has been the case for most pandemics, and there was growing recognition that much more needed to be done to address the root causes of such crises.

To that end, MSF Operational Centre Geneva had adopted 'planetary health' as their new strategic priority. The aim, Martha explained, was to improve MSF's understanding of the health impacts of the interactions between humans, animals and the environment, in order to be better informed and equipped to respond to future emergencies.

I listened, nodding along and gazing out of the window as she spoke.

'Pretty ambitious,' I commented drily. 'I'm glad to hear it, though. Sounds like things are moving in the right direction. Anyway, it's good to hear from you. Thanks for the call. Let's grab a beer some day when this pandemic shit settles down.'

'Wait, Lachie, don't hang up, I haven't finished. We've got this position I wanted to chat to you about. Tropical Diseases and Planetary Health Advisor. New role. Clean slate. Help us figure out how to find a way out of this mess. What do you think? Would you be up for it?'

Fuck me.

ACKNOWLEDGEMENTS

Viri, for bringing joy and meaning to my life.

Ma and Bob, for a lifetime of love and support.

Stephen Carver, for teaching me how to write a book.

Tim Flannery, Damien Brown and Aaron Smith, for inspiring adventures and literary advice.

The Geneva Writers' Group, for making me feel like a writer, and The Literary Consultancy in London, for treating me like one.

Lucy Morris and Tara Wynne at Curtis Brown, for being outstanding agents, and Claudia Connal at Octopus and Robert Watkins at Ultimo, for being such insightful editors.

Tony McMichael, Steve Iddings, Diarmid Campbell-Lendrum and Greg Elder, for taking a chance on me and enabling me to 'learn by doing'.

Sam Jones, Pat Giddings, David Campbell, Bonnie Ward, Dan Manahan, Brooke Fallon, Brett Cowling, Jill Benson, Brett Dale, Lisiate 'Ulufonua and all of our Rocketeers, for sharing the Rocketship vision and joining the wild ride.

All my treasured medical mates who've been part of the adventure but are not mentioned in this book (mostly for their own protection): Ash, Blackers, Brooksy, H-bomb, Mikey, PD, Penoir, Schuller, Skip, Tank, WD40 and all the rest, you know who you are.

A NOTE ON FLYING

As an environmental activist and, if I may be permitted a moment of immodesty, something of an 'expert' in the field of climate change and health, I am very aware that it doesn't look good – nor is it good for the planet – that I travel so often by air.

I have grappled with this dilemma a great deal over the years.

I have questioned how I can be more disciplined in limiting my personal carbon emissions while still providing care for my patients in rural and remote areas and counsel for the governments of other countries who request my advice. I have come to the imperfect conclusion that, in order to be most effective in my roles as a rural generalist and public health physician, some travel is inevitable. Digital technology is fast evolving, but for most of my career, I have needed to be physically present with the patients I am treating, and see with my own eyes the problems I am being asked to help address.

I feel I can, to some extent, justify the harmful impact of my carbon emissions by pointing to the positive impacts of my work. However, I acknowledge that this is hypocritical, at least in part, especially when I am so outspoken about the weak governance and flawed political leadership that has hitherto limited the essential, drastic action required to combat global heating.

It is but a token assurance, but I do pay to offset all my flights, work-related or not, and I travel by train or other forms of public transport whenever feasible.

We each have to take personal responsibility for our actions and make our own decisions about this issue. I believe the best we can do is make those decisions in the most informed, honest and conscious way we can. I hope to be able to continue making constructive contributions to the ongoing debate about how we can together resuscitate our dying planet.

FURTHER READING

There are many excellent publications to which readers may wish to refer for further information on topics included in this book, such as the health impacts of climate change, antimicrobial resistance and the role of psychedelics in clinical therapy. It would be impossible to provide an accurate and up-to-date list of the best references, but I offer below some suggestions of non-fiction books and scientific articles as potential starting points for those who would like to know more. A complete list of the research papers and textbooks that I have written and co-authored is available via my website: www.drlachlanmciver.com.

Climate change and health

Books

Epstein, P and Feber, D. *Changing Planet, Changing Health*. University of California Press, 2011.

McMichael, A J, Campbell-Lendrum, D H, Corvalan, C F, Ebi, E L, Githeko, A, Scherega, J D and Woodard, A (eds). *Climate Change and Human Health*. World Health Organization, 2003.

Articles

Hanna, E and McIver, L. 'Climate change: a brief overview of the science and health impacts for Australia'. *Medical Journal of Australia* 208(7) (2018): 1–5; DOI: 10.5694/mja17.00640.

McIver, L, Kim, R, Woodward, A, et al. 'Health impacts of climate change in Pacific island countries: a regional assessment of vulnerabilities and adaptation priorities'. *Environmental Health Perspectives* 124 (2015): 1707–14.

Watts, N, Amann, M, Arnell, N, et al. 'The 2020 report of The Lancet Countdown on health and climate change: responding to converging crises'. *Lancet* 397 (2021): 129–70.

Antimicrobial resistance

Books

Blaser, M. *Missing Microbes: How the Overuse of Antibiotics Is Fueling Our Modern Plagues*. Picador, 2015.

McCarthy, M. *Superbugs: The Race to Stop an Epidemic*. Avery, 2019.

Articles

Marston, H D, Dixon, D M, Knisely, J M, et al. 'Antimicrobial resistance'. *Journal of the American Medical Association* 316(11) (2016): 1193–1204.

'Tackling Drug-resistant Infections Globally: Final Report and Recommendations'. The Review on Antimicrobial Resistance, chaired by Jim O'Neill, 2016; https://amr-review.org/sites/default/files/160525_Final%20paper_with%20cover.pdf.

Psychedelic medicines

Books

Miller, R L. *Psychedelic Medicine: The Healing Powers of LSD, MDMA, Psilocybin, and Ayahuasca*. Park Street Press, 2017.

Pollan, M. *How to Change Your Mind: The New Science of Psychedelics*. Penguin, 2019.

Articles

Belouin, S J and Henningfield, J E. 'Psychedelics: where we are now, why we got here, what we must do'. *Neuropharmacology* 142 (2018): 7–19.

Chi, T and Gold, J. 'A review of emerging therapeutic potential of psychedelic drugs in the treatment of psychiatric illnesses'. *Journal of the Neurological Sciences* 411 (2020): 116715; https://doi.org/10.1016/j.jns.2020.116715.

Palhano-Fontes, F, Barreto, D, Onias, H, et al. 'Rapid antidepressant effects of the psychedelic ayahuasca in treatment-resistant depression: a randomized placebo-controlled trial'. *Psychological Medicine* 49 (2019): 655–63.

Perkins, D, Sarris, J, Rossell, S, et al. 'Medicinal psychedelics for mental health and addiction: advancing research of an emerging paradigm'. *Australian and New Zealand Journal of Psychiatry* (2021); https://doi.org/10.1177/0004867421998785.

Zeifman, R, Palhano-Fontes, F, Hallak, J, et al. 'The impact of ayahuasca on suicidality: results from a randomized controlled trial'. *Frontiers in Pharmacology* 10 (2019): 1325.